Time, Language, and Ontology

OXFORD STUDIES OF TIME IN LANGUAGE AND THOUGHT

GENERAL EDITORS: Kasia M. Jaszczolt, *University of Cambridge* and Louis de Saussure, *University of Neuchâtel*

ADVISORY EDITORS: Nicholas Asher, *Université Paul Sabatier*; Johan van der Auwera, *University of Antwerp*; Robert I. Binnick, *University of Toronto*; Ronny Boogaart, *University of Leiden*; Frank Brisard, *University of Antwerp*; Patrick Caudal, *CNRS*; Anastasia Giannakidou, *University of Chicago*; Hans Kronning, *University of Uppsala*; Ronald Langacker, *University of California, San Diego*; Alex Lascarides, *University of Edinburgh*; Peter Ludlow, *Northwestern University*; Alice ter Meulen, *University of Geneva*; Robin Le Poidevin, *University of Leeds*; Paul Portner, *Georgetown University*; Tim Stowell, *University of California, Los Angeles*; Henriëtte de Swart, *University of Utrecht*

PUBLISHED

Time: Language, Cognition, and Reality
Edited by Kasia M. Jaszczolt and Louis de Saussure

Future Times; Future Tenses
Edited by Philippe De Brabanter, Mikhail Kissine, and Saghie Sharifzadeh

Time, Language, and Ontology
by M. Joshua Mozersky

Time, Language, and Ontology

The World from the B-Theoretic Perspective

M. JOSHUA MOZERSKY

UNIVERSITY PRESS

OXFORD
UNIVERSITY PRESS

Great Clarendon Street, Oxford, OX2 6DP,
United Kingdom

Oxford University Press is a department of the University of Oxford.
It furthers the University's objective of excellence in research, scholarship,
and education by publishing worldwide. Oxford is a registered trade mark of
Oxford University Press in the UK and in certain other countries.

First Edition published in 2015

Impression: 1

Published in the United States of America by Oxford University Press
198 Madison Avenue, New York, NY 10016, United States of America

British Library Cataloguing in Publication Data
Data available

Library of Congress Control Number: 2014939571

ISBN 978-0-19-871816-1

Printed and bound by
CPI Group (UK) Ltd, Croydon, CR0 4YY

To Carol-Anne and Jacqueline
In eternal love

Contents

General Preface

The series *Oxford Studies of Time in Language and Thought* identifies and promotes pioneering research on the human concept of time and its representation in natural language. Representing time in language is one of the most debated issues in semantic theory and is riddled with unresolved questions, puzzles, and paradoxes. The series aims to advance the development of adequate accounts and explanations of such basic matters as (i) the interaction of the temporal information conveyed by tense, aspect, temporal adverbials, and context; (ii) the representation of temporal relations between events and states; (iii) human conceptualization of time; (iv) the ontology of time; and (v) relations between events and states (eventualities), facts, propositions, sentences, and utterances, among other topics. The series also seeks to advance time-related research in such key areas as language modelling in computational linguistics, linguistic typology, and the linguistic relativity/universalism debate, as well as in theoretical and applied contrastive studies.

The central questions to be addressed concern the concept of time as it is lexicalized and grammaticalized in the different languages of the world. But its scope and the style in which its books are written reflects the fact that the representation of time interests those in many disciplines besides linguistics, including philosophy, psychology, sociology, and anthropology.

Philosophical discussions concerning the nature and properties of time underlie many different kinds of inquiry in contemporary metaphysics, linguistics, logic, epistemology, psychology, and anthropology among others. In this volume Mozersky addresses fundamental temporal questions, defending the objective conception of time. In particular, he supports the view that past, present, and future events are all equally real (*eternalism*), challenging in the process some proposals developed in the philosophical literature such as that only the present exists, or only the present and the past but not the future exist. He presents arguments in favour of the *tenseless* theory of time, according to which tenseless propositions, that is propositions whose truth values are not relativized to time, constitute the meaning of tensed (in the semantic sense of the word) sentences. The fact that *tense*, understood in philosophy as temporal location in the past, present, or future, is evidently present in thought and language is explained by appeal only to earlier-than/later-than relations, which places this account within the B-theoretic camp in the ongoing debates between A-theorists (supporters of *tensed* reality) and B-theorists (supporters of *tenseless* reality). Finally, Mozersky successfully attempts to combine his tenseless theory with the view that time really passes, without resorting to such problematic explanantia as the non-relative past, present, or future: everything to do with time and change derives from the temporal ordering of events.

Kasia M. Jaszczolt and Louis de Saussure

Acknowledgements

This book would not have been possible without the generous assistance of many people. I would like to thank the following for their comments, criticism, and encouragement on various versions of the manuscript in whole or in part: Rachel Barber, Octavian Busuioc, Andrew Butler, Staphane Carini, Martin Caver, Yual Chiek, Jennifer Cornick, Frederic Cote-Boudreau, Jacob Erola-Channen, Kyley Ewing, Frank Gairdner, Omid Hejazi, Matthew Hodgetts, Tim Juvshik, Arash Farzam-Kia, Heather Kuiper, Joshua Landry, James Marton, Storrs McCall, Ryan McInerney, Ulrich Meyer, Jon Miller, Patrick Moran, Sharday Mosurinjohn, Scott Nicholson, Brendan O'Grady, Tara Ostner, Elyse Platt, Nolan Ritcey, Shitangshu Roy, Peter Saczkowski, Mastoureh Sadeghnia, Steven Savitt, William Seager, Jamie Shaw, Rubin Sozinho, Adam Sproat, James Stuckey, Kijin Sung, Radhika Tikku, Michael Vossen, Jun Wang, Peter West-Oram, V. Alan White, and Michel-Antoine Xhignesse. I am also indebted to numerous audiences on whom I have tried out several of the arguments below.

A few people deserve particular mention. Kasia Jaszczolt read the penultimate draft and provided very valuable suggestions for finishing touches. Henry Laycock is a regular source of philosophical insight and wisdom, and I thank him for our many conversations on ontology, semantics, and related issues. Calvin Normore read an early draft in its entirety and I am grateful to him for his insightful comments. I am in Crawford Elder's debt for his engagement with an earlier draft that resulted in a greatly improved manuscript and a greatly encouraged author. Many, many thanks go to Nathan Oaklander for his perceptive and constructive criticism over many years. My debt to James Robert Brown and Bernard D. Katz can hardly be repaid; they were instrumental in guiding me as I began my philosophical journey and without their support this project would never have been started, let alone completed. I take full responsibility for any errors and confusions that remain after such generous and astute advice from so many excellent philosophers.

Finally, I would like to thank Carole-Anne and Jacqueline for putting up with me as I worked on this book; I dedicate it to them.

Some sections in Chapters 2 and 3 use material from my 'Bourne-Again Presentism', which originally appeared in L. N. Oaklander (ed.), *The Philosophy of Time: Critical Concepts in Philosophy* (Routledge 2008). I am grateful to Routledge and the editor for permission to reprint that material here.

An earlier version of Chapter 4 appeared as 'Tense and Temporal Semantics' in *Synthese* 124 (2000): 247–69 and an earlier version of Chapter 5 appeared as 'A Tenseless Account of the Presence of Experience' in *Philosophical Studies* 129 (2006): 441–76. I am grateful to Springer for permission to reprint material from those essays here.

1

Introduction

Time, tense, and the objective conception

John Campbell writes:

There is a distinction that philosophers and psychologists have tried to draw between different ways of thinking about space...It is sometimes called, and I will call it, the distinction between *absolute* and *egocentric* space. But it is not a distinction between different types of regions. It is a difference between ways of representing, or thinking about, a particular region...Intuitively, the distinction is between thinking about space as a participant, as someone plunged into its center, as someone with things to do in that space, on the one hand, and, on the other hand, thinking about the space as a disengaged theorist. (Campbell 1994, p. 5)

A similar distinction can be drawn with respect to time. To think about time as a participant is to think of time in a way that is centred on the present. For example, past actions can be remembered and future actions anticipated, but to act is to do something right *now*. When time is examined from the point of view of the disengaged theorist, however, the present seems to fade way, not into oblivion but, rather, into a sea of similar moments. So, from the egocentric, or subjective, point of view, the present is unique or at least special in some way; from the absolute or objective[1] point of view, the present is just one time amongst other equals.

Since our language draws the distinctions between past, present, and future by the use of grammatical tense, these two perspectives on time are often called *tensed* (in place of egocentric) and *tenseless* (in place of objective) theories or accounts (see, for example, Oaklander and Smith 1994). The philosophy of time, however, contains a debate that has no real analogue in the philosophy of space, namely whether or not time is *in fact* centred; that is, whether or not the present is unique in some way as opposed to merely being experienced as such. Philosophical disputes over the nature of space long ago left behind the idea that space contains a privileged position or

---

[1] Because 'absolutism' is the name given to the view that space or time exists independently of objects and events, I will use 'objective' to refer to a view of time that does not privilege any moment.

centre, so one would be hard pressed to uncover a recent account of space that attempts to single out the 'here' as anything more than that location amongst similar others that happens to coincide with a speaker or some other reference point.

This is not to say, however, that the egocentric and objective perspectives of space are easily or simply integrated. As Campbell continues:

The idea of absolute space sometimes appears in discussions of self-consciousness. When self-consciousness is conceived in this way, it can seem dizzying. What it demands is that one should build up a synoptic picture of the world, one that wholly abstracts from one's own place in the throng, and then somehow identify one of the people so pictured as oneself. What is dizzying is the kind of complete objectivity, the degree of abstraction from one's own busy concerns, that is required. A first interpretation is that what is wanted is a kind of top-down view, so that we think in terms of a kind of aerial photograph, and then one has to identify oneself as one of the people shown in the photo. But that would not be enough, for it would only give the viewpoint of the photographer, and we need a picture of the world that is objective, in that it is not from any viewpoint at all. (Campbell 1994, p. 6)

If self-consciousness requires a view from nowhere (Nagel 1986), then it might seem that self-consciousness is impossible. One approach would be to suggest that:

we do not need any kind of objective conception in order to be self-conscious. Immersed, as we are, in the thick of things, we have no need or use for such a conception in our everyday lives, whereas self-consciousness in commonplace. So an objective conception is not demanded by self-consciousness. (Campbell 1994, pp. 6–7)

Campbell thinks that we need and use the objective conception of space (Campbell 1994, p. 7). Note, however, that this is a problem of reconciling two systems of representation and neither Campbell, nor anyone else I am aware of, seriously considers that the objective conception is impossible because a particular region is singled out by nature as objectively centred or 'here'. Such a response is simply not a live option in debates about the structure of space and our representations of it.

Again, the situation is different in the philosophy of time. Not only do philosophers ask whether we can coherently form a tenseless conception of time (e.g. Teichmann 1998, Stoneham 2009), but they regularly debate whether time itself could be tenseless; that is, whether or not the present time could be just one time amongst many, similar others, or whether the present is both experientially distinguished from other times, as is the here, and *ontologically* distinguished as well. For example:

One common way to present the issue is in terms of what is required for a complete description of reality. Suppose we provide a complete tenseless description of reality; we say what happens when, and in what order, but without any appeal or orientation towards the present time. We may then ask: is the description complete? Or is it a further fact, not implicit in the description itself, that I am *currently* sitting, for example? (Fine 2005, p. 265; see also Mellor 1998, Oaklander and Smith 1994, Sider 2001)

So there are two issues that need to be considered. The first is ontological: is the objective conception of time true; that is, is time like space in lacking a 'centre' or privileged position? The second is conceptual/representational: is the objective conception of time possible?

Note that the answer to the latter question might be negative even if the answer to the former is positive. That is, it may be that, as in the third quotation from Campbell above, though time itself has no position of privilege, it is nonetheless impossible to form this perspective on time. On the other hand, one might argue that while the present is ontologically distinct from other times, we are able to abstract from this fact and form an objective conception of time; in this case, the objective conception might be a useful heuristic for some theoretical purposes but ultimately must be treated as a metaphor or an approximation. Others (e.g. Craig 1996, Ludlow 1999, Smith 1993) argue that the semantic and ontological questions cannot be separated: an utterance of 'it is very bright now' *entails* that the time of utterance is mind-independently present, so we can only avoid commitment to an egocentric vision of time on pain of denying the possibility of speaking truthfully about it (see Chapters 4 and 5 for further discussion).

The goal of this book is to defend both the possibility and truth of the objective conception of time and then to examine some of the implications of this viewpoint.

I begin with the ontological question. Eternalism is the view that all times and their contents exist equally; in other words, position in time is not existentially relevant. I defend this view negatively, that is by examining the various ways one might go about denying it. Broadly speaking, there are two families of views here: those, first, according to which the present and past exist, but the future does not; and those, secondly, according to which only the present exists.

Chapter 2 addresses the first family of views and argues that they all suffer from a similar kind of problem: they are unable to bear their own ontological weight. What I mean by this is that these views are built around models of the world that are, I argue, incompatible with propositions about time that are essential to these very views.

Chapter 3 considers presentism, the second kind of denial of eternalism. I argue that presentism suffers from a problem much like that of the empty future views: a model confined to what exists now simply cannot support all the claims about time that the presentist wishes to make. Hence, I conclude that attempts to temporally restrict ontology are unsatisfactory. Before proceeding, however, I consider two additional rivals to eternalism that do not fall neatly into the division above. First, I address the 'moving spotlight' view (Skow 2012) according to which all times exist equally but the present is highlighted, singled out as objectively NOW, as if a universal spotlight shines upon it; I argue that this view is in fact analogous to eternalism but with additional difficulties, so should be rejected. Secondly, I consider a recent suggestion from Kit Fine (2005, 2006), according to which there is no unified reality so there can be no single model that is adequate to it; while this may seem like an extreme view, Fine argues that the reality of temporal passage strongly suggests it. I agree wholeheartedly that the passage of time is a real phenomenon, but I argue that Fine's way of preserving it is unpersuasive.

So I conclude that the objective conception of time is true. Nonetheless, I grant that we couldn't do without tensed thought and language because they are essential to timely interactions with the world. How can we account for this if eternalism is correct and reality is not demarcated along tense lines? A second worry arises here as well: if tensed language and thought are ineliminable, can we be sure that a tenseless conception of time is available to us after all; might we be fooling ourselves if we suppose we can think ourselves outside the confines of the present moment? To answer these questions we must address the relationship between tensed language and the world; we must, in other words, turn to semantics.

In Chapter 4 I present an account of tensed language that is both compatible with its ineliminability and, I argue, entirely tenseless. By the latter I mean that the truth conditions of our utterances involve only the temporally invariant, B-series relations 'x is earlier than y', 'x is simultaneous with y', and 'x is later than y' (McTaggart 1908). These relations suffice to define a temporal order on all events, including our utterances and thoughts, but they fail to pick out any time as ontologically privileged or objectively NOW; hence the proper semantic account of tensed language is tenseless. I conclude that we in fact possess the linguistic tools to express the eternalist model.

In Chapter 5 I address the question of why the present is privileged in perception and action. I present an account that is limited to the eternalist ontology but, I argue, explains why we plan and perceive the way we do; all that is required is a tenseless, temporal ordering of events and some basic assumptions about our causal inter-actions with the world.

The conclusion I draw from these two chapters is that tenseless theories offer the best explanations of why we speak, think, and act as we do—i.e. in tensed terms—with respect to time. We can fully explain why it is that at any moment at which we are thinking or speaking, that particular moment is privileged in language and thought, and we can do this without ontologically privileging any moment. It is in this sense that I consider the view from nowhen to be coherent and the objective conception to be possible for us.

The notion of indexicality features prominently in the arguments of Chapters 4 and 5. I argue that tensed thought and action are fully explicable in terms of different relations speakers and thinkers bear to one and the same temporal context (and, indeed, content), which is a view that draws heavily on classic work in the semantics of indexicals (such as Perry 1979 and Kaplan 1989) and applies it to a variety of temporal considerations. This is important because the indexical account of the subjective point of view can, I believe, be extended to the cases of spatially and personally centred language and thought, thus promising a unified, objective account of human perspective; in other words, an objective account of subjectivity (see Chapter 8).

Chapters 2 to 5 constitute my defence of the objective view of time, which is the combination of eternalism with an entirely tenseless account of temporal language and thought. This combination is usually referred to as the *B-theory*, which is the term I shall use from this point onward (the *A-theory* is any view that rejects one or both components of the B-theory). One of the interesting features of the B-theory, as I defend it, is that it contains only relational temporal predicates. This suggests a solution to the ancient puzzle of change, and Chapters 6 and 7 explore and defend this solution.

Because the extensions of tenseless relations do not vary with time, the B-theory is often accused of entailing a 'block universe' that is devoid of any dynamic character (e.g. McTaggart 1908). In Chapter 6 I address this concern by focusing on temporal predication more broadly. I argue that ordinary predicates, such as 'x is red' or 'x has mass m' (what Lewis (1986) calls 'temporary intrinsics'), are, in fact, relations between objects and times. This leads to the conclusion that genuine change is relational in character and, therefore, that the B-theoretic account of language does not commit us to a universe without change. The most important objections to this view derive from David Lewis, and a large portion of this chapter is dedicated to the response to his views, though other important objections are considered as well.

The relational, B-theoretic account of change opens up conceptual space for an under-appreciated view: that even though the B-theory is correct, *perdurance theory* is not. Perdurantists argue that objects persist in virtue of having temporal parts that are located at different times. Traditional proponents of this view (e.g. Quine 1950, Smart 1963, Heller 1984, Lewis 1986) consider objects to be temporally extended entities that are composed of temporal parts. A recent variation, however, is *stage theory* or *exdurantism* (e.g. Hawley 2001, Sider 2001) according to which objects *are* instantaneous temporal parts and 'persist' only in virtue of standing in a *counterpart* relation to other temporal parts, located at later times. On the former view, an object persists in virtue of spanning different times, while on the latter an object persists in virtue of being appropriately related to distinct, temporally instantaneous entities of a similar kind. The views are united by the propositions that temporal parts exist, are the primary bearers of (at least most) predicates, and that *persisting* objects are extended *four-dimensional* entities. *Three-dimensionalists*, on the other hand, believe that objects are not composed of temporal parts and persist by *enduring*: retaining their strict, numerical identity before and after a change.

The differences between the two four-dimensionalist views are not especially relevant in the arguments to follow, so I will use 'four dimensionalism' or 'perdurantism' as general terms that may refer to either view, and only distinguish them as need be (e.g. by reference to the 'stage theorist').

In a sense, the B-theory views space and time as a four-dimensional, perduring whole. Perdurance theorists, typically, accept this view of time and space but they err, I argue, in thinking of ordinary objects in the same way. If, however, persisting objects are not 'spread out' in time, as perdurantists of both stripes argue, then how are we to think of them? It is typical to claim that for the three-dimensionalist objects are 'wholly present' at each moment that they exist, in contrast to perdurance theory according to which only a part of a persisting object is ever present at a given time (e.g. Mellor 1998, Sider 2001, Crisp and Smith 2005). This turn of phrase is, I think, a misleading one, and in Chapter 7 I employ the resources of the relational account of temporal predication to explain why, and also why I believe we have no good reason to believe in temporal parts, and how an endurantist can account for persistence.

In Chapter 8 I present what I take to be perhaps the most significant payoff of the view that I defend to that point: that the B-theory provides the resources for an objective account of the passage and direction of time. One of the primary reasons philosophers offer for resisting the B-theory is the belief, in fact encouraged by many B-theorists, that this view is incompatible with temporal passage and must relegate this concept to the status of illusion or some other form of cognitive error (e.g. Mellor 1998, Prosser 2007; see, also, Jaszczolt 2009 for an alternative, interesting take on the relationship between time and our experience of passage). This, I argue, is a mistake. It is simply incredible to suppose that time doesn't pass. It is important, however, not to *inflate* the concept of temporal passage so that it requires an incredible ontology or an implausible semantics. It is, rather, the B-theory that supplies the appropriately deflated account of temporal passage, one that can do the necessary explanatory work without relying on fantastic metaphysical manoeuvres. Defending this position is the task I take on in the final chapter of the book.

The upshot, I conclude, is that the B-theory provides a compelling, unified picture of both time itself and the human understanding of time. The power of the B-theory is grounded not only in the arguments in its favour but also in its ability to reconcile the subjective and objective temporal conceptions by explaining the perspectival, tensed aspects of time in non-perspectival, tenseless terms.[2] Not everyone believes that the subjective and objective points of view can, in general, be reconciled (e.g. Jackson 1986, Nagel 1986). I think, however, that the B-theory is an example of success on this score, as I hope to establish in the following.

---

[2] It might seem that this is unfair to the A-theorist. If reality itself is tensed, then explaining the experience of time in tensed terms may very well be to explain it in mind-independent terms. Agreed. I argue below, however, that one cannot make sense of a world that is objectively divided along tense lines. Nonetheless, I grant that we need to carve up the world this way in our thought and language. So this aspect of our experience must be explained in tenseless terms. Accordingly, while this paragraph may seem to characterize the A-theory tendentiously, I hope to make good on this characterization in the arguments to follow. (I thank Kasia Jaszczolt for bringing this potential objection to my attention.)

2

The reality of the future

2.1 Introduction

It is compelling to suppose that there is more than one possible future course of history. Many philosophers have argued that this proposition entails that there is simply no fact of the matter as to what will occur.[1] The suggestion, in other words, is that there is good reason to suppose that there are genuine, distinct future possibilities open to us and that if there are, then there is no determinate truth concerning what will occur. We ought, therefore, to modify our semantics for the future tense; when we speak of the future we can at best guess or speculate, but we cannot claim to be uttering truths and falsehoods, for there is nothing determinate to speak about. The future is 'unsettled', 'open', 'yet to be written', 'unknowable', or otherwise indeterminate.

In chapter IX of his *De Interpretatione*, Aristotle famously considered whether an adequate account of future contingents demands a revision of classical logic (see, e.g., McKeon 1941). John MacFarlane provides a nice, contemporary version of the affirmative case:

Suppose that at some moment m_0 there is an objectively possible future history h_1 in which there is a sea battle the next day, and another h_2, in which there is no sea battle the next day...Now suppose that at m_0 Jake asserts 'There will be a sea battle tomorrow'...Given that nothing about the context of utterance singles out one of the histories of which it is a part, symmetry considerations seem to rule out saying either that the utterance is true or that it is false. Thus, it seems we must count it neither true nor false. (MacFarlane 2003, p. 323)[2]

The primary semantic consequence of this view is that future contingents either take on a third truth-value, 'indeterminate', or else fall within a gap between 'true' and 'false'. In other words, the position entails, and can perhaps be identified with, *future-tense semantic indeterminism* or, more briefly, FSI.

---

[1] Unless there are some necessary truths concerning the future; I shall restrict the discussion to future contingents.

[2] Note that MacFarlane defends a hybrid view that attempts to capture the strengths of both the indeterminist and determinist positions. I discuss his account below.

Those drawn to FSI tend to argue that it is underwritten by a particular ontological stance concerning the future. This can be spelled out in a couple of ways. The future may, for instance, simply be 'empty', containing no future histories, though waiting to be 'filled in' as time passes (see, for example, Tooley 1997, Broad 1923). On the other hand, the future may consist of many distinct but non-actual series of events—originating in the present much as branches fan out from a tree trunk—one of which will be actualized (Bourne 2006a, 2006b, MacFarlane 2003, McCall 1994, Thomason 1970).

In what follows I examine the branching future and empty future ontologies. I conclude that neither view is compatible with a system of semantic principles known as the truth-value links.[3] As a result, the underlying metaphysical pictures turn out either not to be coherently expressible or else expressible only at great ontological cost. Hence, neither theory is preferable to eternalism.

2.2 Preliminaries

There are a number of principles that will play a significant role in the arguments below. They provide structure to debates about the reality of the non-present in the following sense: each of them is sufficiently plausible and well grounded that if any of them is contradicted by a theoretical—not limited to but including a metaphysical—hypothesis, then this provides some reason to be suspicious of the theoretical hypothesis. In other words, any conflict with these principles can only be rendered reasonable if the benefits of doing so are sufficiently high. The principles are the following:

a) There are true propositions about non-present times and a metaphysical theory ought, as much as is possible, to preserve our views about which such propositions are true and which false.

b) True propositions have truthmakers and a metaphysical theory should not render obscure or mysterious what the truthmakers are for those propositions.

c) Propositions about various times are bound by truth-value links that a metaphysical theory ought to accommodate.

Principles similar to these are expounded by Craig Bourne (see Bourne 2006a, pp. 1–2). I shall have more to say on all three of these as the discussion progresses, but it is appropriate to expand on them a little at the outset.

It is, I think, uncontroversial that at least some propositions about the past and future are true. For one thing, to deny this would be to commit to a kind of solipsism of the present moment that would have us reject many of the well-supported findings

---

[3] See section 2.2.

of archaeology, palaeontology, history, astronomy, and other fields. For another, not all propositions about the past and future can be false because some pairs contradict each other; nor can they all be indeterminate, for in that case it is *not true* that what is present was once future and will be past, which must be true unless this is the first, last, or only moment of time. So, (a) seems secure.

The truthmaker principle is intended to capture the idea that what is true depends on what exists. Simon Keller (2004) makes a helpful distinction between a stronger and weaker interpretation of the principle. The stronger reading is that there is a distinct entity, *the* truthmaker, for each true proposition. The problem with this view is that there appear to be no plausible truthmakers for true negative existential propositions, such as that there are no leprechauns. One solution is to posit negative facts, such as *the fact there are no leprechauns*, for each true negative existential, but this is a rather unwieldy and controversial move. Moreover, it is an unnecessary one, for there is a weaker reading of the principle according to which truth merely *supervenes* on being: no two worlds can differ in what is true in them without a difference in what there is in them (see, for example, Lewis 1992, Sider 2001, pp. 35–42). A world in which it is true that there are no leprechauns and one in which it is false that there are no leprechauns must not have identical inventories. Nothing so robust as a negative fact is needed, but truth still depends on, and is grounded in, what exists.[4] Accordingly, (b) may be accepted.

The truth-value links are a set of semantic principles that bind (propositions expressed by) sentences that differ only in tense.[5] For instance, suppose that Socrates is sitting. This appears to entail that (i) it was the case that Socrates will sit and that (ii) it will be the case that Socrates sat. Let us follow convention and suppose that propositions about the past and future have the logical form of a tense operator attached to a core, present-tense proposition. In other words:

(1)   Socrates sat

and

(2)   Socrates will sit

have the structure of:

---

[4] Keller argues that one ought to take the truthmaker principle as a commitment to a particular order of explanatory priority, i.e. as an obligation to appeal to what there is in explaining what is true, rather than the other way around (Keller 2004, p. 86). That is, he thinks that we should not think of the principle as naming some sort of natural kind or mind-independent relation between propositions and non-propositional entities. I remain agnostic, but have no objection to this view.

[5] I assume that sentences or their utterances are true or false in virtue of the truth or falsehood of the proposition that they express. In what follows, where I speak of the truth or falsehood of sentences I mean the truth or falsehood of the propositions they express, though I try to be as explicit on this point as possible.

(1′)   It was the case that Socrates is sitting.

and

(2′)   It will be the case that Socrates is sitting

respectively. Letting p represent the proposition that Socrates is sitting, 'P' = 'it was the case that', and 'F' = 'it will be the case that', then the logical forms of (1) and (2) can be represented by the following respective formulas:

(1*)   **P**p
(2*)   **F**p.

The truth-value links can now be represented as follows:

(TV1) $p \Rightarrow$ **FP**p
(TV2) $p \Rightarrow$ **PF**p

As I point out in section 2.5, on some models of time there may appear to be well-motivated reason to doubt (TV2). (TV1) is, however, more secure. The key point, as I argue in section 2.5, is that models that render the future ontologically open or indeterminate depend on (TV1), even though they are incompatible with it. So for now, I will assume (TV1) holds and employ it in the arguments to follow.

With these three principles in hand, we can assess the prospects of the two metaphysical theories that differentiate the future from the past and present both ontologically and semantically: the empty future model, and the branching future model.

2.3 The empty future model

To account for indeterminate propositions, Łukasiewicz (1970) famously proposes the following truth tables for the familiar logical connectives (where '1' = 'true', '0' = 'false', and '½' = 'indeterminate'):

~	
1	0
½	½
0	1

&	1	½	0
1	1	½	0
½	½	½	0
0	0	0	0

∨	1	½	0
1	1	1	1
½	1	½	½
0	1	½	0

⊃	1	½	0
1	1	½	0
½	1	1	½
0	1	1	1

In the tradition of C. D. Broad (1923), Michael Tooley (1997) has defended the application of this system to the evaluation of future contingents:

Some statements fail to be true at a time simply because there is nothing that is actual, as of that time, that makes them true, while others fail to be true at a time because there is, as of that time, a positive truthmaker for some logically incompatible statement. And given that this is so, to hold that there are only two truth-values—namely truth and falsity—would seem unsatisfactory...A three-valued logic with truth, falsity and indeterminateness provides a vivid representation of this fact. (Tooley 1997, p. 129)

Let us examine some of the consequences of such a view.[6]

---

[6] In what follows I focus on the Łukasiewicz logical system because that is what Tooley employs in his defence of the empty future ontology. As I argue, in the end I think this system is inadequate for Tooley's purposes, but I also argue that his view is self-undermining, and hence that there is no logical system that

Suppose that p is a contingent proposition. Fp is, accordingly, logically indeterminate; so too is its negation, ~Fp. Fp ∨ ~Fp will, therefore, also be indeterminate. Similarly, Fp & ~Fp will be indeterminate, as will ~(Fp & ~Fp). So on this system, propositions of the form p ∨ ~p and ~(p & ~p) are not generally true. Accordingly, if one adopts Łukasiewicz's tables to deal with future contingents, then one must reject the laws of excluded middle and non-contradiction.

This is clearly a significant, *prima facie* drawback of Tooley's approach, and might, for many, be reason enough to reject his view. Note, however, that for Tooley future contingents are neither true nor false *because* there exists nothing later than the present: the future is, simply, devoid of existence. Accordingly, there is no fact of the matter as to what will occur. Given this outlook, one might wonder whether sacrificing excluded middle and non-contradiction is such a high price to pay. After all, for any moment it is logically possible that it is the last moment of time. It is, therefore, possible that there will be neither a truthmaker for Fp nor one for ~Fp so that it won't, in the future, be the case that either p or ~p has a truthmaker. Similarly, there may not, in the future, exist anything that is incompatible with the truth of (p & ~p): since there may not exist anything later than right now, it is possible that it is not the case that there will exist anything that is incompatible with any proposition; so ~(p & ~p) is not guaranteed to hold universally. It seems appropriate, therefore, to combine an empty future ontology with the denial of excluded middle and non-contradiction as logical laws.

Another important feature of Łukasiewicz's tables, which is also endorsed by Tooley, is that material conditionals with indeterminate elements are true. It follows that a proposition such as Fp ⊃ Fq, where p and q are contingent, is true. This, however, combines *unnaturally* with the underlying metaphysics, for if p and q are contingent propositions, then it is possible for the future to unfold in such a way that p will be the case and q will *never* be the case, which would seem to falsify Fp ⊃ Fq (here I am equating 'it will be the case that' with 'it will be the case at some time that'). This strikes me as problematic. Suppose that on the basis of a scientific theory, someone makes the following prediction: 'if it will be the case that I mix chemical compounds A and B together at t, then it will be the case that there is an exothermic reaction R at $t + n$'. Now suppose that A and B are mixed at t but R is not observed at $t + n$. It seems to me that this shows the material implication to be false.

Tooley might reply that the material conditional has changed in truth-value, from true to false. I don't think this view is very plausible, however. After all, the initial proposition, Fp ⊃ Fq, is deemed by Tooley to be true even though the occurrences it is about do not exist; in other words, it is true even though there exist (present tense) no facts or conditions in the world that make it true. Later on, the conditional

will resuscitate it. As a result, I do not consider how other three-valued systems might combine with Tooley's ontology.

becomes false because certain facts or conditions materialize. This, however, appears to be a case of shifting the grounds of evaluation: initially, it is true for purely formal reasons (i.e. it has the form of a material conditional with indeterminate components); later it is false for factual reasons (i.e. in virtue of the way the world is). This, however, just suggests that there are no good reasons for viewing the material implication as having, initially, the form of a truth: propositions that are true in virtue of form ought to remain true regardless of the contingent facts.

The claim that, in general, material conditionals with indeterminate components are true appears, therefore, to be a mistake for the empty-futurist. Rather, it seems preferable to insist that they are logically indeterminate since, when one expresses $Fp \supset Fq$, it is possible that the world will evolve in such a way that is compatible with the antecedent but not the consequent, and since the implication concerns what will occur, there is little motivation to consider it to be true. Why not, then, reject the determinate truth of material conditionals that have an indeterminate antecedent and consequent?

Notice that, in setting up his defence of three-valued logic, Tooley writes:

> If one thinks of the truth-value [indeterminate] as really indicating a truth-value gap, then it is natural to consider how the truth-value of the disjunction will turn out given the different possible ways of filling in those truth-value gapes. If the same truth-value results for every possible filling-in, then one can take that truth-value as the appropriate entry. Thus, for example, in the case where p has the truth-value [true] and q the truth-value [indeterminate], the appropriate truth-value for the disjunction is [true], since that will be the truth-value it will receive when q's truth-value gap is filled in either by the truth-value [true], or by the truth-value [false]. (Tooley 1997, p. 131)

If, in light of this, one considers a proposition of the form $p \supset q$, where each element is indeterminate, then on one 'filling in' of truth-values (i.e. the value taken on by the proposition that p is *true*, the value taken on by the proposition that q is *false*), the proposition expressed is false; on the three others, it is true. So why follow Łukasiewicz here, if one is an empty-futurist? It seems better to modify the truth-table for the material conditional.

This would, however, render propositions of the form $p \supset p$ indeterminate whenever p takes on a future contingent as a value, and this is hard to swallow. But since we are considering a system that rejects the general truth of propositions of the form $p \vee \sim p$ and $\sim(p\ \&\ \sim p)$, this may not be much of an additional cost.

No *additional* cost, perhaps, but the price is high. That which began as an attempt to find space for future contingency has, in the end, eliminated future necessity. There no longer appear to be sufficient formal constraints on reasoning about the future to render it possible to understand what people in fact do when considering what will be the case. Moreover, there are plenty of implications that concern future, contingent occurrences that we know to be true on the basis of scientific evidence. It seems better, therefore, to look for a way to preserve the traditional logical laws while employing a three-valued logic for future contingents. This is what Tooley in fact does (Bourne too, as I explain in section 2.4.1).[7]

To recover the logical laws, Tooley denies that the logical connectives are truth-functional (Tooley 1997, p. 135). Certain propositions are true in virtue of their logical form, for example $p \vee \sim p$, $\sim(p \,\&\, \sim p)$ and $p \supset p$ (Tooley 1997, p. 137). Such propositions do not depend on the world (at a time) for their truth; other propositions differ since their truth or falsehood depends on how the world is at the time they are expressed, i.e. on whether there exists a truthmaker for it then (Tooley 1997, p. 137). For example, $Fp \vee \sim Fq$ is true only if the world contains something that suffices for the truth of one of the disjuncts. Since, however, the future is empty, there (currently) is no such truthmaker. Hence, not only is each disjunct indeterminate, the disjunction is as well.

On the other hand, $Fp \vee \sim Fp$ is a disjunction with two indeterminate disjuncts that is nevertheless true because it is a 'logical truth', i.e. true in virtue of having the form $p \vee \sim p$. For Tooley, accordingly, the truth-value of a disjunction depends on more than the truth-values of its disjuncts; it depends on whether the disjunction is a 'logical truth', and so is true in virtue of its logical form, or a 'factual truth' and so is true only if there exists something in the world (at the relevant time) that renders it true (Tooley 1997, pp. 137–44).

Now, Tooley suggests (1997, pp. 144–6) that it is natural to take factual truth-functionality as basic. The reason is that factual truth-functions reduce to traditional truth-functions in the context of bivalent logic: if every atomic proposition is either true or false, then there exists something to suffice for the truth or falsehood of any compound proposition. Hence, if eternalism is correct, then one needn't adjust one's understanding of the logical connectives, for in that case it would turn out that factual truth-functionality and truth-functionality coincide. If, on the other hand, the empty future metaphysics pans out, then factual truth-functionality can be employed for all but the logical truths.

But then, given that factual truth-functionality is the logically basic notion, it becomes difficult to understand why the forms that are, traditionally, logical laws come out as logically true on Tooley's account. After all, as I have noted, it is logically possible that the world might evolve (or, better, not evolve) so that no future truth-makers come into existence and, therefore, neither a truthmaker for p nor one for $\sim p$ comes to be. Given this, a commitment to, for example, the law of excluded middle, when applied to future contingents—$Fp \vee \sim Fp$—seems simply *ad hoc*; better to admit that it does not always hold.

---

[7] Thanks to Bernard Katz for discussion on the issues discussed in this and the previous five paragraphs.

In the context of Tooley's arguments, the desire to preserve traditional logical laws is unmotivated. It is unclear what recommends calling a propositional form such as $p \vee \sim p$ a 'logical truth' when substitutions into the non-logical parts of the formula can result in propositions that are not true.[8] On a bivalent, truth-functional logic, certain logical forms turn out to be true no matter what the truth-values of their non-logical components. Why, however, should one wish to resuscitate these laws in a system that is neither bivalent nor truth-functional? It is difficult to see the motivation for Tooley's stance.

Tooley does argue that even in a dynamic world where the future is non-existent, there is need for a notion of truth *simpliciter*, which is two-valued and, therefore, truth-functional. For example, consider the proposition that there will never be a twenty-foot tall human. Such a proposition can never be 'true at a time', argues Tooley, since it is always possible for a state of affairs that falsifies it to come into existence. Still, the proposition could be true (since it is not contradictory), so the notion of truth used here is not that of truth at a time (Tooley 1997, p. 152). Similarly, truths about abstract objects, if possible, will not supervene on temporal truthmakers, so in discussing their (possible) truth, we must have truth *simpliciter*, not truth at a time, in mind (Tooley 1997, pp. 149–52). Finally, logical truths are not made true by anything that obtains at a particular time but, rather, by 'the totality of what is actual' (Tooley 1997, p. 149); hence, the notion at play here is truth *simpliciter*.

Whether or not these examples are convincing, they are of no use against the charge of *ad hoc*ness. The first two examples—universal negatives and abstract entities—really just increase the concern, for the logical laws remain selectively applied, and one is left wondering why they should apply to future contingents. The final example is just a reiteration of Tooley's stance that, since logical laws are true in virtue of their form, they are true tenselessly rather than at a time; but given that our concern is over the question of *why* the logical laws should be taken as universally true, this answer is hardly to the point.

So, in sum, the attempt to deal with future contingents via an application of Łukasiewicz's three-valued logical system comes at a high cost. On the one hand, one may choose to jettison such logical laws as excluded middle, non-contradiction, and $p \supset p$. There is some motivation for doing so, if one considers the future to be non-existent, as Tooley does, but this seems to me to give us more reason to reject the empty future view than to revise classical logic. On the other hand, one may attempt, as Tooley does, to rescue the logical laws at the expense of the truth-functionality of logic. This manoeuvre, however, comes off as unmotivated. The empty future view is caught between a rock and hard place.

---

[8] Thanks to Bernard Katz for discussion on this point.

Let us, however, imagine that one is willing to accept one of the horns of this dilemma. There nevertheless remains a fundamental problem with Tooley's system, whether in its truth-functional or non-truth-functional guise: in either case, the truth-value links are broken. Consider an utterance, at t, that expresses the proposition Fp. Now consider the meta-proposition:

(3)   Fp is logically indeterminate at t.

If we follow Tooley, then (3) is true (assuming, as I shall from here, that p is contingent). Suppose that a day later, at $t + 1$, a truthmaker comes into existence that suffices for the truth of p. At this point, the world has 'grown by accretion of facts', and now includes both (i) an utterance, at t, that expresses Fp; and (ii) a truthmaker for p at $t + 1$. Now consider the following question: is it true, at $t + 1$, that Fp *was* indeterminate at t?

It seems that it cannot be, for the universe is no longer such that its structure suffices for the truth of:

(3*)   P(Fp is logically indeterminate at t).

As of t, the universe contains an utterance that expresses Fp and, a day later, something that suffices for the truth of p. So if (3*) is true, then there must exist—as a truthmaker for it—an earlier stage of the universe, one that contains nothing later than t. Such a stage does not, however, exist. If we could examine the universe in its entirety at $t + 1$, we would search in vain for a state that consists of everything up until t but nothing else.[9]

This is problematic because the transition from (3) to (3*) is no more than an instance of a truth-value link, (TV1). Hence, even if one wishes to accept one of the horns of the above dilemma one is faced with the rather serious problem of denying the truth-value links. Indeed, this is a particular instance of a much deeper problem with the empty future ontology.

To see this, imagine that Tooley is asked: what makes it true that the universe was once smaller than it is? There exists (now) nothing to make that claim true because reality includes everything that is present or earlier. We also ask, what makes it true that the universe will be bigger? The answer is that there now exists nothing to make that claim true. Since both of these conditions apply to times generally, it follows that it will never be true to claim that the universe grows by accretion of facts. Hence, if the implications of the dynamic model of reality provided by Tooley are true, then the model itself is not true. The model does not appear to be coherently expressible.

---

[9] It is there as a logical or mereological part, i.e. we can abstract away all reality after t; but that won't help. After all, there exists an arbitrary part of me, right now, that weighs 5 lbs, but that does not suffice for the truth of the proposition that I once weighed 5 lbs. I can have a part that weighs 5 lbs even if I came into existence, *ex nihilo*, at 6 lbs.

Tooley does, as noted above, distinguish between factual truth at a time and factual truth *simpliciter*. Might he say that the dynamic picture is never factually true at a time, but it is factually true *simpliciter*? I think not, for he writes:

in the case of factual truth *simpliciter*, a proposition (or statement, or sentence, etc.) is factually true if, and only if, there is some external truthmaker for it—that is, if and only if there is some fact outside the proposition itself that suffices to ensure that the proposition is true. Similarly, in the case of factual truth at a time, a proposition is factually true at a given time if, and only if, some external truthmaker for it is actual as of the time in question. (Tooley 1997, p. 137)

This is quite odd. On the dynamic view Tooley advocates, the only truthmakers that ever exist are those that exist now or in the past. So what can this distinction amount to, unless we admit the existence of truthmakers that don't (yet) exist? To do so, however, would violate the dynamic model itself, which asserts that nothing future exists. So Tooley's position requires that we admit past and future phases of the universe into our ontology, which again is to render his account self-refuting.

It seems that in order to discuss the empty future model itself, Tooley needs to employ concepts that allow him to step outside of that model at any particular time; he requires something that enables him to conceive of the universe *sub specie aeternitatis* (or, alternatively, from the point of view of a fifth dimension). Tooley is aware of this:

besides being able to speak of what is actual as of the present moment, one needs also to be able to make sense of propositions about what was actual, and about what will be actual, and, more generally about the totality of what is actual at some time or other. In short, one needs to be able to offer an account of the concept of a total, dynamic world, as contrasted with the history of a dynamic world up to some point in time... *X* is an actual, temporal entity or state of affairs means the same as *X* is part of the mereological whole that is composed of every state of affairs that is actual as of some time *t* or other. (Tooley 1997, p. 40)

The question I have been raising regards the coherence of such a position. How can there be a mereological whole that consists of every state of affairs that is, was, or will be, given that the future lacks existence, so much so that any proposition about what will occur turns out to be semantically indeterminate?

Tooley attempts to help himself to the notion of such a mereological whole:

The immediate upshot is that on any dynamic view of the world that holds that not all temporal states of affairs are actual as of all times—such as the view that I shall be defending here—one can give an account of the idea of a whole, dynamic world only if one employs both the concept of being actual as of a time and the concept of the totality of existence... it seems that, on *any* dynamic view of the world, there are two concepts that need to be taken as primitive. (Tooley 1997, p. 41)

It is precisely this that highlights the sense in which I find the empty future model to be self-undermining. On the one hand, Tooley insists that any future tense claim is untrue because when uttered, thought, or considered there quite simply exists nothing later than the time of utterance. On the other hand, in order to propose the model itself we must assume that there exists a sum total of reality, which consists of all states of affairs, including future ones. The model is, therefore, self-contradictory.[10]

Tooley could, I suppose, opt for an ontology that includes indefinitely many universes, each corresponding to a moment of time. These 'snapshots' of the universe would all exist and form a five-dimensional array (as each is itself a four-dimensional entity). There would, as a result, exist the requisite truthmakers for all the claims we wish to make about other times, including future ones. For instance, it is true that the universe was once smaller than it is because there exists a past universe that contains fewer entities; similarly, there exists a future version that contains more entities.

I think, however, that there are at least three good reasons for resisting this move. First, it is ontologically explosive, committing to indefinitely many universes just like the one that exists right now, each of which contains more or fewer events, objects, or persons; note, moreover, that events will appear repeatedly in different universes, for they exist in all universes that correspond to later times. Secondly, it commits one to the view that reality is in fact five-dimensional, including the three spatial dimensions, one temporal dimension, and another dimension along which all the various universes are ordered; it is difficult to believe that we can know this about the world *a priori*. Thirdly, it is difficult to see how one captures the 'dynamic' aspect of time on this view, for all the various stages of the universe exist tenselessly; rather than being a single entity growing by accretion of facts, the universe consists of indefinitely many sub-universes each of which differs from the others in size.

Notice, moreover, that eternalism suffers none of these disadvantages; it is committed neither to indefinitely many universes nor to higher dimensions (though it is consistent with both theses if they turn out to be necessary for other reasons). Tooley's view suffers significant comparative disadvantages.

So, I think that the attempt to rescue the empty future ontology from self-contradiction commits one to an ontology that is less preferable than eternalism. If there were overwhelming reason to resist eternalism, then it might very well be worth paying these ontological costs. Is there such overwhelming reason? It is the burden of this book to argue that the answer to this question is 'no': eternalism supports the best semantics for tensed discourse (Chapter 4); is consistent with our experience of time (Chapter 5); makes sense of attributions of change and persistence through time (Chapter 6); does not commit to exotic entities such as temporal parts (Chapter 7); and is compatible with objective temporal passage and direction (Chapter 8). If not

---

[10] Oaklander 2004 (chapter 12) raises similar concerns.

convinced here that eternalism is preferable to the empty future view, I hope the reader will be by the end of the book. Next, I turn to the branching future model.

2.4 The branching future model

Though typically rejecting bivalence, branching future theorists, in contrast to Tooley, generally wish to formulate semantic theories for future contingents that preserve the traditional logical laws of excluded middle and non-contradiction. Some authors (e.g. Bourne 2006a, 2006b) defend an ontology in which branches exist as abstract or ersatz future histories; others (e.g. McCall 1994) consider branches to be concrete entities. Though the problems facing them are similar, there are some interesting differences, so I shall comment on both in the following.

2.4.1 *Ersatz branches*

Craig Bourne (2006a, 2006b) defends an ontology in which multiple future histories exist as abstract entities. He also argues that past times exist only as abstract entities, but in a single branch, since his view is a version of presentism (a theory I consider in detail in Chapter 3). So, his view serves as an ersatz version of the branching future ontology and an examination of his theory will lead to some general lessons.

Bourne argues that times are maximally consistent sets of propositions; propositions that do not contain tense operators. Intuitively, these can be viewed as sets of propositions that completely describe a moment. These times, i.e. sets of propositions, are assigned a date; therefore, an analogue of the 'is earlier than' relation can be defined on them (Bourne 2006a, pp. 10–11). A time is, therefore, any member of the set of maximal proposition sets over which the 'E-relation' is defined:

> The E-relation is not the genuine *earlier than* relation since it does not relate spatio-temporal objects, but it does *represent* the *earlier than* relation in the way it relates times. The properties of the E-relation match whatever we take to be the properties of the genuine *earlier than* relation. This allows presentists to have a time series related by 'earlier than' without being committed to the existence of real, or rather, concretely realised *relata*, something anathema to presentism. (Bourne 2006a, p. 11)

An initial concern with this view is that if times are abstract, then the present, being concrete, is not a time. Bourne replies:

> Ersatzer Presentism is the view not that only one time exists, but that only one time has a concrete realisation. This is a mere nominal difference, equivalent to saying that presentists do not believe in any times other than the present. (Bourne 2006a, p. 11)

The ontology that Bourne defends is, then, one of many existing but abstract times, one, and only one, of which is (ever) concrete.

There is one final piece of Bourne's puzzle. He suggests that one take the *E*-relation to be

a one–many relation in the direction from the present to future... but only one–one in relation to the direction from the present to the past. The reason is simple: we all need a way of distinguishing the past from the future. (Bourne 2006a, p. 12)

According to Bourne there are, at a given time, many possible future branches, only one of which will become concrete. In contrast, there is, from any moment in time, only one path toward the past. This is, therefore, an ersatz version of the branching future ontology.

Bourne writes that:

'It will be the case that *p*' is neither determinately true *simpliciter* nor determinately false *simpliciter*, given the branching structure, when *p* is contingent. (Bourne 2006a, p. 15)

For Bourne, a proposition is true *simpliciter* if and only if it is true at the present time (Bourne 2006a, pp. 12–13). So, on this view, future contingents are neither true nor false.

Bourne (2004) defends a three-valued logical system that is, he argues, capable of handling logically indeterminate future contingents consistently with the classical laws of excluded middle and non-contradiction. He suggests that in order to accommodate future indeterminacy, we replace the classical truth table for negation with the following modification:

~	
1	0
½	1
0	1

The justification is as follows: if some proposition, for example F*p*, is indeterminate, then it is not the case that F*p*; so, not-F*p* is true (Bourne 2004, p. 124). F*p* is true *simpliciter* if and only if every branch from the present contains a time with *p* as a member; it is false *simpliciter* if and only if no branch from the present contains a time with *p* as a member (Bourne 2006a, p. 15; see also Thomason 1970). This system allows Bourne to combine indeterminacy for future contingents with the laws of excluded middle and non-contradiction.[11]

---

[11] Excluded middle is secured because if *p* is indeterminate, then ~*p* is true; so *p* ∨ ~*p*, having a determinately true disjunct, is true. Non-contradiction is preserved because if *p* is indeterminate, then, though *p* & ~*p* remains indeterminate, ~(*p* & ~*p*) is, as the negation of an indeterminate proposition, true.

Bourne continues:

[A]ccording to the branching view, future contingents are presently indeterminate precisely because only *one* branch of the possible branches *will* get realised, but...there *is* no branch in particular that is presently that branch...branching does not conflict with our ordinary presupposition that we *will have* a single future, although it does conflict with the idea that we *have* a single future. (Bourne 2006a, p. 16)

So, Bourne maintains that it is untrue *of any particular future branch* that it *is* (i.e. is now) the one that will be realized. If we let *b* be a variable that ranges over future branches and '*Cx*' = 'is concretely realized', then the following is denied by Bourne:

(4) $(\exists b)\text{F}(Cb)$.

If (4) were true, then we would *have* a single future.

Yet, Bourne claims that it is true right now, so true *simpliciter*, that it will be the case that one branch is realized. How are we to understand such a proposition? Obviously (4) is ruled out, but, as Bourne writes in the quotation above, what is true is that 'we *will have* a single future', i.e.:

(5) $\text{F}(\exists b)(Cb)$.[12]

Since it is metaphysically and logically possible that the present is the last moment of time, (5) appears to be a future contingent; so the question is how it can be true, given that (4) is not. The answer lies, I think, in the idea that, for Bourne, F*p* is true when *p* is a member of every future branch. The Ersatzer might, therefore, insist that the embedded proposition in (5), i.e. a proposition of the form:

(6) $(\exists b)(Cb)$,

is a part of each future branch, thus rendering (5) true *simpliciter*.[13] The idea, then, is that though each future branch contains a proposition of the form of (6), it remains indeterminate *which* branch—and hence which instance of (6)—will be realized. Perhaps, for example, each future proposition (6) entails that a *different* branch is concretely realized. Presumably, then, the passage of time is required before it is settled which of the currently existing branches becomes concrete.

---

[12] In both (4) and (5) it is technically necessary to add a uniqueness clause to capture the claim that exactly one branch is realized. For instance, (5) might be better construed as:

(5*) $\text{F}(\exists b)(Cb \,\&\, [(\forall b^*)(Cb^* \supset [b^* = b])])$.

Similar modifications would be required of (4), but I will avoid this complication for the sake of expository ease.

[13] If this strategy is to succeed, then each proposition of the form of (6) must *not* entail that one particular branch is such that it will be concretely realized; otherwise, (6) will come out as true *simpliciter*, which would violate indeterminacy.

How are we, however, to understand the passage of time on this model? The natural suggestion, found, for example, in MacFarlane (2003) or McCall (1994), is that 'branch attrition'—the process whereby all the possible futures from a moment, except for one, disappear from existence—defines the passage of time and explains why only one branch is ever realized and why, on Bourne's view, we have a single past. It turns out, however, that branch attrition cannot in fact be used to define the passage of time. The problem can be seen by a consideration of the truth-value links.

To see this, consider the following questions: once, at time $t + n$, a single branch from earlier time t has been concretely realized, what happens to all the other ersatz histories that branch from t? Do they continue to exist, abstractly, in the past, or do they disappear from reality entirely?

Suppose that one utters, at t, 'there will be a sea battle tomorrow'. Assume that there are two branches from t: one, b_1, contains an ersatz sea battle; the other, b_2, does not. According to Bourne, the utterance expresses, at t, an indeterminate proposition. Assume that a sea battle occurs the next day, at t_1. We decide, at t_1, to ask the following question: was the t-utterance of 'there will be a sea battle tomorrow' true, false, or indeterminate *then*?

The truth-value links recommend the answer 'indeterminate'; that the utterance expresses an indeterminate proposition entails that it will thereafter be the case that the utterance expressed an indeterminate proposition. If we accept this reasoning, then, since indeterminacy is underwritten, indeed defined, by the existence of abstract b_1 and b_2 branching from the time at which the original utterance was made, it would follow that those branches still exist at t_1. If not, there would be nothing at t_1 to ontologically ground the proposition that the utterance was indeterminate at t, which would violate (b) in section 2.2. In short, if it is true that an utterance expressed something that *was* indeterminate, it is true that branches from the time of utterance *exist*. It is not, of course, that they exist *now*, in the sense of branching from t_1, for the retroactive assessment to be grounded.[14] The branches must, however, be part of the world in order for there to be something to ground an assessment of 'was indeterminate' of (the proposition expressed by) the earlier utterance. In other words, the branches must exist *tenselessly*; otherwise propositions about the past structure of the model will simply lack any ontological grounds.[15]

What this shows is that the combination of the truth-value links and branching future histories *conflict with* branch attrition.[16] The explanation as to why only one

---

[14] Thanks to L. N. Oaklander for drawing my attention to this potential confusion.

[15] The ersatz presentist might try to ground the truth of 'branches from t existed' in current entities, but the problem, as we shall see in the next chapter, is that there appear to be too few present entities for this strategy to work.

[16] Another difficulty with the branch attrition view, suggested by L. N. Oaklander (personal communication), is that it is difficult to understand how the disappearance of branches can define a temporal process or, indeed, be dependent on time in any way. After all, branches are abstract entities, so they would, it seems, be incapable of standing in temporal relations at all. I am tempted to agree.

branch will be realized cannot be that, in time, all branches between t and t_1 except for one are eliminated from existence. To preserve the truth-value links, branches from t must persist (tenselessly) at later times. This, however, leads to various difficulties.

First, it is unclear what explanation the branching-futurist—ersatz or otherwise—can provide for the passage of time, once branch attrition is eliminated. Perhaps it must remain a primitive feature of the branching model, a brute fact that is not otherwise grounded in the model. In that case, however, it is hard to see what work the branches are doing in the theory.

Secondly, if, despite this, we respect the demand for truthmakers (i.e. (b) in section 2.2), then the Ersatzer branching future model becomes ontologically explosive (much like Tooley's view). Consider that on the branching future model the past utterance of 'there will be a sea battle tomorrow' (expressed a proposition that) was indeterminate because it was the case that both branches from t were then non-concrete. There must, therefore, be some truthmaker for the proposition that both b_1 and b_2 once were non-concrete. But there appears to be none. The Ersatzer model of the world at t_1, without branch attrition, contains one branch from t that is concretely realized and one that remains abstract/ersatz. One would search in vain for any part of the model that contains two ersatz branches from t; as time has passed, the universe has changed such that it is false that there is no concretely realized branch from that moment. If (b) is to be maintained, then the branching-futurist will have to suppose that a past configuration of the world exists and grounds the truth of the proposition that both branches were once non-concrete. In other words, there must exist as many worlds as there were once arrangements of the branching structure of the world. There are, therefore, very many more entities in Bourne's ontology than in the eternalist's (or else Bourne must drop at least one of (b) or (c), in section 2.2).

Thirdly, once the Ersatzer is committed to this array of world-configurations, it becomes difficult to see how the model can do what it is in part designed to do, namely single out a particular moment as the unique present. After all, in each world-configuration, a different moment is present (i.e. a different moment is concrete), so no time is ontologically privileged. In order to regain an ontologically unique present, the Ersatzer will require an additional, *meta*-notion of 'concrete' that will single out one from the vast array of world-configurations, i.e. the one that represents the present. This meta-concreteness must then move from one configuration to another as time advances. But a renewed conflict with the truth-value links reasserts itself, for now that the meta-present has moved on from a past time t, we must ask: in virtue of what is it true that t once was meta-concrete? It appears that we will need meta-meta-concreteness, and so on *ad infinitum*. The model is becoming increasingly cumbersome and unwieldy; in short, increasingly unbelievable.

In sum, I think that Bourne's version of the branching future ontology doesn't succeed. To retain the truth-value links he must commit to indefinitely many ersatz universes (what I've called 'world-configurations') that serve to ground propositions about the past. Despite all that, it remains unclear how the view is to explain the passage of time—the successive concrete realization of one branch at the expense of others—without running into regress problems. It seems that Bourne may have to surrender the truth-value links or the demand for truthmakers after all, a choice the eternalist can avoid.

2.4.2 Branch attrition and contextual truth

John MacFarlane (2003) defends a branching future ontology that commits to concrete branches and robust branch attrition. He does so by arguing for a new method of assessing the truth of utterances. Let us examine the prospects of such a view.

Imagine that we look back two days in time and consider an utterance of 'There will be a sea battle tomorrow' that occurred then. Since one branch has been actualized at the expense of the others, we may assume that the sea battle came to pass. Accordingly, it seems wrong to assign any semantic value other than 'true' to the utterance at that time. MacFarlane calls this the 'determinacy intuition':

> Those who have tried to save the determinacy intuition have typically resorted to the following expedient. Out of all the possible futures at the moment of utterance, one is marked out as 'the actual future', as if with a 'thin red line'... The thin red line is an objective feature of the context of utterance, but not an epistemically accessible one, except by waiting. Positing such a thin red line looks like a way to eat our cake and have it too. By supposing that there are many objectively possible future histories, we hang on to objective indeterminism, and by positing the thin red line, we get the determinate truth-values we need for 'retrospective' assessments of utterances. We are not forced to say, as the supervaluationist does, that assertions of future contingents are neither true nor false. (MacFarlane 2003, p. 325)

MacFarlane resists the thin red line for, he argues, it renders indeterminacy merely epistemic (MacFarlane 2003, pp. 325–6). Instead he argues that the determinacy and indeterminacy intuitions can both be accommodated if we give up the idea that 'utterance truth' is absolute, i.e. independent of the time at which the utterance is *assessed* (MacFarlane 2003, pp. 328–32). Instead, he argues that the truth of an utterance is evaluated on the basis of all the histories that are common to both the time of utterance and the time of assessment (MacFarlane 2003, p. 331).

Suppose again that S utters, at t_0, 'there will be a sea battle tomorrow' and that there are two future branches from t_0: one, h_1, with a sea battle the next day (call this time t_1); and another, h_2, with no sea battle the next day (call this time t_2). Since utterance truth depends on both the context of utterance and the context of assessment, the following all hold: the utterance is true if the context of assessment is t_1 (because there is a sea battle on h_1); false if it is t_2 (no sea battle on h_2); and neither true nor false if it is t_0 (both future histories are possible). In this way, both the determinacy and indeterminacy intuitions, each of which is compelling to MacFarlane, are preserved.

MacFarlane is concerned with *utterance* truth rather than the truth of the proposition expressed by an utterance. There is a thought, expressed by Evans (1985), that unless we aim, in our utterances, at stable truth-values, the point of making an assertion becomes incomprehensible. If, to put it briefly, S is unsure which context of assessment will be relevant for the truth of her utterance, and if her aim is to state the truth, then there is no way for her to determine what she is to assert.

MacFarlane's response is that, when committing oneself to the truth of one's assertions, one is:

committed to producing a justification, that is, giving adequate reasons for thinking that the sentence is true (relative to its context of utterance and the asserter's current context of assessment), whenever the assertion is challenged. (MacFarlane 2003, p. 335)

So assertions are provisional: if one can't meet a challenge, one must withdraw it. At t_0, S must withdraw her assertion of 'there will be a sea battle tomorrow', for there is nothing she can point to that can meet the indeterminacy objection. At t_1, on the other hand, the *original* assertion can be defended against challenges by pointing to the raging battle. As long as one can meet a challenge at the time at which it is raised, the assertion may stand; otherwise, it must be withdrawn.

This is an interesting way to maintain two apparently competing thoughts about the future tense. It is, however, ultimately unsatisfactory in a familiar way: it conflicts with the truth-value links and grounding.

At first blush it appears as if context of assessment sensitivity ('a-contextuality', as MacFarlane puts it) in fact rescues the truth-value links. After all, from the perspective of, say, t_1, not only is the past utterance of 'there will be a sea battle tomorrow' true, it is clear that it will be the case that it was true at t_1, since all future histories will include t_1. Similarly, from t_2, the same utterance is not only false, but will continue to be false, at t_2, from all future a-contexts.

The problem arises, however, when we attempt to recover what we want to say about the utterance *when it was initially made*. Imagine that the time is t_1. From this a-context, it turns out that the original utterance, u, is now true. Since, according to MacFarlane, future contingents are necessarily indeterminate, we must also agree that when u originally occurred, at t_0, it was not true; i.e. from the a-context of t_0, u is indeterminate. But MacFarlane rejects the thin red line: today, from a-context t_1, there exists no branch from t_0 that does *not* contain a sea battle the next day: branch h_2 has disappeared from existence. But it was the existence of objective possibilities that justified the claim that utterances about the future are logically indeterminate. Hence, the ground for the claim that u is indeterminate at t_0 no longer exists at t_1. There is, in other words, no longer any good reason to say that u *was* indeterminate.

We are compelled to conclude not only that u is true, but that it was true as well, thus contradicting the claim that the future was once indeterminate.

This undermines MacFarlane's semantics, which include the claim that even at t_1 we can say that u is indeterminate at a-context t_0; this cannot hold at t_1, since at t_1, t_0's a-context lacks future indeterminacy. So it turns out that MacFarlane must reject the truth-value links, which inform us that if a proposition is (currently) indeterminate, then it will be the case thereafter that it was indeterminate. Unless all t_0-branches continue to exist at t_1, i.e. unless we accept the existence of the thin red line, this simple formula is invalid.

We can now see that the metaphysical view that underlies MacFarlane's compromise position—namely, branch attrition—cannot be straightforwardly stated. It is supposed to be the view that while at a given time, t_0, the future contains many equally possible future histories that branch from t_0, at a later time, t_1, all branches between t_0 and t_1, except for one, no longer exist. But then, at t_1, the ground for the claim that there once was more than one history that branched from t_0 has ceased to exist, and there is nothing that can meet the challenge to withdraw that claim: even evidence that all parties, in the past, *agreed* that future branches (then) existed is insufficient; since we are raising the challenge now, we are forced to admit that the claim is ungrounded.

If we suppose that it is now time t_1 and that the universe nevertheless contains branch h_2, then there exists something to ground the claim that u was indeterminate at t_0. But then we must conclude that h_2 continues to exist, and this is precisely the view that MacFarlane wishes to deny, for it removes genuine branch attrition.

The general challenge for the defender of branch attrition, then, is to ground the truth of a proposition that is central to defining branch attrition itself, namely:

(A)   That the universe once contained more branches than it does today

This appears to be a central meta-thesis of the view, necessary for the branch-attritionist to describe her theory. However, branches that were real but have been eliminated no longer exist, so there is nothing to ground the truth of (A). The question, then, is: can this view consistently describe itself?

Storrs McCall, a prominent defender of the branching future ontology with branch attrition, insists that, though past branches no longer exist, they are nevertheless available to us for our analyses. For example:

If Napoleon had won the battle of Waterloo, he would not have died on St Helena. Assuming the conditional is true, what makes it true? Letting W = Napoleon wins at Waterloo, and H = Napoleon dies on St Helena ... [t]he truth of $W \rightarrow \sim H$ consists in the fact that every W-branch in the model is a $\sim H$-branch. Since W is false and H is true in the actual world, the branches on which the truth of $W \rightarrow \sim H$ depends no longer form part of the branched model today. They are not, however, lost to counterfactual analysis, but can be resurrected, since they formed part of past branched models depicted in 'snapshots' of the universe which date back to 1814 and earlier. (McCall 1994, pp. 173–4)

What, however, does it mean to claim that past branches are available for counterfactual analysis?[17] It suggests that past branches are to be considered members of our ontology, something to which we ontologically commit:

> Though past branches do not exist today in the sense of forming part of today's branched model, they used to exist... This past existence is entirely 'objective', and will be appealed to and made use of for the purpose of evaluating counterfactuals... A complete semantics for conditionals of all sorts, including counterfactuals, will require as model structures not only the *present* form of the universe tree... but all its *past* forms as well. (McCall 1994, p. 174)

This is, however, hard to combine with what McCall claims elsewhere:

> Consider the story of Nerlich's 1959 daughter who never got conceived or born... Before conception in 1959, each gamete had a chance to win the race; by chance one won and the other lost, meaning that the branch containing the XY zygote became part of the past trunk and the branch containing the XX zygote vanished. Furthermore, it vanished without trace. The past contains only those things that succeeded in achieving actuality, with no record of those that failed. (McCall 1998, p. 318)

This leads to an unhappy dilemma. On the one hand, to model the dynamic features of time, branch elimination must be a genuine, ontological process; particular branches are supposed to vanish without any ontological trace; on the other hand, to describe the branch attrition model itself, unactualized future histories must persist after their chance at actualization has passed. If the former is the case, then the universe, at any given time, contains insufficient structure to ground the truth of (A), in which case it is impossible to describe the model on its own terms.[18] If the latter is the case, then branch attrition is not genuine: we are either back at some kind of thin red line view, or else past world-configurations (and, perhaps, meta-configurations, etc.) must persist to ground propositions about the branching

---

[17] Whatever account the eternalist wishes to give of counterfactuals, she can rest assured that her analysis will not put her at an ontological disadvantage compared to the branching future model of time. To see this, consider that it is generally agreed that the most ontologically extravagant analysis of counterfactuals would be one done in terms of David Lewis's modal realism (Lewis 1986). On such a strategy the truth of, for example, $H \rightarrow \sim W$ is grounded in the fact that every H world is a $\sim W$ world. The branching-futurist is hardly in a position to object to this because it is hard to see what ontological scruples would counsel *against* non-actual concrete worlds but in *favour* of non-actual concrete world histories; indeed, since the set of possible worlds is unchanging, there is no grounding problem for modal realism analogous to the one for the branching future ontology. So, eternalism is not going to incur greater ontological costs than McCall's theory, however it analyses counterfactuals.

[18] McCall writes of something he calls 'Big-W' (see McCall 1998, pp. 317–18) which contains sub-models which undergo branch attrition while Big-W remains unchanged. The various sub-models allow for relativistic variation in the ordering of events. I don't see how this set-up can help. After all, each sub-model will face the same dilemma: do the branches disappear entirely or do they persist? Either way it will be impossible to combine both temporal passage and the correct semantic principles. If they disappear from the sub-model but persist in Big-W, then it seems to me that Big-W simply represents all the indefinitely many universe configurations that exist, and the branching ontologist does indeed have an explosive ontology.

model itself. The thin red line view renders branches superfluous and the world-configuration view entails an ontological explosion.

It is possible, I suppose, for McCall to argue that branch attrition is a primitive, inexplicable process, but this would clash quite obviously with (b) from section 2.2, for the truthmaker of a central thesis of the view is rendered mysterious. Moreover, this move shows eternalism in a very favourable light, for it need rest on no such primitive, unexplained notion.

It appears, therefore, that there is no satisfactory branching model on offer. Given the serious difficulties with the empty future view, it is best to reject the notion that the future is either ontologically or semantically distinguished from the past and present. Eternalism not only avoids the problems of these two ontological theories, but is seen to be ontologically simpler and subject to fewer primitives.

2.5 More on the truth-value links

In this section I defend the truth-value links in more detail. The phrase 'truth-value link' comes from Dummett (1978a):

If I now (2:45 p.m. 12 February 1969) say, 'I am in my College room', I make a present-tense statement which is, as I say it, true: let us call this statement *A*. Suppose now that exactly one year later someone makes the statement (call it *B*) 'A year ago Dummett was in his College room'. Then it is a consequence of the truth-value link that, since the statement *A* is now true, the statement *B*, made in one year's time, is likewise true. (Dummett 1978a, p. 363)

In this quotation Dummett mentions what I have referred to as (TV1), but most discussions include (TV2) as well.[19] In a linear eternalist system, both principles will probably appear persuasive, but what about in the context of branching time?

Anybody drawn to a branching future ontology with genuine contingency concerning which branch is realized may be inclined to reject (TV2): that a particular branch *is* realized won't entail, on such a view, that in the past it *was the case* that such a branch *will be* realized. So, the branching future ontology may be seen as *motivating* the rejection of the second truth-value link.[20] In what follows I argue both that there is good reason to accept (TV1) and that the branching future ontology cannot in fact motivate the rejection of (TV2), so that both links are secure.

In most cases, the branching-futurist doesn't deny (TV1). Once, for instance, a particular event occurs, the event will remain part of every future history, so it will be the case thereafter that the event occurred. However, I argue above that there are many cases in which the branching-futurist will have to deny (TV1) and the question

---

[19] See, for example, Bourne (2006a, 2006b), Gallois (1997), Ludlow (1999), Sider (2001), Weiss (1996), and Wright (1993).

[20] Thanks to an anonymous referee for pressing this point. For more on branching futures see Lucas (1989), and Belnap, Perloff, and Xu (2001).

is whether such denials are well motivated. The primary kind of case in which the branching-futurist denies (TV1) consists of explanations of the branching future model itself. In particular, *retroactive indeterminacy* appears to be ungrounded on any model that includes genuine branch attrition. Hence, the branching-futurist is forced to reject (TV1) but in so doing undermines the model itself because certain, important past facts about the universe have, at any given time, no ontological grounding on this model. Put another way, for each time, t, some allegedly past features of the model lack truthmakers, and therefore the model will always lack grounds for allegedly true self-descriptions. A similar problem, as argued above (section 2.3), plagues the empty future model. In other words, the cost to the branching- or empty-futurist of denying (TV1) is the inability to ground her own model.

Now I think there is very strong independent reason to accept (TV1), for it rests on two very appealing ideas: (i) that the past is fixed; and (ii) that what is present becomes past (unless the present is the last moment of time; more on that in a moment). To see why (i) must be true, suppose it was the case at some past time, t, that p (perhaps p is the proposition that Socrates is sitting and he was sitting at t); in other words, Pp is true now. If we reject the fixity of the past, then it follows that, even though Pp is true, it is somehow possible for it to come to be in the future that p *was not* the case at t; i.e. ~Pp. But ~Pp entails that there was never an earlier time at which p was the case, which contradicts the assumption that Pp is true now (here I assume 'P' to be equivalent to 'at some past time...'). This means that so long as Pp is true, it will always be true thereafter.

We can look at it the other way around: suppose that even though Pp is true today, tomorrow ~Pp will be true. If ~Pp is true tomorrow, then p was never the case before that day (i.e. 'it is not the case that: at some past time, p'). This, however, contradicts the assumption that Pp was true the day before. Once again, given Pp it will always be the case that Pp. So, the past is fixed. This is, of course, a common assumption, but here is one representative expression of the idea:

The second ingredient is again a very appealing, natural idea—one is tempted to say an assumption of common sense. It captures the intuitive idea that the past is currently 'fixed' and 'out of our control'... if a person's performing a certain action would require some actual fact about the past *not* to have been a fact, then the person *cannot* perform the act. (Fischer 1994, p. 9)

It is worth noting that one way around the fixity of the past condition is to adopt a branching *past* ontology according to which new past histories come into existence with the passage of time. On such a view, it might be the case now that all past branches include Socrates sitting at t, but in the future those branches disappear and new past histories come into existence that lack any sitting by Socrates at t. I have more to say on this below, but for now note that whatever this view is, it is not a branching *future* or empty *future* model, each of which includes a single, fixed past history. So while a branching past view may, for now, be taken to be logically possible, it cannot be used by the branching- or empty-futurist to motivate a rejection of (TV1).

Now to (ii): could the past be anything other than the formerly present? Is it possible, for example, for a sequence of events, all located earlier than today, to come into existence tomorrow, not having existed before then? On the face of it, this appears to be a contradiction: some set of events, {E}, both exists earlier than today but also never existed prior to tomorrow. At the very least, such a scenario would violate the fixity of the past condition since it could be true on, for example, Tuesday that at no earlier time does an event, *e*, exist but true on Wednesday that at some time earlier than Tuesday, *e* exists.

The one way I could imagine one wishing to object to this argument would be to argue that truth is relative to a time. This will not work, for familiar reasons: suppose, on Wednesday, one wishes to express the proposition that on Tuesday *e* did not exist on Monday, a proposition that is by hypothesis true. Such a proposition is ungrounded, for the world, on Wednesday, contains *e* occurring on Monday. Either the Monday that lacked *e* has disappeared from existence, in which case no ground for the proposition exists, or else *two* pasts exist, one with a Monday that contains *e*, another with a Monday that does not. This, of course, is back to the branching *past* ontology, so is of no use to McFarlane and McCall. Moreover, as I argue below, a branching past ontology will suffer from the inability to coherently describe itself just as the branching future view does. Finally, if two pasts exist, then it is not *true* that on Tuesday *e* did not exist on Monday but, rather, *indeterminate*, which is not what is needed to correctly describe the situation.

I conclude that whatever has occurred at some past time, *t*, has never not occurred at *t*. So, if *e* is present and the present is not the last moment of time, then *e* will be past simply because the present is past relative to all later times. Hence, (ii) is true.

If we put (i) and (ii) together, then it follows that whatever is the case right now will forever after be the case. Again, not an uncommon view, but here is one nice expression of it:

...whenever something happens, no matter how trivial...[it] will always be that this once was, even if people in the future may not *remember*, and even if no evidence remains that would enable them to find out. (McKinnon and Bigelow 2012, p. 254)

So, I conclude that (TV1) has excellent independent motivation.

So much for (TV1); what about (TV2)? Recall that the reason that the branching-futurist denies (TV2) is that in the past there *existed* branches (from, say, past time *t*) that don't exist today, and it is in virtue of those once extant branches from *t* that propositions about what would happen later than *t* *were* indeterminate. As I have argued, however, the branching-futurist *has no ontological ground* for the proposition that past branches once existed and, therefore, no ground for the claim that propositions about what would happen after t were indeterminate then (the only alternative is to reject branch attrition, which neither MacFarlane nor McCall want to do). In other words, there are no ontological grounds for the denial of (TV2) on this model.

Similarly, the empty-futurist may deny (TV2) on the grounds that when some past time, t, was present, there existed nothing later than t, which rendered any proposition, Fp, about what would be the case after t indeterminate then. Now, however, there exists nothing to ground the proposition that it once was the case that nothing existed later than t. So, there is no ontological ground for the proposition that it was once, i.e. at t, indeterminate whether or not p will be the case; that is, the grounds for rejecting (TV2) are missing. In sum: (1) there is independent motivation for (TV1); (2) the rejection of (TV1) will entail that the branching future and empty future models lack grounds for the description of certain aspects of the past *as it is according to these models*; and (3) the lack of these grounds undermines the rejection of (TV2).[21] I see, in short, no reasonable way for *either* truth-value link to be denied on the basis of the branching future or empty future ontology.

I want now to return to two issues noted in passing above: first that (TV1) fails for a model that includes a last moment of time (and, similarly, that (TV2) fails for models that include a first moment of time); secondly, that branching past ontologies may motivate rejection of the fixity of the past.

Suppose that the universe ends at a particular time, T. Suppose further, and for simplicity, that all that occurs at T is a single event, E, perhaps a bright flash of light. If P is the proposition that E occurs at T, it seems false to suppose that it will be the case that it was the case that P, simply because nothing is the case after T.[22] One thing that can be said right away is that while (TV1) may not hold of every time, nevertheless the fixity/inalterability of the past will entail that (TV1) holds for all times prior to T. In particular, even on the empty and branching future models, if e occurs at t, then it remains the case for any time later than t that e occurs at t. So, in neither model is there any retroactive alteration of past events, even if there is a last moment of time.

---

[21] Here is a further reason to be suspicious of the rejection of (TV2). Suppose that at t there exist multiple future branches and it is, allegedly, indeterminate which will be realized. Suppose further that at $t' > t$ a particular branch, B, is realized. Why isn't it a fact even at t that B *will* be realized? While there is, by hypothesis, no fact of the matter *at t* as to which branch will be realized, there is a fact of the matter at t'; and why can't future facts be included in one's ontology? Notice that, if the arguments above are right, the branching-futurist must insist that there are facts about the past structure of the tree even though there exists nothing right now to ground those facts. But here is an analogous move for the future: while nothing *currently* grounds the fact as to which branch will be realized, there *will* be such a fact and this renders propositions about the future true even today. Unless one thinks that all facts must be grounded in what is present (which the branching-futurist must deny), I think that the rejection of (TV2) is not well motivated on the branching future (or empty future, *mutatis mutandis*) model.

[22] Thanks to an anonymous referee for bringing this point to my attention.

Accordingly, I don't think that the existence of models in which, for some times, (TV1) fails undermines the above arguments against the branching and empty future models. Note, first, that the empty and branching future models *presuppose* the existence of more than one time because any model that contains only one time will not be a model that exhibits either growth by accretion of facts or else branch attrition. Since, therefore, any branching or empty future model worth considering contains more than one time, the fixity of the past entails that (TV1) applies to at least one time in either model. In that case, however, either the past once contained fewer events than it does now (empty future model) or the past once contained branches that no longer exist (branching future model). As I have argued, neither of these dynamic, structural features of the model have ontological grounds, as they ought to have if the past is fixed. So even branching future and empty future models that contain a last moment of time will be ungrounded. The same applies, *mutatis mutandis*, to the failure of (TV2) on models with a first moment of time: so long as more than one time exists, genuine branch attrition and growth by accretion of facts will be ungrounded and, therefore, so will be the rejection of (TV2).

The fact that the truth-value links may fail for some times gives us a clue to their content. We can't assume that for each time there exists a time later than it, but if the past is fixed then we can commit to the following:

(TV1*) If p is a true proposition about the present time, t, then if there is a time, t', such that t' is later than (future with respect to) t, then it will be the case that it was the case that p.

(TV2*) If p is a true proposition about the present time, t, then if there is a time, t', such that t' is earlier than (past with respect to) t, then it was the case that it will be the case that p.

(TV1*) and (TV2*) are, I think, undeniable. First, it is trivial that if t' is later than (or future with respect to) t, then t is earlier than (or past with respect to) t', and vice versa; so if p reports some occurrence at t, then it is trivial that that occurrence is past relative to a later time and future relative to an earlier time. Secondly, note that these truth-value links, being conditional in form, hold for models of time that include a last or first moment: if there is a last moment of time, T, then when $t = $ T the consequent of (TV1*) will be true because it (the consequent) has a false antecedent, in which case the entire conditional, (TV1*), is true; similarly, if T is the first moment of time, then when $t = $ T, (TV2*) is true because its consequent has a false antecedent, in which case it is true. Hence, (TV1*) and (TV2*) can be used justifiably to evaluate any empty and branching future models that include more than one time and can be substituted for (TV1) and (TV2) in the arguments above if so desired.

Now to the second issue, namely that one might suppose that (TV1) fails because the past is ontologically indeterminate; that there is no fact of the matter as to what has occurred. As I have noted, such a route is not available to defenders of the

Tooley–Broad or MacFarlane–McCall models, both of which include a single, onto-logically determinate past. Indeed, the difference between determinacy and indeter-minacy is what distinguishes the future from the past on such views. However, I would like to briefly comment on the possibility of a temporal model that includes an indeterminate past.

Consider, first, the hypothetical inverse of the Tooley–Broad ontology, what we might call the 'empty past' model, according to which the present and future exist as a single timeline but in which the passage of time consists of the continual extinction of slices of reality from the 'back' ('the universe shrinks by the *deletion* of facts'). On this view, something is present in virtue of having nothing *earlier* than it while having something later than it, and as time passes, what is present disappears from existence. Such a model will face the same problem that the empty future model faces, namely that it cannot describe itself: once the universe has shrunk by deletion of facts, there will no longer exist a truthmaker for the proposition that the universe once contained entities that no longer exist. Similarly, at no time is there a truthmaker for the proposition *that soon the universe will contain fewer entities than it has now*. In short, the empty past model is self-undermining.

Next, consider the inverse of the branching future model, in which the past consists of multiple, unrealized branches while the present and future form a single history. On such a view, the passage of time will have to consist in branch *acquisition*, which leads to a familiar problem: in virtue of what will it ever be true that the universe once contained fewer branches than it does now? At time *t* the past will consist of the full array of possible histories and there will be no ontological ground for the claim that some of those branches were once unreal. Similarly, the model will lack ontological grounds for the proposition that the future will contain branches that it currently does not.

In sum, the inverse of the empty and branching future models appear to be as unsatisfactory as the originals. Any view in which only the past and present are ontologically determinate is unsatisfactory, as is any view in which only the future and present are ontologically determinate. Of course, the various combinations of such views will be unsatisfactory as well (e.g. an empty past combined with a branching future; a branching past and branching future; a branching past and an empty future; etc.) since each part will inherit both sets of difficulties outlined above.

There is one potential argument against the truth-value links that I haven't yet considered: an argument based on verificationism. The idea here is that since (i) truth is not evidence transcendent and (ii) evidence can disappear, it can be the case both that *p* is true and that in the future *it was the case that p* is false. Since such a position does not ontologically distinguish the past and future (after all, we can lack evidence for both), I will postpone discussion of this objection until the next chapter, where I consider presentism, the doctrine that only the present is real.

2.6 Conclusion

There are two prominent families of theory that attempt to ontologically distinguish
the future from the present and past: the empty future view, according to which the
future is a realm of non-being, and the branching future view, according to which the
future is a realm of multiple, unrealized histories. I have argued that both kinds of
theory fail because they are committed to, and based on, models that are incapable
of grounding central aspects of those very theories, namely that what is present will
be past and that what is present was once future. This completes one half of the
argument for eternalism.[23] The other half is to reject presentism, the view that
ontologically distinguishes the future *and* past from the present by denying the
reality of *both* the past and future. If presentism is found to be unsatisfactory, then
the only remaining model of time is one in which all regions of time are on an
ontological par, i.e. eternalism.[24] I turn next, therefore, to a consideration of
presentism.

---

[23] I shall mention, though I think it is obvious, that eternalism does not entail that the future is
predictable. This is because neither ontological nor semantic determinacy entails current epistemic
accessibility. For example the proposition that 'the exact number of hairs on the first member of *Homo
sapiens* is *n*' may be determinately true but in principle unknowable at this time. Similarly, propositions
about the future can be semantically determinate but unknowable now (they are most likely unknowable
now because our cognitive faculties evolved in the context of the second law of thermodynamics, which
entails that later states of a system are closer to equilibrium than earlier states, or because knowledge entails
causally interacting with one's environment and causation is temporally asymmetric; both relations can
hold, however, between equally real relata, so the eternalist can appeal to either to explain the knowledge
asymmetry (see e.g. Horwich 1987 or Price 1996).

[24] Well, not quite. In Chapter 3 I consider two other alternatives as well, deriving from Skow (2012) and
Fine (2005, 2006).

3

Restricting reality to the present

3.1 Introduction

According to *presentism*, neither the past nor the future exists.[1] This may seem trivial. For instance, though Caesar existed, he is dead so he does not exist; similarly, those who are yet to be born will exist but do not. The problems arise when we consider propositions about the past and future: in virtue of what are they true? A natural answer is that they are true in virtue of the past and future: it is true that Caesar crossed the Rubicon because he in fact did just that. But if that crossing event doesn't exist, then there is nothing to ground the truth of the proposition, so it seems it cannot be true, which is absurd. So the argument goes. Put more generally, the past did exist, and the future will, hopefully, exist, but in virtue of what is this general proposition about the universe true, if only the present exists?

3.2 Tense and presentism

Consider the following:

[P]resentism is the claim that it is always the case that, quantifying unrestrictedly, for every *x*, *x* is present. (Crisp 2007, p. 107)

According to Presentism, if we were to make an accurate list of all the things that exist—i.e. a list of all the things that our most unrestricted quantifiers range over—there would be not a single non-present object on the list. (Markosian 2004, p. 47)

I am using the sentence 'Only presently existing things exist' and its companions, such as 'Only presently red things are red', to distinguish the presentists from the eternalists. To serve this purpose, these 'test' sentences must be given a particular interpretation. The quantifiers should be read as unrestricted quantifiers; the tokens of 'exists' should be understood as tokens of a nonindexical 'exists' and as tokens of the same word; and 'presently' should be read as an indexical tense operator. Working under these stipulations, we can see that the sentence 'Newton exists' will express the same proposition at different times, and the sentence 'Newton

---

[1] For some examples, see Bigelow (1996), Bourne (2006a, 2006b), Chisholm (1990), Craig (1998), Crisp (2005, 2007), Hinchliff (1996, 2000), Markosian (2004), Prior (1962, 1970), Sider (1999), Zimmerman (1998).

presently exists' will express different propositions at different times. (Hinchliff 2000, pp. 576–7)

In each passage, appeal is made to an *unrestricted* quantifier, in particular a *temporally* unrestricted quantifier. There is a good reason for this. For the presentist, only what is present exists. If 'exists' is in the present tense, then 'only what is present exists' is equivalent to 'only what is present exists now'. This is a trivial truth. If 'exists' is in the past or future tense, then 'only what is present exists' is equivalent to 'only what is present did/will exist', which is obviously false (Caesar doesn't exist, but he did). What is needed, to express an interesting version of presentism, is a sense of 'exists' that is not restricted to the present or any temporal region. Such a sense would be insensitive to when things occur, including its own utterances, and could be contrasted with the ordinary, present-tense 'exists', which entails that something is present. A temporally unrestricted quantifier is supposed to supply this unrestricted sense.

To exist (present tense) is to exist now. To exist in the temporally unrestricted sense is to exist *at some time or another*. Let us use 'exists$_1$' for the tensed version of 'exists' and 'exists$_2$' for the temporally unrestricted, or tenseless, sense of 'exists'.[2] It might be helpful to think of exists$_2$ along the lines of the existential quantifier in standard first order logic.

With these distinctions in hand, we can try to formulate presentism as follows:

(1)   Only what is present exists$_2$.

Alternatively:

(2)   Only what exists$_1$ exists$_2$.

We might think of this as follows. The temporally unrestricted quantifier passes its gaze over all of time as a whole: it invites into its domain anything that is past, present, or future. According to the presentist, however, this quantifier is perennially disappointed.

One more modification is required. Presentism is a metaphysical thesis. It is not, in other words, that it just so happens that nothing non-present exists (that is exists$_2$). This is not supposed to be an empirical discovery. Rather, it is, according to presentism, a necessary truth:

A presentist thinks that everything is present; more generally, that, necessarily, it is always true that everything is (then) present. (Sider 1999, p. 326)

So the following more completely captures the presentist doctrine:

---

[2]   We can also distinguish two senses of the copula is$_1$ and is$_2$ such that 'x is$_1$ F' entails 'x is now F' but 'x is$_2$ F' does not.

(3)   Necessarily: only that which exists$_1$ exists$_2$,

where the necessity is understood as metaphysical.

Tom Stoneham brings up an interesting point:

while 'Mary laughs at midday on the 14th July 2006' conveys no information about whether the date in question is before, after, or contemporary with the utterance, it is not thereby tenseless because it is simply elliptical for 'Mary laughs, laughed or will laugh on the 14th July 2006'... 'Mary laughed' tells us that there was a laughing by Mary prior to the assertion of that sentence. Consequently, one might think that the failure to convey such information would be sufficient for tenseless predication. But this would be a mistake, for a disjunction of tenses conveys no such information, but is not the sort of tenseless predication required to state the conflicting theses of presentism and eternalism. (Stoneham 2009, p. 203)

This is worth taking seriously. If tenseless existence, existence$_2$, is just existence *at some time or another*, then 'x exists$_2$' would seem to be equivalent to 'x is, was, or will be' (for any time you wish to consider as present). But if that is true, then (3) is equivalent to the following:

(3')   Necessarily: only what exists now exists now, did exist, or will exist.

This, as noted, is obviously false, in which case it is unclear that an acceptable description of presentism has been provided.

There is a solution to this problem. We could take the temporally unrestricted quantifier to be *absolutely* unrestricted, in which case to exist$_2$ is to exist *simpliciter*, even outside of time, as an abstract entity. Tenseless existence, then, should be thought of as existence *simpliciter* applied to entities that stand in relations to time, while abstract existence is existence *simpliciter* applied to entities that lack such relations. On this understanding, (3) is more like:

(3'')   Necessarily: only what is present has being, in any sense.

This might seem unsatisfactory as well, however, as it suggests that the presentist is committed to denying that abstract objects could exist since presumably they don't exist in the present; this seems unfair. Indeed, ersatz presentists (see section 3.3.2) take past and future times to be abstract entities.

I think the presentist can reply that abstract objects are at no temporal 'distance' from the present: they aren't present, but they aren't past or future either. In that case, presentism becomes the view that only things that are at no temporal distance from the present exist:

(4)   Necessarily: only what exists$_1$ or is atemporal exists$_2$.

In other words, the presentist insists that a complete inventory of the world, at any given time, includes only those things that exist at that time and whatever abstract entities there are. The eternalist believes that such an inventory also includes the entities that exist at times other than the one under consideration.

Stoneham remains unconvinced. He thinks that we lack an atemporal concept of existence:

So imagine that we are talking about Pythagoras, then we might quite intelligibly say '$\sqrt{2}$ was irrational, though he did not know it'. So tensed predication of necessary properties to numbers does make sense and we have no compelling reason to think that '3 is prime' is an uncontroversial example of tenseless predication. (2009, p. 205)

I have to admit that, to my ears, '$\sqrt{2}$ was irrational' sounds improper unless we are talking about a proof procedure or a set of numerals; as a claim about a number, I don't see how it can properly be said to *have had* certain properties, for this would imply that the number instantiates temporal relations. Moreover, I am not sure that the fact that it 'makes sense' to predicate necessary properties of numbers using tensed language shows that '3 is prime' is not an example of tenseless, atemporal predication. After all, how can we be sure that '$\sqrt{2}$ was irrational, though he did not know it' isn't elliptical for 'we now know that $\sqrt{2}$ is (tenselessly) irrational even though Pythagoras did not know this'? Perhaps, when speaking of Pythagoras, we fall into the habit of putting everything in the past tense and keep it up even when discussing the mathematical propositions he pondered. We do this without worrying about the fact that those propositions can't be temporally modified; after all, we can always substitute a more appropriate alternative if need be.

Stoneham counters:

Given that English predication is always tensed, can we really understand the notion of tenseless predication used in the debate? (2009, p. 208)

The fact that our language is tensed does not, however, entail that it is only capable of representing a tensed reality or concept. Even if it is true that *we* need to use tensed language in order to capture this concept, this doesn't mean that there is no concept whose extension is that of existence$_2$ and it even more certainly doesn't mean that reality can't consist of that domain. To argue otherwise is to come dangerously close to the position that features of our language must be features of reality, a fallacy I discuss in section 3.4 (see also Dyke 2008). In the meantime, I simply see no reason to draw the conclusion that tenseless, atemporal concepts are unavailable to us because of grammatical features of our language, so I shall assume in the following that there exists a concept, existence$_2$, that is unrestricted, and that presentism is to be understood along the lines of (4) above.

This does, however, leave the worry about *grounding* intact. In particular, as I have noted, I worry about the statement of presentism itself. Notice that presentists are not, in general, solipsists of the present moment: they believe that time passes and this seems to entail the following:

(5)   What is past was present and what is future will be present.

These are, after all, just general instances of the truth-value links and it seems that if the present is constantly changing, as the presentist can hardly deny, then (5) must be true. I suspect that the presentist model is unable to ground (5); I turn now to the development of this objection.

3.3 The grounding objection

If propositions about the non-present can be true, then it is reasonable to ask the presentist for an account of what exists *in the present* upon which such truths supervene. Consider a proposition such as:

(6)   Anne was Queen of England.

Arthur Prior argues that (6) can be true even if nothing non-present exists because:

the fact that Queen Anne has been dead for some years is not, in the strict sense of 'about', a fact about Queen Anne; it is not a fact about anyone or anything—it is a *general* fact. Or if it is about anything, what it is about is not Queen Anne—it is about the earth, maybe, which has rolled around the sun so many times since there was a person who was called 'Anne', reigned over England, etc. (Prior 1962, p. 13)

If truths about the past and future are about what exists in the present, then the present must be ontologically rich enough to support the true propositions of history. But it appears that the past and future are *underdetermined* by the present, and that is the problem for presentism.

Consider the following propositions:

(7)   There are determinate truths and falsehoods about the past and future.
(8)   Truth supervenes on being.
(9)   The present underdetermines what is true in the past and future.
(10) All and only that which is present exists.
(11) Therefore, there are no determinately true or false propositions about the past or future.

The grounding objection is, in a nutshell, that of all the premises in this *reductio*, (10) is the weakest, so it should be rejected. Let us examine how presentists have responded.

3.3.1 *Property presentism*

John Bigelow argues that one ought to reject premise (9) above:

We do not need to suppose the existence of any past or future things ... only the possession by present things of properties and accidents expressed using the past or future tenses ... What exists in the present is a tract of land which has the accident, of being the earth on which a spark of love kindled a dazzling blaze of pitiless war. Or, what exists in the present is a region of space which has the accident, of being the space within which a Wooden Horse set the towers of Ilium aflame through the midnight issue of Greeks from its womb. (Bigelow 1996, p. 46)

I think, however, that such a view either begs the question against the grounding objection, or else is problematically *ad hoc*. Consider that the state of the world right now is compatible with Caesar crossing the Rubicon and his not crossing the Rubicon: the position, momentum, state, etc. of every physical particle in the universe could be exactly what it is right now, even if Caesar never existed. So, there could be a world indistinguishable from ours today but with a different history. So, if some parcel of land, *p*, has the property *being the place where Caesar crossed the Rubicon*, the having of this property cannot supervene on the structure of the world today. But all tensed properties must do so, for there is nothing else for them to supervene on, according to presentism. Hence, it begs the question to suppose that the world contains such properties.

I imagine Bigelow might reply that there *is* something that distinguishes our world from one in which Caesar never existed, namely the property of *being the place where Caesar crossed the Rubicon*. The problem, however, is that this property would have to be detached from all the physical and mental properties of the world. Imagine a future world in which Roman history is long forgotten: all physical traces and memories of Rome are gone. Even *perfect* knowledge of the state of every physical and mental system on the surface of the Earth at that time would be compatible with the proposition that Caesar never existed. If such a world can still be one in which the property *being the place where Caesar crossed the Rubicon* exists, such a property is of a very unusual kind for it is independent of the entire physical and mental structure of the only reality that exists, i.e. the present (I consider the possibility of appealing to abstract structures elsewhere). This is a suspicious kind of property that looks to be an *ad hoc* posit to rescue the presentist ontology.

An alternative is proposed by Ross Cameron, who writes:

the challenge is to locate properties that do two things at once: make a difference to how their bearers are while they are instantiated, thus being unsuspicious, but also settle how they were, thus providing the required grounding for historical truths. What properties could do both things at once? (Cameron 2013, p. 363)

His response is to propose that:

each thing has the following two properties: a temporal distributional property (TDP), and an age. A TDP describes how its bearer is over time, just like a spatial distributional property describes how its bearer is across space. A thing's having the TDP it has settles the B-theoretic truths about it: that it is at some time this way, and before that it is another way, and after that it is another way, etc. But of course, this is not enough: we need to be able to say how a thing is *now*, and how it *was* and *will be*. (Cameron 2013, p. 363)

So, TDPs are combined with *ages*: 'a property that says of thing simply how far along in its life it is' (Cameron 2013, p. 363). A TDP could be something like the following: *being a child then being an adult then being an old man*. If we combine such properties with an age, we settle the past and future history of the thing.

In order to get clear on my concern with TDPs, it will be necessary to take a look at Cameron's motivation for postulating them. He writes:

> The suspiciousness of properties such as *being such as to have been a child* consists in their not making a contribution to the intrinsic nature of their bearers at the time at which they are instantiated. I think everyone can agree on this as being what is suspicious about Lucretianism [i.e. Bigelow's view] . . . I propose, then, that we constrain the properties we admit into our ontology by only admitting those properties—call them *difference making properties*—the instantiation of which at a time makes a difference to the intrinsic nature of the bearer at that time.
>
> *Intrinsic Determination*: For all objects x and properties F and times t, if x instantiates F at t, then x has the intrinsic nature at t that it has partly *in virtue of* instantiating F at t. (Cameron 2011, pp. 60–1; original emphasis)

This is, as Cameron points out, particularly appealing to the presentist, because if only the present is real, then '[m]y present intrinsic nature is my intrinsic nature *simpliciter*' (Cameron 2011, p. 60).

My worry is that Cameron's intrinsic determination (ID) schema only considers one side of the equation. If something's current intrinsic nature just is its intrinsic nature, *period*, then I think it is clear that it instantiates the difference-making properties it does in virtue of its intrinsic nature. In other words, the instantiation of a difference-making property entails something about an object's intrinsic nature; that's what makes it a difference maker. I think, in fact, that an object's difference-making properties can be equated with its intrinsic nature, but at the very least they will co-vary.

As written, (ID) misses this and it gives the impression that, just so long as a property makes a contribution to an object's current, intrinsic nature, that object can instantiate that property even if it 'points to' or depends on how things were in the past or will be in the future. But what I take to be the central question remains unaddressed, namely, how there can be truths about how things were in the past or will be in the future if presentism is true. Merely *stating* that there are properties such as *having been a child, being an adult, and going to be an old man* doesn't mean that such properties could exist without past and future times, events, states, etc.; so the underdetermination worry hasn't been addressed.

The way an object is, and certainly the way it is intrinsically, cannot depend on the unreal. This principle strikes me as undeniable. A science fiction writer may imagine that the cells in her body are controlled by tiny, powerful alien spacecraft, but if there are no such things, then her intrinsic, cellular nature does not depend on them (that is not to say that her intrinsic nature can't depend on her *imaginings*). A child may believe that the size of the stack of presents in her living room depends on how many items Santa Claus can carry at a time, but if Santa Claus doesn't exist, then the size of the pile of presents cannot depend on his capacities. And so on.

If the past is a species of unreality—not just diminished reality or a different kind of reality, but genuine non-existence—then the current nature of an entity cannot depend on the past. That is what the principle above entails. I believe, as do most presentists, that an object's current nature, even its current intrinsic nature, can depend on the past; that is in part why I believe the past to be real. When presentists insist that an object can depend on the past because the past *was* real, I believe they are, implicitly, taking the eternalist stance: assuming that past properties or states can be appealed to in explaining the current state of things. My response is to insist that the presentist must take the non-existence of the past more seriously: past existence is non-existence; therefore the nature of what exists right now can't depend on the past, which is, of course, unacceptable.

If, on the other hand, the presentist wants to take a different stance toward the past, to assume, for example, that past existence is still a kind of existence, then I have no general objection to the view; it will be the details that matter (see, for example, the discussion of Ersatzer presentism in section 3.3.2). The kind of presentism that I think this principle rules out is one according to which past (and future) existence is non-existence *simpliciter*, in which case past and future events, objects, and properties are on an ontological par with imaginary aliens and Santa Claus, and can have no effect on how things are right now or any other time.

Cameron responds:

> The presentist should grant that I am a temporally extended entity, but deny that my existence thereby requires there to be a region of time in which I temporally extend. The presentist should hold that I can exist even if there is only one instant of time, despite the fact that my existence, shall we say, 'points beyond' that instant. (Cameron 2011, pp. 72–3)

But how can something be temporally extended if only the present (tenselessly) exists? This response strikes me as simply rejecting the principle that an object's intrinsic nature cannot depend on the unreal. If one defends presentism at the cost of rejecting this principle, then I think the presentist can at most win a pyrrhic victory.

3.3.2 *Ersatz times*

Instead of tensed properties, Thomas Crisp (Crisp 2007) posits the existence, in the present, of non-present but *abstract* times. These times are sets of maximal, consistent propositions:

> x is a time $=_{df.}$ For some class C of propositions such that C is *maximal* and *consistent*, $x = [\forall y$ $(y \in C \supset y$ is true)$]$ (Crisp 2007, p. 17)

Informally, these abstract, maximal propositions represent the entire state of the world—i.e. what is true—at a particular moment (Crisp 2007, p. 99).

Crisp argues that abstract times are temporally ordered by a (semantically primitive) 'earlier than' relation. This doesn't add up to a B-series but, rather, an 'ersatz B-series', i.e. an ordering of abstract times/representations that represents a genuine B-series. Though standing in the equivalent of a temporal order, non-present times are at no temporal distance from the present so they can be quantified over and serve as truthmakers right now (Crisp 2007, pp. 98–105). Accordingly, properties such as *being an x such that x ate improperly cooked food one hour ago* are properly viewed along the lines of *being an x such that the proposition that x eats improperly cooked food is included in an earlier time* (Crisp 2007, p. 105).

As a result, Crisp views presentism as the following: only one time, namely the present, is ever *concrete*. Since times are propositional, one could put the same point as the claim that only the present is ever true; all other times are abstract, or false. Of course, which time is true is a constantly changing matter, because time passes. The abstract times, ordered in an ersatz B-series, serve as the grounds for truths about the past and future. So, concludes Crisp, it turns out that the present does not underdetermine the non-present, proposition (9) above may be appropriately denied, and the grounding objection eluded.

The point of Crisp's view is to provide truthmakers for propositions about the past and future. There are, however, some truths that such ersatz times simply cannot ground. For instance, consider an Ersatzer version of (5) above:

(12)   Past (future) ersatz times once were (will be) concrete, present times.

If ersatz-presentism is true, then (12) must be true; otherwise, time doesn't pass. The problem, however, is that the existence of past and future *abstract* times cannot ground the truth of (12): if the existence of ersatz dinosaurs in an ersatz time suffices for the truth of the proposition that there once were dinosaurs, then the proposition that there once were dinosaurs can be true even if there never were concrete dinosaurs, for nothing concrete is needed for the truth of that proposition.

Consider another example: the proposition that Caesar was assassinated. On Crisp's view, the existence of an ersatz time, which includes an abstract Roman ruler and an abstract assassination, is the truthmaker for this proposition. If, however, it is true that Caesar was assassinated, then, because what is past was present, Caesar was once a concretely existing individual and the assassination was a concrete event, existing in actual space and actual time. None of this is entailed by the ersatz time that grounds the truth of the proposition that Caesar was assassinated. An ersatz Caesar can be the subject of an ersatz assassination that is located in an abstract time that is related to other abstract times by a primitive temporal ordering *without* it ever having been true that the ersatz entities were once concrete/true. In short, if an abstract, ersatz time can suffice for the truth of the proposition that Caesar was assassinated, then that proposition can be true even if nothing past was ever concrete. So all instances of (12) remain ungrounded on the ersatz view, even though such instances are essential to presentism.

Now I suppose one may respond that the above reasoning is incorrect: there can only exist an ersatz Caesar suffering an ersatz assassination if Caesar concretely existed. The problem with this reply is that the proposition *that Caesar concretely existed* remains ungrounded on this view: ersatz times are supposed to be what truths about the past supervene on, so unless the existence of an ersatz time can make it the case that Caesar concretely existed, appeal to the latter fact has no place in the theory. Accordingly, the ersatz view does not escape the grounding objection.

3.3.3 Haecceities

It has been suggested that the presentist can reply to the grounding objection by arguing that there currently exist haecceities of non-present entities (Keller 2004; McKinnon and Bigelow 2012). A haecceity is commonly understood to be the property of something's being the thing that it is. It is the property of 'thisness' as Adams puts it (Adams 1979, 1989) that, some argue, can exist even when the thing does not.

Keller writes:

When the [eternalist] talks about Anne Boleyn, he is talking about a person—a concrete thing—but when the presentist talks about Anne Boleyn, she is talking about a property—an abstract thing. (Keller 2004, p. 98)

But this response just seems to provide the wrong kind of truthmaker for past and future propositions. When discussing or thinking of Anne Boleyn, we are talking or thinking about a past *person*, not an abstract entity. Hence, this version of presentism simply seems to mischaracterize the subject matter of tensed thought and talk.

A more pressing problem is that the grounding objection is not in fact circumvented by haecceity-presentism. Indeed, this view faces the same problem as do those of the property-presentist and ersatz-presentist. For consider that if the existence of Caesar's haecceity is sufficient for the truth of the proposition that Caesar existed, then it can be true that Caesar existed even if a concrete Caesar never existed; all that is required is the abstract entity. Or, to take Keller's example, if the referent of 'Anne Boleyn' is an abstract property and this property, and other abstracta, can make 'Anne Boleyn existed in 1536' true, then what need have we to suppose that a concrete Anne ever existed? The current truth of the proposition that Anne Boleyn existed is consistent with her never having existed *concretely*.

It seems that the haecceity-presentist must suppose it to be a primitive metaphysical truth that a past or future entity's haecceity exists if and only if that something did or will exist concretely. Keller, for instance, argues that Anne's haecceity as well as its relations to other haecceities must 'make it the case that on the 19th of May, 1536, Anne did exist' (Keller 2004, p. 99). But if what is meant here is *concrete* existence, then just why and how this is the case is left unexplained, for the existence of an abstract entity does not entail the earlier or later existence of a concrete entity. So, once again, the proposition that the past was concrete and the future will be concrete remains ungrounded.

3.3.4 *Epistemic presentism*

Imagine a presentist who adopts an epistemic theory of content for past and future tense utterances. She may suppose that instead of truth conditions such utterances have verification conditions; they are made true or false by the evidence that exists when they are made. For example, even if Caesar and his stabbing no longer exist, one can have conclusive reason to assert 'Caesar was stabbed' in virtue of the evidence that exists today. Existing documents, artefacts, predictions, photographs, etc. will combine, on this view, with principles of inference to warrant various tensed assertions without committing to the existence of past things.

The difficulty for such a view concerns the truth-value links:

(TV1) $\phi \Rightarrow FP\phi$
(TV2) $\phi \Rightarrow PF\phi$

Anyone defending an epistemic theory of semantic content is going to have a very difficult time motivating the denial of these links for, as Michael Dummett argues (Dummett 1978a), we learn linguistic tense by, in large part, coming to accept the truth-value links. Nonetheless it is precisely these truth-value links that are threatened by an epistemic theory of tensed utterances. The reason is straightforward: there may very well be plenty of evidence available at one time to justify an utterance even though there will be (or was) no evidence that will justify (or did justify) the future (or past tense) of that utterance. Dummett notes the problem:

For you [the epistemic theorist] must surely agree that if, in a year's time, you still maintain the same philosophical views, you will in fact say that, on the supposition we made, namely that all evidence for the truth of the past-tense statement *B* is then lacking, and will always remain so, *B* is *not* true (absolutely). And surely also you must maintain that, in saying that, you will be correct. And this establishes the sense in which you are forced to contradict the truth-value link. (Dummett 1978a, pp. 372–3)

One response to this is to focus on the meaning of the truth-value links in the present. Suppose, in other words, that in accepting the links one does no more than commit *right now* to there being evidence in the future that will justify an utterance in the past tense of a currently justified utterance. It doesn't follow that one will be committed *in the future* to the presence of evidence then. If meaning is tied to evidence, and the evidential basis of utterances changes in time, then perhaps it follows that what is meant by our words varies with time so that what one means now by an utterance doesn't entail a particular future meaning. Dummett writes:

that over which I quantify now when I say, 'There *is* something in virtue of which ...', is not the same as that over which I shall be quantifying when I use the same expression in a year's time. The anti-realist need not hang on to the claim that the meaning of the expression alters: he may replace it by the explanation that he cannot now *say* what he will in a year's time be saying when he uses it. (Dummett 1978a, p. 373)

In other words, if, at time t, evidence warrants acceptance of an utterance, 'u', then there is evidence at t for an utterance of 'PFu' and 'FPu'. So, at any given time, one is committed to the links. If, however, semantic content depends on evidence and evidence changes, then the meaning of an utterance, at $t + n$, of 'Pu' might differ from an utterance, at t, of 'u' so that the link to which one is committed today cannot be assumed to hold across time. In that way, to deny the link at a future time is, in fact, to deny a *different* principle from what is accepted today. Hence, one is never in a position of committing to a contradiction.

This won't, however, work. After all, one knows *right now* that evidence may be lost and, therefore, one knows now that what one asserts in the future by uttering 'Pu' may not mean the same as the utterance, today, of 'u'. Hence, one cannot assume, as Dummett suggests, that evidence for the current truth of 'u' commits the verificationist right now to the truth of a future utterance of 'Pu'; to do so would just be to ignore the impermanence of evidence. If a present-tense utterance, 'u', is true now, then 'Pu', uttered in the future, will only be justified if the requisite evidence survives. But the epistemic-presentist knows that the evidence may not survive. Since that in virtue of which 'u' is now true is not the same as that in virtue of which 'Pu' will be true (if it indeed is), there is no guarantee that the truth of the former will transfer to the latter. The epistemic-presentist knows all this today so she cannot commit to the truth-value links after all.

As I have noted, the truth-value links embody a core commitment of presentism: that the past is the once present and the future the soon to be present. To commit to the links *in the present*, the epistemic-presentist must commit to the inevitable persistence of evidence, which is simply not credible. She must, then, reject the truth-value links after all, and this is simply not a plausible position for her to be in.

3.3.5 *Will quasi-truth do the trick?*

While it may seem that (7) is the strongest part of the grounding objection, some have argued that it can be denied so long as truth, for propositions about the non-present, can be replaced with something 'close enough' to it. For example, Markosian (2004) and Sider (1999) develop the suggestion that propositions about the past and future can be 'quasi-true' even if untrue. If quasi-truth is indeed close *enough* to truth, then perhaps it is less absurd than initially thought to deny that propositions about the past and future are true.

The idea is that a false proposition can be quasi-true if it is false for non-empirical, philosophical reasons. For example, a presentist does not believe that the world today differs *empirically* from how it would be were eternalism true. But since, argues the presentist, eternalism is false for *metaphysical* reasons, it turns out that propositions about the past and future are only quasi-true (Markosian 2004, p. 69).

Sider's version is as follows. Suppose that *P* is false but *Q* is true. Suppose further that *Q* is such that were ontological view *T* true, then *Q* would still be true and would entail *P*. In that case, *P* is quasi-true (Sider 1999, pp. 332–3). Here is an example. Suppose that the presentist denies the existence of singular propositions about Caesar but accepts that there exist general propositions about him. Let *P* be the false, singular proposition that Caesar was bald:

(P)   Bald(Caesar, *t*)

where *t* is a time earlier than the present. *Q* is the general proposition that somebody named Caesar was bald:

(Q) $P[(\exists x)(x = \text{the referent of 'Caesar' and } x \text{ is bald})]$

Let us note three points. First, (Q) is, according to the presentist, true (let us suppose so at any rate). Secondly, (Q) would have been true had eternalism been true. Thirdly, had eternalism been true, (Q) would have entailed (P). Hence, (P) is quasi-true, but false. The idea then is that the presentist can allow that propositions about the past and future are false but quasi-true and that this is sufficient. I don't think this strategy will succeed, for three reasons.

First, as Crisp (2005) points out, the notion of quasi-truth is flawed for it allows almost any proposition to count as quasi-true. To see this consider some arbitrary ontological theory, *O*, such as: necessarily, undetectable peanut butter sandwiches exist. There is at least one proposition that is both true and would be true were *O* true, namely the proposition, *R*, that everything is self-identical (since this proposition is a logical truth it is true in our world and any other metaphysically possible world). Let us now consider a proposition, *S*, that I shall assume is false: that at least one undetectable peanut butter sandwich exists. To use Sider's framework, there is a proposition, *R*, that is not only true but, secondly, would have been true had *O* been true and, thirdly, would have entailed *S* (because if *O* were true then *S* would be a necessary truth and every proposition would entail it). But the proposition that at least one undetectable peanut butter sandwich exists should not have the same alethic status as the proposition that Caesar was bald. If it does then quasi-truth isn't 'near enough' to truth after all.

Secondly, suppose *w* is a world in which only the present exists and in which (Q) is somehow true. It still would *not* be the case, in *w*, that were eternalism true, (Q) would be true and would entail (P). To see this, consider two eternalist worlds, w' and w''. In w' the Caesar of our world exists in the past; w' may be our world, for example. In w'', on the other hand, Caesar does *not* exist, but another person exists in the past who was called 'Caesar' and was bald. In w'' (Q) is true but does not entail (P), for (P) is the proposition that *Caesar* was bald yet Caesar does not exist in w''. So it would seem that (P) is not quasi-true after all.

The third worry is less formal and centres on the concern that there is something simply unbelievable about any view that denies that propositions about the non-present can be *straightforwardly* true. It is simply hard to accept that a simple proposition such as that I drove to work this morning is not *true*. This morning's drive does not seem sufficiently distinct from, say, my current typing such that it is, strictly speaking, not true that the former occurred but true that the latter is occurring:

there is not the same metaphysical distance, intuitively speaking, between the present time and other times as there is between the actual world and other worlds. The entirety of what goes on at the present time and at other times is somehow part of the same all-encompassing reality in a way in which what goes in the actual worlds and in other possible worlds is not. (Fine 2006, p. 401)

This seems right and, if so, then it is hard to see why claims about the past can't simply be true. Combined with the technical difficulties attaching to quasi-truth, I think this spells the end of this proposed way out of the grounding objection.

3.4 More on truthmaking and grounding

Let me pause to take stock. I have argued that presentists are unable to properly ground their theory: there must be truths about the past and future that are simply not accounted for in the presentist model because what exists on that model underdetermines what was and what will be; most importantly, it underdetermines the general class of propositions to which presentism itself is committed.

Now, some have argued that arguments such as those miss the mark because the presentist has the right to insist on a *tensed* version of the requirement that truth supervenes on being. In other words, a proposition, p, is grounded so long as there existed, exists, or will exist something upon which its truth supervenes. If we accept this tensed version of grounding, then:

The presentist can then hold that while *that there were dinosaurs* lacks a truthmaker, *that there are dinosaurs* used to have a truthmaker...this is sufficient for treating *that there were dinosaurs* as grounded. (Baia 2012, p. 346)

Others have put the point in terms of *explanation*, but the gist is similar:

When explaining the truth of a proposition about how things were, one needs to appeal not to how things are, but rather to how things once were... This explanation does not point to what there is... It 'points beyond' reality, to describe how things once were. (Sanson and Caplan 2010, p. 38)

The idea is that the presentist can agree that the present underdetermines the past and future but deny that past and future entities exist tenselessly or as ersatz entities. Rather, propositions about the past or future will supervene on the past or future existence of truthmakers.

I think that the problem for the tensed truthmaker principle can be seen if we ask what makes it the case that *that there are dinosaurs* used to have a truthmaker? Baia considers the meta-proposition *that (that there are dinosaurs) has a truthmaker* and argues that the presentist need only say that this proposition *had* a truthmaker (Baia 2012, p. 349). Sanson and Caplan make a similar point: 'Arnold now bears the *once having instantiated* relation to *being pale* because he *once bore* the simple *instantiating* relation to *being pale*' (Sanson and Caplan 2010, pp. 34–5). But on what basis is the presentist entitled to assert that such propositions *had* truthmakers? Isn't this ontological cheating, getting something for nothing?

Baia thinks not:

For imagine that the grounding advocate makes the following demand: 'Please explain why *that there were dinosaurs* is a true proposition. How is its truth value explained by the world?' Now suppose the presentist responds: 'Well, let me tell you how the world was some 100 million years ago: Dinosaurs existed. So that explains the truth of the proposition.' Should the grounding advocate be satisfied with this explanation? I see no reason why she should not be satisfied. (Baia 2012, p. 348)

It is beyond serious doubt that the world is such that dinosaurs existed 100 million years ago. But can the presentist simply help herself to that fact if she insists that all truthmakers for propositions about dinosaurs are unreal? I don't see how.

Consider the case of propositions about fictional characters, such as Sherlock Holmes; for example the proposition *that Sherlock Holmes lives on Baker Street*. While some may suppose that proposition is true, it is unclear how it could be true if one supposes that fictional characters don't exist (i.e. there isn't a part of reality that contains the relevant fictional entities). One way to handle this worry is to place the above proposition about Sherlock Holmes within the scope of an operator, e.g.:

(SH) According to fiction: Sherlock Holmes lives on Baker Street,

which is ontologically non-committing (and opaque in the sense that the substitution of co-referring terms may not preserve truth-values). But can the entire proposition (SH) fail to have a non-fictional truthmaker? I suggest that the answer to this question is no: the 'according to fiction' operator cannot be divorced from what is, i.e. what is non-fictional. In order for (SH) to be true, there must exist a story of some kind, either written in ink on paper, stored as digital bits in a computer, in the memory of a storyteller, as electromagnetic waves in space-time, or what have you. In other words, (SH) can only be true if there is, *non-fictionally*, a story.

Imagine, on the other hand, that one were to insist not only that Sherlock Holmes, being merely fictional, doesn't exist but also that all the stories in which he appears are mere fictions and hence don't exist; in other words, nobody composed those stories. Would it be sensible on these suppositions to conclude that (SH) is true? It might be, if there existed a story in which it is written that somebody wrote a series of books about a character named Sherlock Holmes; there can be fiction within fiction. But then the story in which the fictional stories are described must itself not be a mere fiction. In other words, it is ontological cheating to suppose that fictional entities can exist independently of anything non-fictional; fictional entities must be tied in some way to the non-fictional world, and propositions about the fictional must ultimately be explained by the non-fictional.

None of this would apply, however, if one conceived of fictional entities as self-subsistent denizens of a particular part of reality, a view that Prior dismissed:

> Philosophers often speak as if the real world were just one of a number of different big boxes in which various things go on, the other boxes have such labels as 'the mind' or 'the world of Greek mythology'. For example, centaurs exist in the world of Greek mythology but not in the real world... I want to suggest... that this way of conceiving of the relation between the real and the unreal is profoundly mistaken and misleading. The most important way in which it is misleading is that it minimises, or makes a purely arbitrary matter, the vast and stark *difference* that there is between the real and every form of unreality. (Prior 1970, p. 129)

Someone who insists that propositions about Sherlock Holmes could be true even in the absence of actual stories that mention 'Sherlock Holmes' is, I think, reasoning in the way that Prior, rightly, rejects here. It is not logically incoherent to suppose that all fictional characters exist independently of the non-fictional world, in a realm of being which our storytellers manage to characterize and to which they manage to refer. Of course, we have no real reason to believe in such a world since we have a far simpler explanation of how fictional characters come into existence: the actual (i.e. non-fictional) efforts of non-fictional people such as Arthur Conan Doyle *create* such characters, who are no more than concepts in people's minds or descriptions on a page (or, perhaps, once created, fictional characters persist as abstract entities; even then, their creation will depend on non-fictional entities). In other words, if you truly think that fictional beings such as Sherlock Holmes do not exist, then any propositions about them will supervene on and entail the existence of something that is non-fictional.

Why, then, is it any different in the case of the past? If the past is truly non-existent, i.e. does not simply exist in some other region of the world (i.e. in those parts that are earlier than now, as the eternalist claims), then why can truths about the past, such as *it was the case that Dinosaurs existed*, be accepted without committing to there existing, *in some sense in which the past does not exist*, something on which this truth supervenes? The italicized clause is important. There is a certain combination of claims that appears to be impossible to hold: (i) that some entity, *x*, is non-existent; and (ii) there are truths about *x* which do not entail the existence of anything that has any more reality than *x* or that is distinct with regard to existence in comparison to *x* itself. For example, the past is non-existent but truths about the past do not entail the existence of anything that is not past.

What I believe lies behind the 'truth supervenes on/is grounded in being' slogan is Prior's suggestion that *every* kind of unreality/non-being is qualitatively distinct from reality/being. It is not just that when we refer to something that is real we refer 'over here' and when we refer to something unreal we refer 'over there'. The unreal just isn't 'there'.

This highlights what I take to be the central difficulty with the Baia/Sanson and Caplan line of response: they suppose that the past can both be unreal and serve as the ground for truths *about itself*. To my ears, this sounds just like claiming that Santa Claus is unreal but that *he* grounds truths about himself. To reply that, unlike Santa Claus, the past *once was* real does not address this issue. The reason is that whatever *once was* real is, if presentism is correct, unreal. So, to say that the past can ground truths about itself because the past *once was* real is to say no more than that that which is unreal can ground truths about itself, and the reason for this is that the proposition that the past *once was* real entails, in the presentist framework, that the past is (tenselessly) unreal.

Many authors point to analogies between tense and modality (e.g. Keller 2004, Markosian 2004). Suppose we think that the following proposition is true: *that Arnold could become president*. One might suppose this is true in virtue of the existence of a non-actual but concrete possible world in which Arnold *is* president (Lewis 1986). Another possibility is that this proposition is true in virtue of Arnold having the property *possibly being president* (Sanson and Caplan 2010, p. 37). Suppose, however, that one were to insist on both of the following: (i) Arnold could become president; and (ii) there *are* no possible worlds or modal properties (assume for the sake of argument that these are the only possible grounds for modal truths; if there are more, the argument can be modified accordingly)? This simply doesn't strike me as a cogent combination: 'the merely possible is not able to assert its independence from the actual' (Sanson and Caplan 2010, p. 37). The same, I would add, goes for the merely fictional.

Imagine now that one were to respond to this by saying that though there *are* no possible worlds or modal properties (or anything else that grounds the truth of modal propositions), there *might be* and that this is what grounds the truth of the proposition. In other words, it is true that Arnold could become president because it is *possible* that the modal property of possibly being president is instantiated by Arnold or it is possible that a non-actual world in which Arnold is president exists, though neither the property nor the non-actual world exists. This is hardly acceptable for it amounts to saying that the possibility that a ground for possibility exists suffices for the ground of possibility to exist; but, of course, just because something might exist it doesn't follow that it does. So, the *possible* existence of a ground for a modal proposition does not ground that modal proposition.

If all of this is right, then an unreal (i.e. fictional) ground for a fictional proposition cannot ground a fictional proposition and an unreal (i.e. merely possible) ground for a modal proposition cannot ground a modal proposition. Why then can an unreal (i.e. past) ground for a proposition about the past ground a proposition about the past? Why is the presentist entitled to appeal to 'the way things were' or 'what once was real' in explaining the truth of propositions when such locutions 'point' to the unreal? Conversely, if she can, why can't we do the same in the case of fiction and modality?

Now it seems that something that is in the background of these presentist challenges to the grounding objection is the idea that the real 'leaves its mark' once it passes out of reality; something that would apply to the present but not, for example, apply to the fictional or the merely possible. For the presentist, the past is the formerly present and, therefore, the formerly real. 'Once real always real' is not the presentist's slogan, of course, but perhaps 'once real, always available for purposes of explanation, analysis, reference, grounding, etc.' could be. The problem of course, is with the 'once real' portion of this slogan. The proposition *that* x *was once real* is ungrounded in the presentist's ontology.

Might the presentist insist that since the present is real, we can conclude that it *will be* the case that the present *was* real simply by application of the truth-value link (TV1)? Perhaps this would be a way of cashing out the idea that the real 'leaves its mark' even once it ceases to exist. However, to do so would be to beg the question against the grounding objection, which is, in essence, the objection that propositions about the past lack truthmakers and, therefore, are not true. Hence, to assume that propositions that will be about the past will be true is to assume that the grounding objection is unsound. If the grounding objection is sound, then it becomes difficult for the presentist to motivate a commitment to (TV1) for there *will be* nothing in the past about which we might have beliefs or to which we might have commitments.

I suppose that one could adopt the stance that (TV1) holds even if propositions about the past lack truthmakers as a result of *quietist* instincts, i.e. the instinct that we should simply avoid metaphysical principles, commitments, and, if possible, debates in favour of some preferable mode of evaluation, such as appeal to common sense, the structure of natural language, logical principles, or the results of natural science. I don't think, however, that quietism is going to be of service to presentism against the grounding objection because quietism gains persuasive force when implemented against an ontologically *bloated* or metaphysically *mysterious* theory. However, the ontological commitments of eternalism are entirely benign; yes, it does commit to many *more* entities than does presentism, but these entities are all of the familiar *kinds*—objects, events, persons—that the presentist accepts anyway[3] so I am hard pressed to see this as a problem. Moreover, there are no metaphysical mysteries that eternalism introduces; in comparison with presentism, which supposes that entities are continually coming into existence then passing out again, eternalism in fact seems quite deflationary. So I don't think the presentist can deflect the grounding objection by brute, quietist appeal to (TV1).

Baia uses the term 'P-Grounding' (short for 'presentist grounding') as a name for the idea I have been challenging above, namely that propositions can depend for their truth on how the world was or will be even if only the present is real, and contrasts it with 'E-Grounding' ('eternalist grounding') according to which propositions depend for their truth on how the world is *tenselessly*. He offers a challenge to the eternalist:

What would be nice to see here—if indeed P-Grounding is inadequate—is some proposed necessary condition on Grounding that is both, (a) genuinely *prima facie* necessary for Grounding, and (b) genuinely supportive of E-Grounding over P-Grounding. (Baia 2012, p. 348)

My response to this challenge is to point to the principle outlined above, that truths about non-existent entities couldn't be grounded in the non-existent; to believe otherwise is to engage in ontological cheating. I think this principle satisfies Baia's (a) in the quotation above. It also satisfies (b), for if the past is truly non-existent (it has no being whatsoever), then truths about the past must be grounded in something non-past, in which case P-Grounding fails.

In other words, the grounding objection to presentism does not presuppose that eternalism is true, only that the unreal can't ground truths about the unreal. Eternalism follows from a *prima facie* necessary condition for grounding and the failure of alternative ontologies to satisfy that condition. The argument against presentism is not question-begging, contrary to what Baia suggests.

In the foregoing I have been using 'existence' and '(has) being' interchangeably, but my argument doesn't depend on it. Suppose, with some versions of free-logic, that existence is a predicate that distinguishes some members in a domain of quantification from others; in other words, the realm of 'being' is larger than the realm of 'existence' so that there *are* some things that *don't exist*. So we can say that

---

[3] Well, perhaps not quite. It might be argued that eternalism introduces B-relations between times that the presentist avoids. I would say two things in response. First, the eternalist needn't reify B-relations: they might be construed extensionally, in which case they add no new kinds to one's ontology. Secondly, B-relations exist, at least derivatively, even for the presentist, because all events in the present are simultaneous with each other (if x is present and y is present, then presumably x and y are simultaneous with each other, even if the latter is analysed in terms of the former). So, while the eternalist ontology does add new sorts of B-relations that the presentist may deny, the general category of B-relations exists either way. Hence, I see this commitment as incurring minimal additional cost (thanks to L. N. Oaklander for pointing this out to me).

all existing things have being, but not everything that has being exists. On this view we need two sets of quantifiers, one that is restricted to those things that satisfy the '*x* exists' predicate, and one that ranges over everything that has being.

Now I want to imagine a presentist who appeals to such a system to explain and defend her view. There is a domain, D, of entities all of which have being, and a sub-set of D, E, containing all the existing entities. Since we are considering a presentist view here, in which case '*x* exists' and '*x* is present' are coextensive, which entities are in E will depend on what time is present. So, for any given time, some things in D are (present tense) future, some are (present tense) past, some are (present tense) existent/present, and some are such that they are none of these (i.e. those things that were, are, and always will be non-existent).

Notice that on such a view, the non-existent but real entities must be temporally structured for at any given time, some of them are yet to exist and some of them have already existed. Merely being in D but not E will not suffice to distinguish the first moon landing as *having* existed from the establishment of the first lunar colony as *yet* to exist. So, on this view, all the non-existents will be temporally ordered (or ersatz temporally ordered) with respect to each other and the present. They will also have being and be available for (wide) quantification. Can this view answer the grounding objection?

It can if we allow entities in D but not in E to be part of the supervenience base for truths about the non-present. But the cost of this view is that it is indistinguishable from eternalism, though it will include an '*x* exists' predicate that is temporally restricted. My question here is, what is the nature of this predicate? In particular, is it monadic or relational? Suppose that it is monadic. In that case, everything that is present satisfies '*x* exists', but since all past and future things in D satisfy '*x* exists' at some time or another, this would result in a situation in which all past and future things in D satisfy '*x* exists', thereby collapsing the view to eternalism.

Suppose the predicate is relational in structure. In that case, it must relate entities in D to a time because each entity exists only at some times and no others:

(EX) $\text{Exists}(x, t)$.

Such a predicate is unable, however, to single out any time over any other. Long after the Battle of Britain ceases to exist, it still satisfies 'Exists(Battle of Britain, 1940)', for example. The presentist who insists on what Baia calls P-Grounding agrees that the proposition *the Battle of Britain was real in 1940* is true today. Since the relational existence predicate holds between anything and the time at which it is present, even past and future entities in D stand in relation (EX) to some times; otherwise there would be no truths about what was once present or what will be present. So, a relational existence predicate cannot uniquely single out the present and what remains is a domain of entities, all of which stand in temporal relation to each other, none of which is uniquely singled out by the existence predicate. In short, this view reduces to eternalism.

My principle is that the unreal can't ground truths about the unreal. There is a view, however, that would seemingly sidestep this principle by flatly rejecting the need for grounds for truths about the non-existent (e.g. Tallant 2009, 2010). Tallant argues that we should favour ontological simplicity over theoretical simplicity. So, while it is relatively theoretically complex to suppose that some truths—those about the present and the actual—have grounds, while others—those about the past and, perhaps, the possible—do not, such a view is ontologically preferable because it resists commitment to past things and possible things.

Ontological cheating is a virtue, however, not only because ontological simplicity is good—'it seems only right to leave the world as simple as can be' (Tallant 2009, p. 429)—but also because in the case of presentism (and modality as well) 'common sense and intuition' (Tallant 2010, p. 506) are on the side of the cheat:

'The past' is, in our pre-theoretical musings, that which has gone; that which has been destroyed and is no more; that which no longer exists—and so on. The natural, intuitive view is that the past is not a part of what exists...just as the natural intuition is that 'lacks' are not to be reified as existents, so our intuition is that 'the past' ought not to be reified, either. (Tallant 2009, p. 425)

Tallant argues that even the robust defender of grounding admits that negative existentials don't require grounds, so if common sense and intuition suggest that a certain class of proposition is about the non-existent, then it is preferable, because ontologically simpler, to deny grounds for true members of that class, just as in the case of negative existentials (Tallant 2009, pp. 424–5). The key thing for truths that lack grounds is the following principle:

CGP: For every proposition, that proposition is true iff it accurately characterizes its subject matter. (Tallant 2010, p. 503)

Propositions about what isn't, such as those about the past or the possible, accurately characterize their subject matter even if—in fact because—there exists nothing that they are about or that grounds them.

I think that Tallant's line of response raises some important points but is ultimately unconvincing. The primary concern I have with his 'cheating' position is in its insistence that ontological simplicity has, *a priori*, some kind of metaphysically preferential status. Tallant writes:

...we have a choice in how we explain the truth of propositions. We can posit more ontology to do the work, or we can make the concept of truth more complicated by admitting of different ways in which explanations can terminate. It seems only right to leave the world as simple as can be. (Tallant 2009, p. 429)

Elsewhere he writes: 'it is better to have complexity in our conceptual framework than it is to have complexity in the world' (Tallant 2009, p. 426). The question I have is: why is this the case?

When Tallant claims it is better to have a simple ontology and complex framework rather than vice versa, the preference is presented as an *a priori* one that can be used to adjudicate between metaphysical theses. But is there any *a priori* justification for the claim that the world is as simple as it can be posited to be? The answer, I think, is no. Ontological theories concern themselves with the structure of reality, but why should the universe have any *preference* (if I may put it metaphorically) for a simple ontological structure over a complex one? It is clear why human beings want simpler *theories* over more complex ones: theories serve to help us understand the world around us and the more complex they become, the harder they are to understand, so unnecessary complexity interferes with a core function of a theory. But when considering the non-human world, why should it be more likely to have fewer entities than more? The world is what it is; whether or not it is ontologically simple strikes me as not a valid *a priori* constraint on ontological theorizing. As the physicist Lawrence Krauss puts it: 'The Universe is the way it is whether we like it or not' (Krauss 2012, p. xii). As I would put it, the universe is the way it is regardless of whether it is, by our lights, ontologically simple or not. Better than 'leave the world as simple as can be' the motto of ontology ought to be 'leave the world as simple (and as complex) as it in fact is'.

Heather Dyke identifies a train of reasoning that she calls the *representational fallacy*, which is the tendency to 'argue from facts about language to conclusions about the fundamental nature of reality' (Dyke 2008, p. 1). She argues, for example, that one of the ways in which the fallacy is committed

... is by conflating claims about descriptions of reality with claims about reality itself. For example, metaphysical realists believe that there is just one way that the world is. Opponents of metaphysical realism often (mis)represent this by saying that metaphysical realists believe that there is just one correct way of describing the world ... The opponent thus conflates reality with descriptions of it. (Dyke 2008, p. 9)

I think Dyke is clearly correct to insist that we distinguish reality from our descriptions of it and, in particular, to emphasize that there may be features of our descriptions of reality that are not features of the reality itself. Indeed, I think this is obvious: we can have colourless representations of red roses, static representations of change, and linguistic representations of the non-linguistic.

Now, Dyke focuses on the relationship between linguistic representations of reality and reality, but I think a broader version of fallacy can be identified, which is the move from features of our *epistemic practices* to features of reality. It may be, for example, that it is part of virtuous knowledge gathering to continually search for the simplest explanation; indeed, it may be an *a priori* justifiable principle that we must always seek the simplest explanation. But, of course, we have *first* to make sure our explanations are adequate to their subject matter, as Tallant points out, and there is no *a priori* constraint that says the world itself is as simple as it can possibly be. Simplicity is *our* preference.

Tallant appeals to the criterion of ontological simplicity to argue against the reality of the past, but this is puzzling to me. After all, past entities are, in general, of the same kind as entities that exist in the present, so the criterion of simplicity amounts to *quantitative* parsimony, not *qualitative* parsimony. But why should reality itself favour numerically fewer entities over more entities, especially when one is already talking about the trillions upon trillions on offer by either the presentist or the eternalist? Unless you believe that the universe is metaphysically constrained to be as amenable to human epistemic preferences as possible, I think there simply is no way to defend such parsimony. The universe has as many entities as it has; it is as structurally complex as it is. Of course our ontological theories do need to feature exactly the same number of kinds as does the universe itself and, amongst all those that do, the simpler theory will be epistemically preferable, but there is no plausible metaphysical principle that says our universe has the fewest *number* of entities possible just because that would be the simplest arrangement.[4]

So, on the one hand, simple theories are preferable to complex ones for straightforward epistemic reasons. On the other hand, we have no reason to think a simpler ontology is metaphysically privileged though, of course, no reason to think a complex ontology is so privileged; this latter dispute is a toss up and we must simply strive to match the categories of our theories with the kinds in the world. Given this, however, Tallant has it backward: all things considered, we should opt for the simpler theory over the complex one, and the simpler theory is that all truths supervene on being; the more complex theory is that all truths except negative existentials have truthmakers or they did have truthmakers, or they could possibly have truthmakers, or ... (see Tallant 2009, p. 426).

If I am right, then the situation is not as Tallant describes it, in which the ontological cheat has both common sense and the metaphysically preferable principle of simplicity on her side, while her opponent has just the grounding principle on hers. Rather, the situation is that the cheat has, allegedly, common sense on her side, while her opponent has both the grounding principle and the preferable, theoretical form of simplicity on hers. Tallant's principle of ontological simplicity doesn't come into play because there is no clear evidence that it ought to be adopted. At the very least, Tallant needs to show that the universe shares our preference for

---

[4] What could be ontologically simpler than solipsism of the present moment? Of course such an ontology leads to tremendous theoretical complexity, but is there any *prima facie* reason to think solipsism of the present moment is more likely to be true than its alternatives? I don't see any.

quantitative simplicity rather than just assuming it; otherwise it appears to be an *ad hoc* principle that is hand-picked to help the cheat overcome her rival.

In this section I have taken a more detailed look at the requirement that truths be grounded in what is real. I have considered the objection that there is no non-question-begging criterion of grounding that succeeds against the presentist because the presentist is within her rights to insist on a tensed version of the principle that truth supervenes on being. I have argued that there is a plausible necessary condition on grounding that does not presuppose eternalism but does count in favour of it. I have also argued that ontological cheating fails to dislodge the grounding principle. Hence, the arguments against the various kinds of truthmakers presentists have proposed are indeed telling.

3.5 Skow's moving spotlight

Let us examine an account of time that distinguishes the present from all other times but not by denying (concrete) reality to the past and future. According to the 'moving spotlight' theory, one and only one time is *singled out* as present even though all times exist equally. As Bradford Skow puts it, this view has three parts:

First, it is a version of eternalism: all times, past present and future, exist. (Here I use 'exist' in its tenseless sense.) Second, it is a version of the A-theory of time: there are non-relative facts about which times are past, which time is present, and which times are future...And third, on this view the passage of time is a real phenomenon. Which moment is present keeps changing...And this does not mean that *relative to different times*, different times are present...No, according to the moving spotlight theory, the claim that which moment is present keeps changing is supposed to be true, even from a perspective outside time. (Skow 2012, p. 223)

As presented, this position doesn't conflict with eternalism, as it presupposes it. It does, however, add something to eternalism that does stand in the way of a tenseless conception of the world, namely the existence of absolute, tensed facts.

I think that this view can be evaluated by reflecting on an initial difficulty it faces; a difficulty whose attempted resolution delimits the view. The difficulty is this. Suppose a particular time, t, is absolutely present. This means that t's being present is not a relation that holds between it and something else. Later, however, another time, t', will be present and it will be so absolutely. But if both t and t' are absolutely present, then both are present despite being distinct times, which is impossible. We can see the problem from a slightly different angle: since the passage of time is a 'real phenomenon', t is not *always* present; it will, for example, be past at some point in the future. If being present is an absolute matter, however, then t is both absolutely present and absolutely non-present.

Suppose we let 'N(x)' symbolize the predicate 'x is present'. The problem is that N(t) and N(t') are both true and in conflict with each other. Unless one has reason to believe that 'N(x)' can never be true, one would be inclined in such a situation to conclude that a parameter is missing in the predicate. That is, 'x is present' ought to be represented as a *relation* between two times, or at least a time and something else, 'N(x, y)'. This, however, is exactly what Skow wishes to avoid for it would reduce tensed predicates to tenseless relations.

If the movement of the NOW from earlier to later times is not to be understood in terms of B-theoretic relations, what is Skow's proposed alternative? He writes:

> Talk of the NOW's motion is to be understood using primitive tense operators. 'The NOW is moving into the future' means (roughly) 'The NOW is located at t, and *it will be the case that* the NOW is located at a time later than t.' 'It will be the case that' here is a primitive tense operator; it is not analyzed in terms of quantifiers over times. (If it were, then the second conjunct above would mean 'there is a future time at which the NOW is located at a future time'; but this makes no sense, since on this theory the property of being NOW is not had relative to times.) (Skow 2012, p. 224)

I must admit that I find the appeal to primitive tense operators troubling in this context. After all, the moving spotlight story appears to land one in the contradiction that something is both absolutely present and not absolutely present. In order to avoid this, we are told by Skow that it is not only that a given time is absolutely present but also that it is a *primitive* fact that it won't always be so. What we aren't told is how these two facts can be coherently combined. The primitive tense operators function, in essence, as contradiction *erasers* but I am left wondering how they are able to do so; perhaps they just paper over the contradiction without removing it.

For comparison, consider whether we would be inclined to accept this style of explanation in other cases. Suppose, for example, that we are evaluating the (imaginary and admittedly implausible) view that spatial relations can at most be two-place. Accordingly, when we come across a situation in which x is to the left of y and x is not to the left of y we are barred from suggesting that there is a (perhaps implicit) place variable, s, with respect to one value of which x is on the left, but with respect to another value of which y is on the left. We are instead to resolve the situation by accepting that while x is to the left of y, it is a primitive fact that x is not to the left of y. The story might go like this: 'x is to the left of y but *it is other-spatially the case that y is to the left of x*' and 'it is other-spatially the case that' is a primitive place operator; it is not to be analysed in terms of quantification over places; it is not equivalent to 'there is another place with respect to which . . .', for if it were, spatial relations would be three-place rather than two-place. Is this a better explanation than admitting an additional variable into one's relations?

Let's consider another example. Imagine a theory according to which being the Prime Minister is an absolute property of individuals. Nonetheless, both David and

Margaret have this property. When faced with this apparent incompatibility, we are told that although Margaret is absolutely the one and only Prime Minister, it is a primitive fact that David is also the one and only Prime Minister. The story is this: 'Margaret is Prime Minister but *it is other-electorally the case that* David is Prime Minister' and 'it is other-electorally the case that' here is a primitive political operator, not to be analysed in terms of quantification over elections; that is, it is not equivalent to 'there is another election with respect to which . . .', for if it were, being Prime Minister would be a relational property not an absolute one. Again, I can't see what would recommend this explanation over one that admits an additional variable into the predicate of being Prime Minister.

The attempt to avoid a contradiction by appeal to primitive operators is worrisome because it introduces obscurity where clarity is needed. That is, it informs us that, despite all appearances, there is no contradiction, but does not indicate what parameter allows us to avoid the contradiction. Without further explanation of the nature of tense operators, 't is absolutely NOW and it will be the case that some other time is absolutely NOW' simply appears to re-write the contradiction that originally threatened the moving spotlight view.

Primitivism about tense operators is, furthermore, odd on the moving spotlight view because this view commits to the existence of future and past times anyway. It weds itself to primitivism in order to make room for the notion of an absolute temporal spotlight. It is, however, hard to see why one would want this; after all, understanding tense operators as quantifying over past and future times is natural and straightforward and Skow's view includes those times. Of course, Skow wants to avoid this because he wants it to be an absolute matter whether some time is NOW, but I think it remains unclear whether that latter desire is worth the cost.

Skow suggests that it might be helpful to think of the movement of the NOW in terms of a higher dimension, supertime, with respect to which the present moves (Skow 2012, pp. 224–5). However, this is merely metaphorical; in reality, there is no supertime:

If we pretend there is such a thing as supertime, then we can pretend to analyze the primitive tense operators that appear in the first presentation of the theory in terms of quantification over points in supertime . . . But this is all pretend; outside of the pretense, the tense operators are still primitive. (Skow 2009b, p. 670)

So far as I can tell, this leaves the worry that primitivism simply papers over a contradiction untouched. This leads to the following question: why go through all this in the attempt to combine eternalism with absolute tense?

I think we can get a clue by focusing on the concept of *change*. It is not uncommon for philosophers to hold that a tenseless B-series, whatever its merits, is insufficient for the existence of real change. For example, McTaggart writes:

Thus we seem forced to the conclusion that all change is only a change of the characteristics imparted to events by their presence in the A series, whether those characteristics are qualities or relations. (McTaggart 1908, pp. 460–1)

C. D. Broad expresses a similar point of view:

As at present advised, then, I am inclined to agree with McTaggart that A-characteristics cannot be analyzed completely in terms of B-relations, and that the notions of Time and Qualitative Change involve A-Characteristics. (Broad 1968, p. 138)

For these two thinkers, the existence of change requires more than the B-theory can provide. Skow seems to be motivated by similar considerations, for on his view the fundamental—he calls it 'pure'—kind of change

occurs when the only difference between p and p' is in the location of the NOW. The universe has all the same properties at each time, according to p and p'; the only difference is a shift in which time is NOW. (Skow 2012, p. 228)

Note that here p and p' are variables that represent points in supertime. For the NOW to move is for it to be at different moments of time at different points in supertime: the NOW is at t_1 at p_1 and t_2 and p_2, say.

The problem with this stems from the following observation: for any entity to be at a given time with respect to a particular position in supertime is for that entity to stand in a relation to supertime. So, for example, for a time, t_1, to be NOW is for t_1 to stand in a relation to p_1. Call this relation 'x is NOW at y', or 'NOW' for short. We can see that for t_1 to be now at p_1 is for the following to hold:

(13) $NOW(t_1, p_1)$.

Similarly, for t_2 to be now at p_2 is for the following to hold:

(14) $NOW(t_2, p_2)$.

The conjunction of (13) and (14) would represent the universe as a whole undergoing pure change.

Let us consider how the B-theorist explains change as variation in time (I say more on this in Chapters 6 and 7). I want to consider two different examples. *Example 1:* suppose a piece of fruit, an orange say, changes from sweet, at t_1, to sour, at t_2. Its being sweet at t_1 would be for the following to hold:

(15) $SWEET(o, t_1)$.

For it to be sour (i.e. not-sweet) at t_2 would be for the following to hold:

(16) $Not\text{-}SWEET(o, t_2)$.

The conjunction of (15) and (16) represents change in the orange.

Now let's consider *example 2*: the universe as a whole changes as follows: at t_1 orange$_1$ is sweet (and orange$_2$ sour); at t_2, orange$_2$ is sweet (and orange$_1$ sour). In that case, part of this change is represented by the conjunction of:

(17)   SWEET(o_1, t_1)

with

(18)   SWEET(o_2, t_2).

So, the pure change of the NOW moving from one time to another, and the 'change' represented by the universe containing one sweet orange and then another, are formally analogous. Both conjunctions—(13) and (14), and (17) and (18)—are of the form:

(CH) $F(x_1, y_1)$ & $F(x_2, y_2)$.

How is it, then, that genuine change has occurred in one case, but not in the other?

One might want to consider the NOW to be an individual that aligns itself with different times at different points in supertime:

(19)   AT(NOW, t_1, p_1) and AT(NOW, t_2, p_2).

This, however, appears to be formally analogous to the motion of an ordinary object in space:

(20)   AT(o, t_1, s_1) and AT(o, t_2, s_2).

So I once again find change in supertime to be formally analogous to ordinary change and therefore cannot see why only the former counts as genuine change.

Now I should note that Skow explicitly combines supertime with an open future theory according to which a given time will be in an indeterminate state relative to some supertimes and determinate at other supertimes (Skow 2012, p. 227): when 1 January 2016 is future it is indeterminate, but when it is present it becomes determinate and remains so thereafter. So we can conceive of pure change as involving a time going from indeterminate to determinate and the motion of the NOW will correspond to this process. It can, I think, be seen that even conceived of this way, pure change will be formally analogous to B-theory change, for it will consist in a particular time being indeterminate with respect to some points in supertime and being determinate with respect to others:

(21)   Not-DETERMINATE (t_1, p_1)

and

(22)   DETERMINATE (t_1, p_2)

Compare (21)-and-(22) with (15)-and-(16). I think that no matter how one conceives of change with respect to supertime, it is analogous to variation within time.

Skow starts from the assumption that variation in time is insufficient for change, but variation in time is logically analogous to variation in supertime. I think there is a general lesson here: no matter how many temporal parameters one has in one's theory, at some point change will have to consist in relations between entities, on the one hand, and the values of one of those parameters, on the other. Logically, there is no advantage to adding a parameter for supertime: time itself will do the trick if supertime does.

So, Skow's metaphorical use of supertime doesn't logically alter the conception of change that he is trying to avoid. This renders the postulation of supertime suspect, I think. These arguments are made, of course, in the context of taking the concept of supertime literally when in fact it is just a metaphorical explanatory tool. The literal truth is that it remains unexplained how we are to avoid the contradiction inherent in the idea of a NOW that is both temporally absolute and temporally variable. I conclude, therefore, that eternalism is preferable to Skow's moving spotlight picture.

3.6 No unified reality: Kit Fine's 'nonstandard' realism about tense

Kit Fine defends an ontological position that is distinct from those considered thus far, and quite radically so. Fine considers the following propositions:

Realism Reality is constituted (at least, in part) by tensed facts.

Neutrality No time is privileged, the tensed facts that constitute reality are not oriented towards one time as opposed to another.

Absolutism The constitution of reality is an absolute matter, i.e. not relative to a time or other form of temporal standpoint.

Coherence Reality is not contradictory, it is not constituted by facts with incompatible content. (Fine 2006, pp. 399–400)

He wonders whether they are compatible. Upon reflection:

these assumptions, when taken together, lead to inconsistency, thereby suggesting that Realism should be rejected. (Fine 2006, p. 400)

The presentist denies Neutrality; if the present alone is real, then the facts, tensed or otherwise, that constitute reality are indeed oriented toward one time over all the others.

Fine, however, suggests an alternative road to preserving Realism, namely keeping Neutrality but rejecting either Absolutism or Coherence. In the former case, the facts are absolute but whether they are part of reality is relative to a time; in the latter case, reality itself is *fragmented* in the sense that it contains facts, all of which are internally coherent, that do not add up to a coherent whole (Fine 2006, pp. 401–2). The key point is that either option entails that reality fails to form a unified, coherent whole:

Each of these nonstandard positions takes there to be many realities where the standard position takes there to be only one. But they differ on how these realities are given. According to the relativist view, there is something beyond the facts themselves by which the different realities are given. The facts belong to different realms of reality, as it were, and these realms have some kind of independent status as the 'locus' of the facts. According to the fragmentalist view, by contrast, there is nothing beyond the facts themselves by which the different realities are given. The facts arrange themselves, so to speak, into different coherent fragments; and there is nothing beyond their coherence that might account for their belonging to one fragment as opposed to another. (Fine 2006, p. 402)

Fine explicitly rejects the idea (2006, p. 403) that these alternative realities should be conceived of as alternative possibilities simply because none of them is intended to be singled out as the uniquely actual world. At the same time, they are not to be conceived of as alternative perspectives on a unified reality. Rather, the idea is to be taken as stated. On the one view, all the facts are absolute (i.e. not temporally relative), but whether a fact is part of reality is a matter that is relative to a time. On the other view, reality itself simply fails to add up to a coherent whole; what there is, in actuality, is a disjointed combination of mutually incompatible realities, each of which settles *all* the facts (Fine 2006, p. 403).

Clearly, then, this is not an eternalist perspective, for what exists at one time—i.e. what the facts are in a given reality—will not be what exists at another. In other words, not all times exist equally because different times belong to different realities. Let me offer some thoughts on this line of thinking.

First, let me note that the denial that there is a unified reality is in many ways what I have just tried to *force* on the presentist. In insisting that the presentist both must provide grounds *in reality* for claims about the past and future and is unable to do so, I mean to suggest that the presentist puts too much metaphysical distance between the present and other times; in particular that what she *wants* to say about what the past was like (or future will be like) when present is incompatible with what the presentist model contains, which suggests a kind of ontological break between the present and the rest. So what Fine is proposing as a feature I simply see as a bug. Concerning Fine's views, I see it as a problem to conclude that my standing beside my office chair a minute ago and my sitting down right now belong not only to different times but to different realities. This not only puts too much ontological distance between potentially very close times; it raises a causal worry: is my sitting right now an *effect* of my decision a minute ago to sit down? If so, then distinct realities can stand in causal relations to each other (or have parts that do, at least), in which case they don't in fact seem like distinct realities as they are causally unified. If not, however, then what possibility is there of bringing together different realities into a single, explanatory framework? It would seem that my current, seated state simply can't be explained by reference to anything else and must just be taken as a rock-bottom fact about this particular reality. But without diachronic explanatory relations, it appears that the larger enterprise of understanding the world evaporates; at the very least, a very radical reinterpretation of the explanatory enterprise will have to be undertaken all in order to avoid the eternalist framework. I don't see the justification for this.

On that point, let me turn to a second consideration. To what does Fine appeal in his attempt to persuade us that giving up Absolutism or Coherence is justified? One is our normal way of thinking:

we are naturally drawn to the idea that the passage of time involves a shift in reality from one moment to the next—now *this* reality is 'on', now *that* reality—even though this way of thinking is at odds with the philosophical conception of reality as unique and unchanging. It is therefore possible that certain philosophical preconceptions of how reality must be have got in the way of our seeing how it genuinely is. (Fine 2006, pp. 403–4)

I have to admit that I have my doubts that this way of putting things captures how we naturally think about the passage of time. For one thing, Fine provides no evidence that this way of thinking is particularly widespread; speaking personally, the above does not reflect my pre-philosophical attitude toward passage as I came to the philosophy of time initially by reading authors such as McTaggart, Prior, and Dummett, and to my mind it was the A-theoretic view that seemed unusual. Secondly, even if it were true that we used phrases or ideas such as 'now this *reality* is on, now that one is', I don't see that this lends particularly strong support to the idea that we are pre-philosophically committed to a disunified, either non-coherent or non-absolute, reality. 'Reality', like any other term, can have multiple meanings, one of which may be something like 'pressing' or 'requiring' action. What someone may mean by saying that a certain 'reality' is 'on' is unclear to me.

However, it is making room for an objective conception of temporal passage that figures most prominently in Fine's thinking:

Whichever nonstandard position [denial of Absolutism or Coherence] we adopt, it can be allowed that presentness is both an absolute feature of reality and one that applies, across the board, to each and every time...there is some hope, at least, of providing an account of the passage of time in terms of tense. The importance of this point is not to be underestimated. For, as I mentioned, one of the primary motivations—perhaps *the* primary motivation—for adopting the realist position was its apparent ability to account for the passage of the time. (Fine 2006, p. 406)

Fine is, of course, correct about motivation. Many authors are drawn to non-eternalist ontologies in order, at least partly, to make sense of temporal passage. I think Fine appeals, however, to the wrong conception of passage:

it has commonly been supposed by realists that the passage of time can be taken to consist in the successive possession of the absolute property of being PRESENT or NOW. This property passes as it were from one moment to the next and it is in its passage, or in some related tensed phenomenon, that the passage of time can be taken to consist. (Fine 2006, p. 404)

He goes on to write that 'the realist has the edge over the antirealist in being able to provide an explanation of this sort' (i.e. by appeal to an absolute property of being NOW (Fine 2006, p. 404) but:

although the realist possesses the right concept of the present in terms of which an explanation of the proposed sort might be given, he does not possess the right metaphysics by reference to which it might actually be sustained. (Fine 2006, p. 405)

The reason for this, according to Fine, is that all the realist about passage can assert is that the present is objectively now; she cannot claim that the past *was* objectively present because to have been present is equivalent to being earlier than now (Fine 2006, 405). In that case, however:

the only distinctive tense-logical content to the claim that each of these times has the tensed status that it does is that the particular time t_0 is present; and so no real progress has been made. (Fine 2006, p. 405)

Now the key move:

The two forms of non-standard realism are not subject to this difficulty since they do not single out any one time as *the* present. (Fine 2006, p. 406)

For the denier of Coherence, each time corresponds to a distinct reality in which that time is absolutely present; for the denier of Absolutism, reality as a whole is constituted, at each time, by the absolute fact that that time is present.

In sum, Fine is led to his unconventional ontological views on the basis of a particular view about the nature of temporal passage: that somehow passage must be made sense of in terms of an absolute property of presentness or nowness. He then notices that it seems impossible to do this coherently and instead of opting for a different conception of passage he decides to bite the bullet and go for a metaphysical conception of reality that cannot be coherently unified into a whole.

Two things seem relevant here. First, while I agree with Fine that we have excellent grounds to believe that time passes, I think we have *at least* equally good grounds to believe that reality is a coherently unified whole. As we perceive and interact with our environment, many obstacles fall in our way and many difficulties of interpretation arise, but the evidence is overwhelming—the relative continuity from moment to moment; the ability to set and achieve long-term goals; the ability to scientifically explain the spatially and temporally distant; etc.—that there is one reality in which we live from moment to moment. Denying this in order to make sense of a particular conception of temporal passage seems to result in no explanatory advantage.

Secondly, what motivates the commitment to the idea that temporal passage must be understood in terms of absolute, i.e. non-relational, properties of presentness or nowness? Sure, we speak and think about what is 'now' and what is 'past' or 'future', but on what basis do we suppose that these are absolute rather than relational predicates? I think there is none, and the fact that, as Fine admits, it appears impossible to coherently describe passage this way, entails not that we should propose that reality itself is incoherent but, rather, that we should accept that temporal passage is *a relational concept*; for time to pass is for events to be temporally ordered; for first one thing to happen, then another. All of this will come out in the chapters to follow, where I argue for a tenseless, relational account of change and passage. For the moment I will note my puzzlement at Fine's decision to opt for a disunified view of reality over some alternative, non-absolute notion of passage.

In sum, I find that Fine's ontological position does not offer a convincing alternative to eternalism. It is not clearly motivated because he does not justify the account of temporal passage on which it is largely based; nor does he give evidence for the alleged naturalness of his account. When this is combined with the other drawbacks of the view—that it is of dubious coherence, as Fine admitted; that it seems to render impossible scientific explanations of how reality evolves; that the unity of reality appears at least as well grounded as the reality of temporal passage—I think that there is good reason to prefer eternalism to either of Fine's nonstandard alternatives.[5]

3.7 Conclusion

The grounding argument against presentism begins by noting that the following set of propositions is inconsistent and concluding that (10) is the weakest member and so ought to be rejected:

(7)   There are determinate truths and falsehoods about the past and future.

(8)   Truth supervenes on being.

(9)   The present underdetermines what is true in the past and future.

(10)   All and only that which is present exists.

---

[5] Fine presents other considerations in favour of his nonstandard form of realism about tense (see also Fine 2005 for a much fuller discussion). In particular, he defends his ontology against the arguments, first, that realism about tense is unable to provide an adequate account of the relationship between what is real and what is true and, secondly, that such realism conflicts with Einstein's Special Theory of Relativity. These parts of his presentation are, however, primarily defensive, aimed at showing that the nonstandard view can respond to objections better than the standard view. So far as I can see, they present no substantially new motivations for the view, that is, no motivation that would stand up if the primary motivation—to make sense of passage—were absent, so I won't consider them here.

I have argued that (8) cannot be plausibly denied and that the presentist herself is committed to (7). The most common defences of presentism against the grounding objection have focused on (9). The general approach is to argue that there are enough abstract entities such as properties, haecceities, or ersatz times to do the grounding work. A verificationist alternative is to point to concrete pieces of evidence as the grounds for truths about the non-present. I have argued that none of these strategies succeeds.

I conclude that presentism cannot reply to the grounding objection in any satisfactory way. If one combines the arguments against presentism, the moving spotlight and the disunified view, with the arguments in favour of a real future (and real past) provided in Chapter 2, one ends up with a convincing case for eternalism; it is the one model of time that can plausibly ground all the propositions about time to which it commits.[6]

3.8 Review and preview

This chapter completes the defence of eternalism, the ontological component of the B-theory, but there is more work to be done, which I turn to next. In Chapter 4 I argue that the semantics of tensed predicates is tenseless and that eternalism is, therefore, compatible with the necessity and utility of tensed language. In Chapter 5 I argue that our experience of time is compatible with eternalism by demonstrating that the semantics of belief, in particular beliefs about the present, is also tenseless. At this point the B-theory that I defend will have taken shape. I then proceed, in Chapter 6, to argue that the B-theory is not only compatible with but provides the most plausible account of genuine change. In Chapter 7 I argue that the B-theory does not entail four-dimensionalism, which is the view that ordinary objects are composed of temporal parts; indeed, the B-theory is the best account of three-dimensionalism available. Finally, in Chapter 8, I argue that the B-theory provides a satisfying account of the passage of time.

---

[6] It is often argued that eternalism ought to be rejected because it entails fatalism, which is the view that if there is a fact of the matter as to what is going to happen, then there is nothing that can be done to either prevent what is to be or to bring about something different (see, e.g., Aristotle's *De Interpretatione* or Taylor (1962)). The key point to note is that in general Fp does not entail that *it is necessary (or unavoidable or inevitable) that* Fp. For example, it is true that I am currently typing on a keyboard, but the proposition that I am so doing is metaphysically contingent. So why should we believe that the proposition that *it will be the case that Josh is typing on a keyboard* entails *it is necessary (unavoidable, inevitable) that it will be the case that Josh is typing on a keyboard*? Note than on the eternalist view, even a random event, e, in the future suffices for the truth of *it will be the case that e*. What grounds the truth of the proposition about the future is the future event, so even free or uncaused events can ground truths expressed at earlier times and there is no reason to suppose that truths about random events become necessary once a tense operator is put in front of them. So, unless some reason is given for the move from p to *necessarily p*, I think that the eternalist can straightforwardly resist fatalism.

4

Tensed predicates

4.1 Introduction

I have argued thus far that temporally restricted ontologies fail. We must, therefore, adopt the eternalist stance, which ontologically commits us to all times. This is one half of the B-theory. The other half is the tenseless account of time, according to which the logical forms of propositions expressed by tensed sentences involve only the B-relations of 'is earlier than', 'is later than', and 'is simultaneous with'. This view combines naturally with eternalism, since according to the latter all times and events exist to stand in temporal relations to one another. Nonetheless, we linguistically carve up the world along tense lines. Moreover, as I grant below, doing so is essential if temporal language is to function properly. So one might feel tempted to adopt a rather sceptical stance toward the claim that B-relations exhaust the logical form of temporal propositions.

Perhaps nobody has done more to articulate and press such challenges than Quentin Smith (see, for example, Smith 1987, 1993) and William Lane Craig (Craig 1996, 2000). Amongst their charges, two stand out and are of note. First, it has been argued that tenseless accounts of time cannot account for the utility and, indeed, need for tensed sentences in language. Secondly, it has been argued that no tenseless account of time can explain obviously valid entailment relations between (propositions expressed by) tensed sentences. In this chapter I address these challenges by proposing a schema for tenselessly analysing propositions expressed by tensed predicates, indicating how it can account for the utility of tensed language and belief, can explain obviously valid entailment relations, and coheres with convincing work on the nature of indexicals and reference.

4.2 Tense and truth conditions

Early defenders of tenseless accounts of time argued that all tensed sentences can be translated into tenseless sentences without loss of propositional content (Russell 1903, Smart 1963). The current consensus is that this will not work. Tensed sentences, particularly those containing temporal indexicals, cannot, it is agreed, be eliminated from language. John Perry has argued persuasively that certain beliefs are *essentially indexical*, i.e. that the cognitive significance of certain beliefs requires that they be irreducibly indexical in character. This includes beliefs about our relations to time (Perry 1979). It seems, then, that an adequate, tenseless theory of time must not only provide a semantic theory of temporal indexicals that avoids tensed predicates, but must do so consistently with the apparent *need* for expressions that, on the surface, include such predicates. In what follows, I present such an account.

To get the discussion going, it will be helpful to begin with the semantic theory presented in Mellor's (1981a) classic account of tenseless time. Consider, for example, a token of:

(1)   The movie starts now

said of a movie that begins at 1:00 p.m. (1) is true, Mellor argues, if, and only if, it is uttered at 1:00 p.m. Since Mellor is a tenseless theorist, this amounts to the claim that (1) is true if and only if its utterance and the movie stand (tenselessly) in the simultaneity relation. This, argues Mellor, is all that one asserts upon uttering (1). So, according to this view, the truth condition of (1) is given by:

(2)   The utterance of (1) is (tenselessly) simultaneous with 1:00 p.m.[1]

(2) is tenseless, as it consists only of: a token utterance; a time that is not characterized in tensed terms; and the relation of simultaneity (Mellor 1981a, pp. 73–88).

If (2) is true, then it is true at all times. Therefore, the belief that (1) is uttered at 1:00 p.m. cannot by itself move one to enter the theatre at 1:00 p.m. rather than any other time. However, the tensed belief that the movie starts *now*, or that it is *now* 1:00 p.m., will, if it is held at 1:00 p.m., cause one to enter the theatre at the right time (I assume, in both cases, that one has the desire to enter the theatre at 1:00 p.m.). Hence, Mellor concludes that though objective reality is tenseless—since tensed sentences have only tenseless, token-reflexive truth conditions—psychological reality is tensed, for we need beliefs whose truth values change with time, and this is precisely what tensed beliefs do. It follows that it is impossible to eliminate all tensed sentences in favour of tenseless translations if language is to continue as a useful tool in our interactions with the world (Mellor 1981a, pp. 89–102).[2]

Mellor's arguments are powerful, in part, because the ineliminability of temporal indexicals from language was previously seen as a devastating challenge to the tenseless position. As Quine (1948), and others (e.g. Zimmerman 1998), have argued,

---

[1] Note that (2) should read 'The utterance of (1) is (tenselessly) simultaneous with 1:00 p.m. *and* 1:00 p.m. is (tenselessly) simultaneous with the start of the movie.' I have left the second conjunct implicit for simplicity.

[2] In Chapter 5 I take issue with Mellor's commitment to tensed beliefs, but for the time being the issue can be bypassed.

perhaps the most compelling way to demonstrate that one is *not* committed to something is to show that one can paraphrase away all apparent ontological commitment to it. The absence of such a paraphrase casts doubt on the resistance to the commitment. To some, the necessity of tensed language may seem to require a commitment to tensed properties, much as, according to Quine, the need for mathematics in science requires ontological commitment to numbers. Thankfully, for tenseless theorists, Mellor demonstrated that one can reconcile the need for tensed predicates with a reality that is not divided along tense lines.

Accordingly, when Quentin Smith (1987, 1993) raised two serious and subtle objections to Mellor's account, hope was revived for tensed accounts of time. By examining Smith's objections to Mellor, the table will be set for the tenseless account of tensed predicates that I prefer. In section 4.3, I consider Smith's argument that it is, in fact, *inconsistent* to maintain both that (2) completely specifies the truth condition of (1) *and* that temporal indexicals are nevertheless needed in language. Then, in sections 4.4 and 4.5, I examine Smith's argument that certain inferential relationships between tensed sentences can be captured neither by Mellor's token-reflexive account nor any other tenseless theory. I conclude that Smith may be right concerning the token-reflexive account, but not as concerns the theory I defend.

4.3 Tense and translation

The heart of Mellor's (1981a) theory is the combination of the following propositions: (i) that (2) completely specifies the truth condition of (1); (ii) that a token of (2) is true any time it is uttered; and (iii) that a token of (1) is true if and only if uttered at 1:00 p.m. In this way, *truth conditions* are seen to be tenseless (in virtue of being temporally invariant) but, at the same time, it is argued, one must utter—and have beliefs characterized by—tokens of tensed sentences in order to keep track of where, in time, events are located with respect to one's utterances and beliefs.

Smith objects: how can two sentence tokens, (1) and (2), that 'state the same fact' differ in the requisite way? This violates what Smith calls the *principle of the identity of truth conditions*:

(PITC) If two tokens of the same sentence or two tokens of different sentences state the same fact, F_1, they have the same truth conditions, i.e. are true iff F_1 and every fact implied by F_1 exists. (Smith 1987, p. 377)

Smith takes (PITC) to follow from claims that Mellor (1981a) endorses: (a) that facts are what make sentences true; and (b) that if a sentence token states a given fact, F_1, the token is true if and only if F_1 and every fact implied by F_1 exists (Smith 1987, p. 376). In other words, there ought to be no difference *of any kind* in the truth conditions of two sentences that 'state the same fact'.[3] But (1) and (2) *do* differ in their truth conditions. After all, (1) is true if and only if it is tokened simultaneously with 1:00 p.m. while tokens of (2) are true whenever they are uttered. Smith concludes that (1) and (2) cannot state the same fact so, if Mellor is right that facts are what render sentence tokens true, (1) and (2) cannot have the same truth conditions.

Smith suggests that the only way for Mellor to resolve this difficulty is to concede that tokens of (1) and (2) have the same truth condition. Indeed, Smith argues that, construed tenselessly, (1) and (2) *do* have the same truth condition: they are each made true by the fact that (1) occurs at 1:00 p.m. If one thinks that that (1) and (2) have different truth conditions, Smith suggests, this is probably because the fact that (1) occurs at 1:00 p.m. is a fact that is *about* a particular token of (1), but *not* about any token of (2). Therefore, (2) has implications for an occurrence of (1), but none for any occurrences of (2) itself. Smith argues, however, that this resolution of the tension created by (PITC) has the effect of reducing Mellor's theory to the classic, tenseless theory of time, which insists on the eliminability of tensed sentences:

Mellor's only grounds for holding that tokens of tensed sentences cannot be translated by tokens of tenseless sentences are that these tokens have different truth conditions, and once these truth conditions are seen to be the same, Mellor is deprived of his reasons for subscribing to the thesis of the new theory that tensed tokens are untranslatable. (Smith 1987, p. 378)

Thus Smith concludes that the only way to rescue Mellor's theory is to reduce it to a position that Perry and others have shown to be untenable.

However, I think that some reflection indicates that Smith's argument rests on a confusion. Mellor is concerned with the truth conditions of dated, particular utterances of (1); that is what makes his account *token*-reflexive. What makes an utterance of (1) true, Mellor contends, is that the movie it refers to starts at the same time as that utterance. Furthermore, we can utter a sentence token that captures this fact by uttering a token of (2). In other words a token, a dated, particular utterance, of (2) has the same truth condition as the 1:00 p.m. token of (1), namely the simultaneity of the utterance of (1) and the movie.

Given this, let us ask what it means to claim that a token of (1) can be uttered truly only at one time while tokens of (2) can be uttered truly at any time. This simply means that at any time other than 1:00 p.m., a dated, particular utterance of (1) is false, but that there are no times at which any utterance of (2) is false. But this does *not* violate (PITC). (PITC) says that for two tokens to 'state the same fact' they must have the same truth conditions. Therefore, so long as *any* two sentence tokens have the same truth conditions, they state the same fact. And this is surely the case with *certain* tokens of (1) and (2). It does not matter, so far as (PITC) is concerned, that

---

[3] I am not committing to any substantial understanding of facts. I am simply using the phrase of Smith and Mellor.

there exist other utterance pairs *of the same types* as (1) and (2) that differ in their truth conditions. In such cases, the two utterances do not 'state the same fact'. For instance, an utterance of (1) that is simultaneous with 1:00 p.m. will have a different truth condition from an utterance of (1) that is simultaneous with 2:00 p.m. What this does not mean, however, is that the token of (1) that occurs at 1:00 p.m. has a different truth condition from a token of (2) uttered at any time. So, if a dated, particular utterance of (1) shares a truth condition with all utterances of (2), then that token of (1) when conjoined with any of the tokens of (2) forms a pair that satisfies (PITC).[4]

According to tenseless semantic theories, the truth condition of any particular utterance of (1) never changes. This is consistent, however, with *different* utterances of (1) differing in their truth conditions since (1) is a sentence type whose tokens can have different truth conditions, while (2) is not such a type. Smith, then, is simply trading on a type/token equivocation in his attack on Mellor.[5] Mellor's position is that we need tensed sentences (i.e. tensed sentence *types*) in our language because they are such that their tokens will have different truth conditions (and, therefore, truth values) depending on when they are uttered, something that is not true of tenseless sentence types. But, he insists, any particular token has a tenseless truth condition, possibly a different truth condition from that of a later token of the same type. In this way, tensed language is reconciled with tenseless reality.

Let us examine Mellor's own words:

[L]et *R* be any token of 'Cambridge is here' and *S* be any token of 'It is now 1980' ... Then *R* is true if and only if it occurs in Cambridge, and *S* is true if and only if it occurs in 1980. If a sentence giving another's truth conditions means what it does, *R* should mean the same as '*R* occurs in Cambridge' and *S* should mean the same as '*S* occurs in 1980'. *But these sentences have different truth conditions*. In particular, if true at all, they are true everywhere and at all times'. (Mellor 1981a, p. 74, italics added)

The highlighted sentence cannot be referring to the token pairs *R* and (a Cambridge occurrence of) '*R* occurs in Cambridge' or *S* and (a 1980 occurrence of) '*S* occurs in 1980'. For one thing, Mellor *insists* that the latter in each of these pairs gives the truth condition of the former, so that the tokens in each pair have the same truth condition (Mellor 1981a, pp. 40–2). Secondly, how can a token, which is a dated particular, be true at all times or at all places? A token is a temporally and spatially localized event. The type can be true at all times, but this simply means that tokens of that type can be truly uttered at any time, as Mellor goes on to write:

---

[4] I shall not assume that truth conditions consist of facts, as Mellor and Smith do. The arguments above are intended to show that even if one accepts facts as truth conditions, Smith's arguments are unable to undo Mellor's position.

[5] Oaklander (1991) also draws attention to the equivocation here. However, his response to Smith's attack on the date analysis of tensed sentences is different from mine (see section 4.5). In particular, my account avoids the objections to Oaklander raised in Smith (1994b) and (1994c).

You need not be in Cambridge in 1980 to meet true tokens of '*R* occurs in Cambridge' and '*S* occurs in 1980'. But you do need to be in Cambridge in 1980 to meet the true tokens *R* and *S*...At all other places and times those tensed sentences would have been false. (Mellor 1981a, p. 74)

The final sentence must refer to *additional* utterances of the tensed sentence types, for a given token cannot find itself any place other than when and where it is uttered.[6]

There is, however, a more fundamental difficulty with Smith's argument. Kaplan has argued persuasively that the truth conditions of an indexical expression are determined by two things: (i) the linguistic meaning or 'character' of the indexical; and (ii) the context of utterance (Kaplan 1989). Therefore, two utterances of the same indexical expression type can differ in content (i.e. have different truth conditions) while two tokens of different sentence types (i.e. types that differ in character) can have the same truth conditions. It follows that two utterances with identical truth conditions can resist intertranslation. To see this, imagine a conversation between two friends, John and Kathy, in which John utters:

(3)   I am six feet tall

and Kathy replies:

(4)   You are six feet tall.

Now, (3) and (4) have the same truth condition, but we could not eliminate sentence type (4) from our language in favour of (3) (nor vice versa) for that would leave one of Kathy or John with no way of conveying the information she or he wishes to convey. Indexicals allow persons with different perspectives to communicate the same information. Identity of truth conditions may be necessary for translatability, but it is not sufficient.[7] Even if Smith's argument did not equivocate on the type/token distinction, it would remain inconclusive.

4.4 Tensed predicates and entailment relations

Smith raises a second objection to Mellor's account; a criticism that I find to be deeper than the first for it is aimed at tenseless semantic theories in general. Smith argues that tenseless theories cannot explain obviously valid inferences between tensed sentences.[8] Consider that:

(5)   It is now 2015

---

[6] These quotations are at odds with the reading of Mellor offered in Smith (1994b). Indeed, I find Smith's interpretation of Mellor on this point to be quite puzzling.

[7] See also Oaklander (1991).

[8] I take entailment relations to hold between propositions expressed by utterances of sentences, but I shall examine the debate in the terms of its participants. Nothing in what follows should turn on this.

entails:

(6)   2015 is present

and vice versa. Smith, rightly I think, takes it that for two sentences to entail each other, their truth conditions must entail each other.[9] Unfortunately for Mellor, a token-reflexive account of the truth conditions of tensed sentences won't live up to this requirement. For the truth conditions of any tokens of (5) and (6) would, on his account, be given by:

(5′)   The utterance of (5) is (tenselessly) simultaneous with 2015

and:

(6′)   The utterance of (6) is (tenselessly) simultaneous with 2015

respectively. But these sentences fail to entail each other. It is quite possible for a token of (5) to be (tenselessly) simultaneous with 2015 without any token of (6) occurring then, and vice versa. Smith concludes that (5) and (6) must 'state facts' *other than* their tenseless truth conditions, facts that account for the entailment relation (see, also, Smith 1994a). The most plausible explanation, he suggests, is that each sentence states the *tensed* facts *it is now 2015* and *2015 is present* respectively. These clearly entail each other and are, he believes, simply the same fact (Smith 1987, p. 379). Smith concludes that only tensed predicates can explain obviously valid entailment relations between (propositions expressed by) tensed sentences, so only a tensed theory of time has the semantic resources to explain tensed language.

Though I think that Smith's criticism is important, and highlights a potential difficulty in Mellor's token-reflexive account, the implications Smith sees for tenseless accounts of time in general are unclear since he has not shown that a tenseless account of the entailment relation between (5) and (6) cannot be found. I believe that such an account exists, and I turn now to a sketch of its details.

4.5 Tenseless predicates and entailment relations

Let us begin by recalling J. J. C. Smart's tenseless account of time, sometimes called the 'date-sentence theory' of time:

When *P* says at *t* 'time *t* is now' his assertion is true if and only if *t* is at *t*, so that if *P* says at *t* '*t* is now' his assertion is thereby true. (Smart 1980, p. 5)

I summarize this account as follows:

(DS)   When *P* says at *t* '*t* is now', *P*'s assertion is true iff *t* is simultaneous with *t*.

---

[9]   However, see Oaklander (1990) for an alternative point of view.

Rather than explaining the truth conditions of tensed sentences in token-reflexive terms, (DS)'s truth conditions are relations between *dates*. At first glance, then, the entailment problem noted above seems not to arise since dates and the relations between them clearly exist whether or not there exist sentence tokens of any kind. In other words, *t* is (or is not) simultaneous with *t* whether or not there are any sentence tokens that express this relation.

Smith, however, rejects (DS) because it sets up tautologies as the truth conditions of sentence tokens that are, he argues, contingent. Consider again an utterance of:

(5)   It is now 2015

that is simultaneous with 2015. If we plug this into (DS) we get the following (with a few minor changes):

(7)   When *P* says in 2015 'It is now 2015' her utterance is true if and only if 2015 is simultaneous with 2015.

But, Smith argues, (5) is a contingent sentence type, so the truth conditions of its tokens must also be contingent. Furthermore, Smith adds, (DS) cannot explain the logical equivalence of 'It is now 2015' and '2015 is present', for each is a contingent sentence type and a tautology can't make two contingent sentences (i.e. their tokens) true in all and only the same circumstances (Smith 1987, p. 386).[10]

What are we to make, however, of Smith's claim that (5) is a contingent sentence *type* (and, therefore, that all its tokens must be contingent)? What does it mean to say that a sentence type such as (5) is contingent? Normally, contingency and necessity attach to the content of a sentence; i.e. the proposition expressed. So, for example, 'snow is white' expresses a contingent truth because it is not necessary that snow is white. Similarly, '2 + 2 = 4' expresses a necessary truth because it is (logically) necessary that 2 + 2 = 4. Therefore, there could be false tokens of 'snow is white'; they occur in any logically possible world where snow is not white (of which there are plenty). The same is not true of '2 + 2 = 4', whose tokens are true in all logically possible worlds, at all times. Smith would be right to point out that 'it is now 2015' is like 'snow is white' in that there are worlds (indeed, times) at which its tokens are false. But this is insufficient to show that *tokens* of 'it is now 2015' are contingent, for that depends on the proposition expressed; or, for consistency with the above, their truth conditions. In fact, there is good reason to deny, as does (DS), that tokens of this sentence express contingent propositions/have contingent truth conditions.

---

[10] Smith argues that so far as the tenseless theory of time is concerned, the truth condition of an utterance of (5) is its occurrence in 2015, something that is specified on the left-hand side of (DS). The fact that 2015 is at 2015 is no part of the truth condition of any utterance of (5); it is a tautology that is trivially implied by the 'real truth condition' of (5), namely its occurrence in 2015. Hence, (DS) is not really a truth condition schema at all and the only remaining, tenseless alternative is the token-reflexive account, which, he argues, reduces to the untenable 'old' theory (see Smith 1987, pp. 385–6).

Thanks to seminal work on the semantics of indexicals (Kaplan 1989, Kripke 1980, Perry 1979, Putnam 1975), it is now common to view indexicals as devices of direct reference. In other words, all that an indexical like 'now' contributes to a proposition is a time. The remainder of the sentence expresses an incomplete 'character' or 'role', which provides a complete thought or proposition only when combined with the time (Perry 1977, p. 493). The insights provided by these theories of reference have been substantial, so I take it to be a virtue of any account of temporal indexicals that it is in alignment with the recent work.[11]

If this is correct, however, then it seems that 'now' *rigidly designates* its time of utterance. Accordingly, a t-token of 'it is now t' ought to express a tautology, and a t^*-token of 'it is now t' ought to express a contradiction. This is perfectly consistent with the claim that sentence *types* such as (5) are such that their tokens can be uttered both truly and falsely, depending on the context of utterance. Tokens of 'it is now t' uttered at t express (necessary) truths; tokens of the same sentence type at t^* express (necessary) falsehoods. Smith's argument would, on the other hand, only go through if the following conditional were true: if a token of a given sentence type is a tautology or a contradiction, then all tokens of that sentence type must express the same tautology or contradiction. But this is clearly implausible in the case of indexical expressions.

Smith protests that even if 'now' is a rigid designator, it does not follow that t-tokens of 'it is now t' express tautologies:

Now for any tautologically true sentence-token, the truth of the token is entailed by premises stating the relevant tautological fact and that the token occurs. (Smith 1987, p. 386)

This certainly seems right; for example, the necessary truth that $P \supset P$ combines with the proposition that a token of '$P \supset P$' occurs to entail that the token is true. But, Smith counters: (i) '2015 is at 2015' and (ii) 'S occurs' (where S is any 2015 token of 'it is now 2015') do not entail that (iii) 'S is true'; after all, perhaps the token S is simultaneous with 2014. So a 2015 token of S does not express a necessary truth after all (Smith 1987, p. 386).

The problem here is that Smith assumes that one can individuate or refer to a particular 2015 token of 'it is now 2015' (i.e. S above) without presupposing that the token occurs in 2015. He takes it that 'S occurs' makes no temporal commitment, i.e. does not refer to S's time of occurrence. He admits that the entailment goes through if the premise, (iv) 'S occurs in 2015', is added to the argument, but this suggests that he assumes that this information is not already contained in (ii) above. However, it is contained there for otherwise S is not a *2015* token of 'it is now 2015' and we, indeed, have no idea which token is being considered at all.

---

[11] I have more to say on indexicals and reference in Chapter 5.

Since a token is a dated, particular occurrence, there is no such thing as a token without an associated time of utterance. Tokens have their spatiotemporal properties essentially: change the properties and we have a different token. Any argument that assumes one can refer to a token, *S*, of 'it is now 2015' assumes that that token has a time of occurrence. Since *S* can only be a real token if it is has a time of occurrence, premise (ii), '*S* occurs', is simply shorthand for (ii*), 'a *t* token of *S* occurs', i.e. '*S* is (tenselessly) simultaneous with *t*'. If *t* = 2015, then the argument consisting of premises (i) and (ii*) does entail (iii) and Smith's claim that even if 'now' is a rigid designator 'it is now 2015' said in 2015 is only contingent, is properly denied. If, on the other hand, *t* ≠ 2015, then *S* expresses the contradiction that 2015 is identical to some time other than 2015, and it is satisfying that the argument consisting of (i) and (ii) does not entail (iii).

So far so good, for the date theory of tense, but Smith has a second, modal objection to (DS). If we assume 'now' is a rigid designator, then a 2015 occurrence of 'it is now 2015' rigidly designates

the set of all and only those events that, in fact, possesses the property of being the twelve-month period that is [2014] years later than the birth of Christ. (Smith 1987, pp. 387–8)

Accordingly, 'it is now 2015' rigidly refers to a particular set of events (call it *A*) and asserts its identity with the twelve-month period that is 2014 years later than Christ's birth. But, Smith argues, this identity is contingent for there are possible worlds in which *A* exists but in which Christ isn't born, or is born a year earlier than in the actual world (though the people of that world don't realize it) and hence *A* is actually 2015 years later than Christ's birth. Therefore, 'it is now 2015', which is equivalent to '*A* is the twelve-month period that is 2014 years later than the birth of Christ', is only contingently true, contrary to the date theory defended here.

This is an interesting but inconclusive argument. There are a number of ways one might block it. First, one could deny that what one refers to by using 'now' is a set of events. Rather, one could insist that 'now' refers to a *time* that contains events but is not identical to them, and that what one asserts with a 2015 token of 'it is now 2015' is that a particular time has a particular place in the timeline, a place that it could not fail to have while retaining its identity. In other words, 'it is now 2015' does not relate a set of events to other events, but a time to itself. This latter relation remains intact across possible worlds no matter how the name for the time in question might change and no matter what events fill that time or any others. This is a substantivalist view of time, which is controversial, but not obviously incoherent. On such an account, any worlds in which the set of events, *A*, bears a different set of temporal relations to other events are not germane to the analysis at hand. For if time is substantive, any worlds that contain time are worlds in which for any *t*: *t* is at *t*. Hence, tokens of 'it is now 2015' may express either a necessary truth or a contradiction, depending on when they (tenselessly) occur.

However, one might wish to refrain from committing to substantive time. Another alternative is not to follow Smith in asserting that '2015' expresses 'the twelve-month period that is 2014 years later than the birth of Christ'. Rather, one might suppose that '2015' is simply a (Millian) *name* for a certain set of events, a name that picks out the same set as a 2015 token of 'now'. If names are rigid designators (Kripke 1980), 'it is now 2015' said in 2015 expresses an identity that holds in all possible worlds. Since speakers can use and understand sentences such as 'it is now 2015' even if they have no knowledge of who Christ is or when Christ was born, it is plausible to suppose that '2015' does not in fact abbreviate 'the twelve-month period that is 2014 years later than the birth of Christ' but, rather, functions simply as a name for a particular set of events.

Of course, we can *describe* 2015 as 'the twelve-month period that is 2014 years later than the birth of Christ', but this does not mean that '2015' is not a directly referential name. After all, I can describe Aristotle as 'the most eminent philosopher of the ancient world' even though 'Aristotle' rigidly refers to a particular individual. Moreover, by naming a year '2015' we can immediately make certain inferences, like 'this year is 40 years later than 1975', or 'in 200 years in will be 2215'. This is because '2015' bears to the names of other years the same arithmetic relations that the number 2015 bears to other numbers. But just as '2015' can be the name of the number 2015, so it can be the name of the year 2015. Hence, 'it is now 2015' uttered in 2015 can serve to refer to a set of events or a time much as 'he is Aristotle' could serve to refer to a certain man without expressing any character of 'Aristotle'. There are, I conclude, good grounds upon which one can rest one's resistance to Smith's modal argument.

So, there is little reason to suppose that (5) and (all of) its tokens are contingent. Recall that Kripke (1980) famously argues that the *a priori* and the *necessary* are not coextensive. For example, water is necessarily H2O in that anything that differed in chemical composition from water would be a different substance. However, that water is H2O is not something that can be known *a priori*: it is an empirical discovery. Now, it is clear that one cannot know *a priori* that it is now 2015. Learning that it is now 2015 requires empirical investigation. But it does not follow that what one learns is thereby contingent. So perhaps—and this is mere speculation—Smith, focusing on the *a posteriori* nature of our knowledge of the time, conflates the empirically learned with the logically contingent.[12]

So, there is no reason to suppose that tokens of a sentence type that can be used to make both true and false utterances express neither necessities nor contradictions as the case may be. This rebuts one of Smith's arguments against (DS). Can, however, (DS) explain the entailment relation between (5) and (6)? Smith, as noted above, thinks not:

---

[12] See Chapter 5 for further discussion of this point.

no tautological fact [such as 2015 is simultaneous with 2015] can make two logically contingent sentences or tokens true in all and only the same circumstances. (Smith 1987, p. 386)

But it is now clear that (5) and (6) are not 'contingent' sentence types in any sense that will support this claim.

Furthermore, just as 'now' directly refers to its time of utterance, so does 'present' (at least in '2015 is present') refer directly to its time of utterance (it functions here as an indexical). So, consider again an instance of (DS) with a 2015 token of (5) substituted into it:

(7)   When *P* says in 2015 'now is 2015' her utterance is true if and only if 2015 is simultaneous with 2015.

Because (5) is uttered in 2015, 'now' rigidly designates 2015 and we get the tautological truth condition noted in (7).[13] Now consider a 2015 utterance of (6):

(7′)   When *P* says in 2015 '2015 is present' her utterance is true if and only if 2015 is simultaneous with 2015.

This follows from the indexical nature of 'is present'. Hence, the truth condition of a 2015 token of (6) is the same as that of a 2015 token of (5). Indeed, it is clear that tokens of either sentence type will be true or false in all and only the same circumstances. In other words, all tokens of either (5) or (6), when uttered in 2015, have the same necessary truth condition, namely *that 2015 = 2015*. Similarly, tokens of either will each express the same contradiction in any other year of utterance. So, given any temporal context, all actual or potential utterances of (5) and (6) will have the same truth value and truth condition. Accordingly, what is expressed by any token of either will entail what is expressed by the other.[14]

So the allegedly troublesome entailment relation has been explained using only tenseless resources. It is easy, furthermore, to see how to apply this strategy to other tensed sentence types; for example, the entailment of:

(8)   The day before today it rained

by:

(9)   Yesterday it rained,

and vice versa. If 'yesterday' directly refers to the day before the day in which it is uttered, and 'today' directly refers to its day of utterance, 'the day before today' and 'yesterday' necessarily refer to the same time, for any given temporal context. Hence,

---

[13] Similarly, if (5) is uttered in, say, 2014, then one utters a contradiction.

[14] One conclusion that is suggested here is that (5) and (6) are *logically equivalent* sentence types which, therefore, entail each other (see Paul 1997).

actual and possible utterances of (8) and (9) will be true on all and only the same occasions. Cases of other tensed expressions can be handled similarly.

4.6 Some advantages of the date theory over the token-reflexive theory

Since a 2015 token of 'it is now 2015' is true if and only if 2015 is at 2015, it follows that any utterance of '2015 is at 2015' and a 2015 token of 'it is now 2015' express logically equivalent propositions. It is tempting to conclude that these sentence tokens express the same proposition (after all, they have the same truth conditions). On the other hand, it is clear that the sentences differ in cognitive significance. One could believe that '2015 is at 2015' is true without believing that 'it is now 2015' is true. Perhaps, then, they express different but logically equivalent propositions.

I argue in Chapter 5 that the tokens do indeed express the same proposition. It seems, then, that to believe that 'it is now 2015' is true, even when this belief is held in 2015, is to be in a different *mental state* than to believe that '2015 is at 2015' is true (believed at any time, including 2015); that much is, however, consistent with what is argued above. That they are different mental states may be thought to follow from the fact, noted above, that the belief that 'now is *t*' is true will, *ceteris paribus*, combine with one's desire to do *x* at *t*, to move one to take steps to do *x*. One's belief that '*t* is at *t*' is true, on the other hand, will not generally combine with one's desire to do *x* at *t*, to move one to take steps to do *x*. So if we insist that both beliefs are beliefs in the same proposition, then we shall have to distinguish the proposition believed from the act of believing that proposition (see Perry 1979). That is, we shall have to explain the noted differences in behaviour by appeal to the difference in cognitive significance between one and the same proposition characterized by 'it is now *t*', on the one hand, and characterized by '*t* is at *t*', on the other.[15]

It is certainly the case that knowing that an utterance of 'it is now 2015' is true in and only in 2015 allows one to use that sentence properly; this is a genuine insight of the token-reflexive account. Nevertheless, it does not follow that the proposition one expresses, in uttering a true token of (5), is *that one utters a token of* (5) *in 2015*. Perry, for example, draws our attention to the distinction between the proposition that is expressed by an utterance and the proposition that the utterance's truth conditions are satisfied. For example, imagine that a speaker says to P: 'You dropped your wallet.' The proposition expressed is *that P dropped her wallet*, which could be true whether or not anything was uttered at that time. On the other hand, the utterance 'You dropped your wallet' could have been true even if someone other than P had

---

[15] We could, on the other hand, follow Mellor (1981a) and distinguish the propositions believed in the two cases on some basis other than their truth conditions. For example, perhaps in one case one stands in the belief relation to a tenseless proposition, while in the other one stands in that relation to a tensed proposition, but with tenseless truth conditions. In Chapter 5, I shall present arguments against this idea.

been addressed. In the latter case, a different proposition is expressed by the same true utterance (see Perry 1988, pp. 235–6). Similarly, to utter 'it is now *t*' at *t* is to express (a proposition equivalent to) the proposition *that* t *is at* t. This differs from the proposition *that an utterance of 'it is now* t' *is true*. These considerations favour the date analysis of tensed sentences provided above over the token-reflexive account.[16]

It is, I think, a strength of the view defended here that temporal statements are, in general, about *times* since we do not, in general, speak about utterances when we speak about times.[17] It is not required that 2215 be 200 years later than an utterance (or belief) for 'in 200 years 2215 will be present' to express something that is the case. All that is required is that 2215 be 200 years later than 2015, which is necessarily true.[18]

4.7 The referential–attributive distinction and the tensed copula

Thus far I have taken the direct theory of indexical reference to be true. Smith, however, believes this theory to be inadequate. His argument begins by considering the following propositions:

(10)   The meeting starts now

and:

(11)   Now is when the meeting starts.

Smith points out that in (10) 'now' functions as an adverb, characterizing the starting of the meeting, and is paraphrased by 'at the present time', but that in (11) 'now' functions as a pronoun, referring to a time, and is paraphrased by 'the present time' (Smith 1990, p. 137). Smith argues that the direct reference theory works well for pronominal uses but not for adverbial uses of 'now'.

---

[16]   See also Williams 1990.

[17]   Smith's claim that '"being present" does not mean (even roughly) "being simultaneous with my utterance"' (Smith 1994a, p. 114) rings true. I hope to have explained this intuition by arguing that one does not express the proposition *that* (5′) in uttering a token of (5), even if the former gives the correct rule of usage for the latter. In Kaplan's terminology, (5′) is not *what was said* by an utterance of (5).

[18]   Heather Dyke argues that the sort of objection I raise in the foregoing two paragraphs commits the fallacy of assuming features of our representations are features of what we represent (Dyke 2008, pp. 57–8). For example, just because a sentence token appears to express something that is about a time rather than a sentence token, it doesn't follow that a token can't be part of the truthmaker for the utterance. Similarly, from the fact that nobody can truthfully utter 'there are no sentence tokens now' it does not follow that it is impossible for the current time to lack tokens. She is certainly right on both counts, but I don't see any reason to suppose that, in general, truth attaches to tokens rather than propositions. In that case, however, why assume that truth conditions or truthmakers generally involve tokens? Still, I am happy to welcome Dyke's token-reflexive view as a viable alternative to my own, as they are both tenseless and nothing essential about the B-theory I defend depends on this point.

According to the direct theory of indexical reference, an utterance of (11) at, say, noon, 1 June 2015 expresses the following (singular) proposition:

(12)   <Noon, 1 June 2015, the character 'is when the meeting starts'>

which suggests that the following translation of (11) will preserve its content:

(13)   Noon, 1 June 2015 is when the meeting starts

which is a well-formed English sentence. Of course, (11) and (13) are sentences that differ in character, but at noon, 1 June 2015 they express the same proposition.[19]

However, if we try the same move with (10) we get the following expressed proposition:

(14)   <Noon, 1 June 2015, the character 'the meeting starts'>,

which leads to the following content-preserving translation:

(15)   The meeting starts noon, 1 June 2015,

and this is syntactically incomplete. Smith's conclusion is that in its adverbial use, 'now' contributes the character of 'at' or 'simultaneously with' to the proposition expressed (Smith 1990, p. 138). Therefore, the direct reference theory is incomplete.

Two comments are in order here. First, as far as Smith's argument might go, it has no bearing on the debate over the status of tense. If we suppose 'now' does introduce a character such as 'at' or 'simultaneously with', these are perfectly tenseless characters, so, even if the direct reference theory were to be modified as Smith's criticism suggests, the temporal debate would remain unaffected. Smith recognizes this point and only uses the distinction between pronominal and adverbial uses of 'now' as a stepping stone to his more fundamental point, which is that 'now' also serves to ascribe the property of presentness to events (the initial distinction simply softens the blow of this more radical manoeuvre).

Second, while Smith's argument is suggestive it is not decisive. To see this, imagine a crime novel in which a murder occurs at a faculty meeting and that the fateful meeting is introduced by the very first lines of the novel as follows:

Noon, June 1 2015. The meeting starts. Professor Jones coughs nervously then begins her opening remarks...

It is perfectly clear what is expressed by the first two sentences in this passage; any competent speaker of English who reads what is written above will understand that

---

[19] I am following Smith and writing 'the meeting' even though, as he notes, it is an improper definite description and cannot serve to introduce a sense (see Smith 1990, n. 3). 'The meeting' should be understood as short for something like 'the one and only 2015 admissions meeting of the Queen's University department of philosophy'.

the author is expressing the proposition that the meeting starts *at* noon, 1 June 2015. To what are we to turn to locate the implicitly contributed 'at'? I suggest we look to 'starts', as Perry suggests (Perry 1977, p. 494). No other word is a candidate. If the first sentence had been left out of the above passage, the reader would assume that the meeting starts *at some time or other*; 'The meeting starts' would be understood as 'The meeting starts [at some time or other]', a time to be determined by subsequent, contextual revelations.

It is not, therefore, at all unreasonable to attribute the character of 'at' to 'starts', even though, as Smith complains, this would make 'Noon is when the meeting starts' and 'Noon is when the meeting starts at' truth-functionally equivalent in extensional contexts, which he believes they cannot be since the latter is syntactically ill formed (Smith 1990, p. 138). However, though the latter sentence may be syntactically ill formed, it is easily understood, and one can conceive of English evolving so that sentences ending in prepositions become grammatically acceptable.[20] Smith is simply taking surface grammar as decisive; but it is logical form that is under investigation here.

However, the real point of Smith's attack, as noted above, is that once we have accepted that indexicals are more than devices for merely introducing referents, we have less reason to reject the subsequent move to 'introduce the sense of "is present" or "has presentness" into the adverbial and pronominal uses of "now"' (Smith 1990, p. 143). But his argument for this conclusion turns out to be question-begging. Smith again draws our attention to an entailment relation, that between (the proposition expressed by):

(16)   The meeting is starting

and (the proposition expressed by):

(17)   The meeting starts now.

Tenseless time plus direct reference can't explain this relation, Smith contends, because (17), uttered at noon, 1 June 2015 would then express the same proposition as is expressed by the following:

(18)   The meeting starts at noon, 1 June 2015.

(18), however, does not entail (16) since (18) may be true even when (the proposition expressed by) (16) is not; assume, for example, that (18) is expressed on 2 June 2015.

---

[20] Similarly, recall that, as Quine points out (1960, p. 118), some languages, such as Russian and Polish, have no articles, and the French phrase 'Il est médecin' translates 'He is *a* doctor'. Different yet successful grammars are possible; the focus here is on the logical form of the proposition expressed.

It seems that the natural move for the tenseless theorist is to paraphrase (16) as:

(16′)   The meeting is now starting,

which is clearly equivalent to (17). Note that (as argued in section 4.5) even though (17) and (18) are different sentence *types*, the noon, 1 June 2015 token of (17) is equivalent to any token of (18). Similarly, assuming the equivalence of (16) and (16′), the noon, 1 June 2015 utterance of (16) is equivalent to any token of (18). Hence, on any given occasion, (16) and (17) have tokens whose truth values are the same so they are indeed equivalent sentence types, whose mutual entailment relations can be understood tenselessly (obviously, any utterances of (16) and (17) that occur at times other than noon, 1 June 2015 are equivalent to a *different* tenseless sentence type than (18), but that is no reason to suppose they do not express tenseless propositions).

Smith insists, however, that (16) is not equivalent to (17). He claims that while a sentence containing a temporal indexical refers to its time of utterance, and hence expresses a different proposition on each occasion of use, the present-tense copula 'is neutral with respect to dates; it does not refer to the date of its utterance or any other date' and, therefore, sentences such as (16) 'express the same proposition on each occasion of use' (Smith 1990, p. 141). Smith also puts the point by saying that the present tense of the copula 'has a constant semantic content' (Smith 1990, p. 141).

On the face of it, this claim is extremely implausible. How can two different utterances of 'The meeting is starting', said at the start of different meetings, perhaps years apart, each express the same proposition? After all, the respective utterances have different truth conditions, and tokens with different truth conditions cannot be understood as expressing the same proposition. But it is precisely this claim that is essential to Smith's position. Smith argues that only the attribution of *presentness* to the meeting in question is a plausible candidate for the constant semantic content of the various utterances of (16). In other words, Smith claims that every utterance of (16) ascribes presentness to a meeting, and this attribution is invariant from occasion to occasion. But, if that is the case, then the only way to explain the entailment relation between (16) and (17) is to claim that 'now', in (17), *also* attributes *presentness* to the meeting (in addition to its referential role). Therefore, the direct theory of indexical reference is incomplete (Smith 1990, pp. 142–4). So it is obvious that without the 'constant semantic content' claim, the argument does not go through. Unfortunately for Smith, the claim is not plausible.

What the claim of constant semantic content amounts to is the assertion that on each occasion of use, sentence type (16) expresses the proposition *that a meeting is present* understood as the proposition *that 'nowness' inheres in a meeting*, without specifying *when* presentness inheres a meeting.[21] However, even if, despite my

---

[21] Thanks to Bernard Katz for conversation on this point.

reservations, this claim were true, it could hardly serve to *justify* Smith's conclusion that the constant semantic content of (16) (and the hidden content of (17)) derives from its attributing *presentness* to an event, for that has been *assumed* to be the constant semantic content from the start.

One ought, then, to refrain from following Smith in asserting that present-tense uses of 'is' are 'neutral with respect to dates'. How *could* this claim be true? When one utters:

(19)   It is raining outside,

how could a listener (or oneself) understand this phrase appropriately if she (one) didn't assume that:

(20)   It is *now* raining outside

or something equivalent was expressed? If we accept Smith's position, and view (19) as *not* implicitly temporally indexed, then why would the listener take the utterer of (19) to be referring to the rainstorm that is outside her window then, which she presumably would do? After all, *each* rainstorm is present while it occurs (i.e. simultaneous with its time of occurrence), so how does the listener know (19) refers to the storm she sees at the same time as she hears (19)? Only by taking (19) as equivalent to (20) can we explain this successful, almost trivial, act of communication. There is certainly nothing other than the copula, i.e. the speaker's setting her phrase in the present tense, that would single out the rainstorm that is simultaneous with her utterance. So, there is good reason to equate the present tense 'is' with 'is now'.

Smith objects. Suppose that at noon, 1 June an utterance of:

(21)   It will be true tomorrow that the meeting starts now

is true. It may very well be, argues Smith, that an utterance, at the same time, of:

(22)   It will be true tomorrow that the meeting is starting

is false. Hence the sentences that follow the 'it will be true' operator must have different semantic contents (Smith 1990, p. 142). This argument lacks force, however, as will become clear upon closer inspection. Smith believes that the utterance of (21) is true because he accepts the claim that a sentence token such as 'the meeting starts now' does refer to its time of utterance and therefore he assumes that the 'now' in (21) refers to the time of utterance *of* (21). Since (21) is uttered at t and the embedded sentence in (21) also refers to t, then what (21) says is that it will be true, even a day after t, that the meeting and t coincide, which is true (for the B-theorist 'coincide' is tenseless while Smith would take it to be past tense; the difference is not important here).

However, Smith takes the embedded sentence in (22) *not* to refer to the time of utterance of (22) but only to predicate presentness of the meeting in a way that is 'neutral with respect to dates'. But now it is hard to see why (22) is false when uttered at *t*. If 'the meeting is starting' simply predicates presentness of the start of the meeting without specifying the date of the presentness, then it is *correct* to say that it will be true tomorrow that the meeting is starting, for one is saying quite truthfully that the proposition *that the start of the meeting is present at some time or another* is true tomorrow as well. If, on the other hand, 'the meeting is starting' asserts that the meeting is *now* present then (22) is not false, as it is equivalent to (21); this is the reading that I recommend based on the arguments above.

What reading of (22) could render its token at *t* false? If (22) were paraphrased as 'it will be true tomorrow that the meeting is starting *then*', or 'it will be true tomorrow that the meeting is present tomorrow', then (22), uttered at *t*, would be false. But this interpretation would come at too high a cost to Smith's argument. First, it would contradict his claim that the present-tense copula is neutral with respect to dates since it specifies the times at which presentness inheres in the meeting. Secondly, and more importantly, since 'the meeting is starting then' and 'the meeting starts now' are obviously non-equivalent sentences, the difference in truth value between (21) and (22) would not, on the above understanding, be telling in the way Smith insists, since it could not be used to show that 'the meeting starts now' and 'the meeting is starting' are not equivalent, as the latter sentence has dropped out of the analysis. There is, then, no reading of (22) that can be used to support Smith's claim concerning the present-tense copula. Smith's arguments against the direct theory of reference for temporal indexicals are inconclusive and the tenseless theorist may, as I have above, combine a date analysis with direct indexical reference.

4.8 The B-theory and the truth-value links

A notable strength of the tenseless theory is that it, when combined with eternalism, entails the truth-value links. According to the tenseless theory defended in the foregoing, 'was', 'is', 'will be', 'past', 'present', and 'future' are all explicated in terms of B-relations, whose extensions do not vary with time. So, for example, if *e* is present at t_2—i.e. simultaneous with t_2—then it is never false that *e* is present at t_2 since the extension of 'is simultaneous with' does not change with time. Similarly, it is never false that *e* is earlier than a later time, t_3 (past at t_3), and never false that *e* is later than an earlier time, t_1 (future at t_1). Put more succinctly, all these propositions are true *simpliciter*; i.e. true tenselessly.

Suppose p is the proposition that some event, *e*, occurs or is at *t*, i.e.:

(p)   *At(e, t)*.

Now consider the truth-value links:

(TV1) $p \Rightarrow \textbf{FP}p$
(TV2) $p \Rightarrow \textbf{PF}p$

They follow straightaway.

On the B-theory, the locution 'it will be the case that it was the case that p', uttered at t, can only express the proposition that: for some time, t', that is later than t, e occurs at a time earlier than t'. In other words, in the case of (p), (TV1), uttered at t, expresses the proposition that there is a time, t', that is later than t and e is at t. So long as the universe doesn't end at t, this is entailed by (p), for it is simply the conjunction of (p) with the proposition that there is a t' later than t. Similarly, (TV2) is equivalent to the conjunction of (p) with the claim that some time t^* is earlier than t, which is also entailed by (p) so long as t is not the first moment of time. So, tenseless time and eternalism entail the truth-value links (for all times other than the first and last, for each of which only one of the links would hold); so the B-theory entails the truth-value links, which is what is wanted.

4.9 Conclusion

I have argued that the tenseless theory of time provides the best semantics for propositions expressed by tensed sentences: (i) it is consistent with the ineliminable need for tensed language; (ii) it can explain obviously valid entailments between tensed claims; and (iii) it entails the truth-value links. So, the tenseless view of time is coherent, explanatorily adequate, and recommends itself as the right analysis of *tensed* language. The case for the B-theory theory of time is shaping up. Still, there remain some important semantic issues to address, especially concerning features of present-tense beliefs. This is the focus of Chapter 5.

5

Experience and the present

5.1 Introduction

The arguments of the previous chapter are intended to establish that the tensed predicates 'is past', 'is present', and 'is future'[1] are semantically tenseless; that is, the logical form of propositions expressed by such locutions includes only the tenseless relations 'is earlier than', 'is later than', and 'is simultaneous with'.[2] This view seems, however, to be challenged by our experience of time. One element of such experience appears to be especially relevant, namely that the present is *experientially privileged*; we are, we might say, only ever capable of experiencing that which occurs in the present.

Since, however, tenseless relations are temporally invariant—if 'x is earlier than (or later than or simultaneous with) y' is true, then it is always true—the B-theory lacks the conceptual resources to describe the uniqueness of the present; for whatever is true of a given time is always true of that time, and there are no new temporal facts to learn upon coming to believe that a time 'is present'. Accordingly, the tense theorist may object as follows: the suggestion, furnished by experience, that the present is metaphysically privileged is compelling; hence there must be more to temporal predication than tenseless relations.

So the question becomes, can the tenseless theory of time account for the obvious facts of human temporal experience? It does no good to deny that we have such experiences. Their occurrence is, as Richard Taylor puts it, a Datum (Taylor 1992). Rather, any semantics of time must be consistent with the experiences we have; after all, such experiences are the starting points for investigation into the world.[3]

In this chapter I present a tenseless explanation of why it is that the present is experientially privileged and why we seem to learn a new fact when we learn that an

---

[1] Temporal indexicals such as 'now', 'today', 'tomorrow', 'yesterday', and, in some uses, 'then', are covered as well.

[2] This is too strict. There are other tenseless relations that a B-theorist can countenance such as 'is before', 'is after', 'is at the same time as', and 'occurs at', since these are definable in terms of the three canonical ones.

[3] For example, even quantum mechanics entails that the macro world behaves much as our experience teaches us. If it didn't, it could hardly be taken seriously.

event is present or now, given that all times stand on an ontological par and all temporal predicates are tenseless. I shall do so via an analysis of the semantics of present-tense belief (or utterance) ascription. I conclude that the tenseless theory of time is consistent with the experiential privilege of the present.

5.2 The problem

The topic is the logical form of the propositions expressed by beliefs and utterances about the present. Suppose I believe that it is now 2015 or that I utter 'now is 2015', believing it to be true. As was argued in Chapter 4, the B-theorist ought to analyse this as follows:

(0)   'now is 2015' uttered at t is true iff 2015 is simultaneous with t.

In general, we employ the following schemata for the truth conditions of propositions expressed by present-tense utterances:

(PT1)   For all t: 'Now is t' said at t^* is true iff $t = t^*$
(PT2)   For all t: 'e is now' uttered or thought at t is true iff e and t are simultaneous.

As noted in the previous chapter, (PT1) and (PT2) entail that the truth conditions of 'now is 2015' uttered in 2015 will be the tautological

(0′)   2015 is (simultaneous with) 2015.

Indeed, I believe this to be the proposition expressed by the utterance.[4]

Consider the following complaint against such an account:

My wedding anniversary is March 12. Suppose that I have memorized this date. Maybe I had it inscribed on my wedding ring. So I know the following: My wedding anniversary is March 12.

Now suppose I am in my office late in the afternoon one day next March. I may say to myself: 'My fifth anniversary is March 12. I should think about buying my wife an anniversary present.' I might then wonder how much time I have. I take out a calendar and find out today's date and discover to my horror that it is March 12! I shout 'My fifth anniversary is today!'

In this little episode it is clear that I had two distinct utterances:

(1)   My fifth anniversary is March 12.
(2)   My fifth anniversary is today.

---

[4] Or the belief; in what follows I shall not worry about the distinction between an utterance of a sentence about the present and a belief about the present since the issue is the logical form of the proposition expressed by either.

It is also clear that when I uttered (2) I had knowledge that I did not have when I uttered (1), and this extra knowledge appears to be reflected in the difference between (1) and (2). Thus, it is arguable that (1) and (2) have different semantic contents. (Ludlow 1999, p. 6)

If the tenseless account of tensed utterances outlined in Chapter 4 is correct, then (2) uttered on 12 March has the same semantic content[5] as (1) uttered any time. But how can standing in the belief relation to one and the same propositional content on two different occasions not only prompt very different responses but do so in a way that enables timely action? We encountered this (kind of) objection in Chapter 4. Here I want to focus on the implications of this kind of argument for the semantics of present-tense belief attribution.

It will help to lay out Ludlow's reasoning in steps:

 I. According to the tenseless view of time, the truth conditions of 'e is at t' believed anytime (Act I) are the same as the truth conditions of 'e is today/now' believed at t (Act II).
 II. So, the two acts of belief are relations to the same content.
 III. But the two acts of believing lead to very different actions, utterances, subsequent beliefs, emotions, concerns, etc.
 IV. It is therefore implausible to assume the two mental states involve relations to the same content.
 V. Hence, (I) is false. The best explanation of the noted differences is that in Act I one is related to a tenseless content while in Act II one is related to a tensed content.
 VI. So, the tenseless view of time (and, therefore, the B-theory) is false; there exist tensed truth conditions.

The first thing to notice here is that Ludlow's argument only goes through on the assumption that the content of utterances/beliefs is transparent, i.e. apprehended directly and not via some sort of mediating entity. In support of this the tense theorist (or A-theorist; I will use the terms interchangeably here) might naturally turn to Frege (1918), who identifies propositions with the meanings of that-clauses found in intentional contexts and belief with the apprehension of propositions. This helps explain why:

(3)   Nancy believes that New York City is in New York State

can be true, while:

(4)   Nancy believes that America's largest city is in New York State

---

[5] i.e. truth conditions; I shall use these two phrases interchangeably in what follows.

is false. Since the meanings of 'New York City' and 'America's largest city' differ, the respective *that*-clauses in (3) and (4) correspond to different propositions and Nancy need not be related to both on any given occasion.

Similarly, it might be argued:

(5)   Peter believes that e is at t

may be false while:

(6)   Peter believes that e is now

is true because different propositions are believed in each case. From here the A-theorist seems well positioned to argue that the logical form of the proposition believed in (6) must involve predicates that are missing from the proposition believed in (5).

However, this is far from decisive as there are clear cases where different Fregean propositions have identical semantic content. The sentences 'I am the happiest person in the room' and 'you are the happiest person in the room' differ in meaning, and so on Frege's account would correspond to different propositions. However, if the proposition expressed by the first is believed by John, and that expressed by the second is believed by Nancy, referring to John, then the two beliefs do not differ in content. Similarly, a difference in meaning between 'e is now' and 'e is at t' does not suffice to show that the truth conditions of any two tokens of these utterances differ. But the latter is precisely what the A-theorist needs if the cognitive features of present-tense sentences are to have semantic bearing. As Perry (1977) has pointed out, the Fregean view has some difficulty explaining indexical belief in general.[6]

These considerations suggest two points. First, there is reason to reject or upgrade the Fregean account of the belief. Secondly, the idea that the truth conditions of believed propositions are directly apprehended is rendered dubious precisely by the case of indexicals. So, a satisfactory account of present-tense belief seems destined to posit something intermediate between a believer and the content of his or her beliefs.[7] Fortunately, there is a stock of items that seems ideally suited for this role: the sentences of natural language.

---

[6] There is in addition the well-known problem facing the Fregean that, for example, John might believe that two weeks is a long time to go without food while not believing that a fortnight is a long time to go without food even though the embedded *that*-clauses have identical meanings, simply because he doesn't know that 'two weeks' and 'fortnight' are synonyms.

[7] This indicates an important difficulty with non-representational accounts of cognition as suggested, for example, in Brooks (1991). If one were directly related to truth conditions then it would be difficult to explain indexical belief.

5.3 Indexicals, linguistic meaning, and semantics

One of the functions of sentences is to facilitate informing ourselves and others of how things stand. At least in the case of indexicals, language serves to mediate between believers and the truth conditions of believed propositions because how truth conditions are presented matters. So belief is a relation between a believer and a propositional content, but a two-part relation: one between a believer and a sentence, the other between that sentence and its truth conditions (here I consider the logical form or content of the proposition expressed by the sentence to be captured by its truth conditions). In other words, to believe that *P* one accepts as true a sentence, '*Q*'. If done correctly, '*Q*' is true iff *P*. But indexical examples teach us that it might also be the case that '*R*' is true iff *P*, and this difference can be significant.

Let me pause before continuing. I am not arguing that in order to believe that *P* one must explicitly think (utter, say, etc.) 'Oh, "*Q*" is true'. On the contrary, one may believe that *P* without adopting a posture of semantic assent. However, some kind of representational item is necessary in order to have a thought with the content that *P*. This item might be a sentence in the language of thought, or even a picture (mental or otherwise). However, even if one thinks at the object level that, for example, protons are heavier than photons, one must have in mind something, call it '*Q*', with the grammatical and semantic properties such that it is true iff protons are heavier than photons. This is why non-linguistic creatures can't have beliefs about atomic physics (or many other things, such as the difference between the A-series and the B-series; they lack representations with the requisite semantic structure). However, so long as '*Q*' is true iff protons are heavier than photons, then it is harmless to equate the belief that protons are heavier than photons with the acceptance of '*Q*' as true.

Let us see how all this applies to Ludlow's example section 5.1:

(1) My fifth anniversary is 12 March
(2) My fifth anniversary is today [believed on 12 March].

(1) is a tenseless sentence so its truth conditions are easily handled using the resources of Chapter 4. Letting e = Ludlow's Anniversary and t = 12 March, (1) is true iff e and t are simultaneous, i.e. iff $\text{Sim}(e, t)$. But, according to the semantics I defend, (2) has the same truth conditions because 'now'[8] refers *directly* to its time of utterance/thought, so that (2) thought or uttered on 12 March is true iff $\text{Sim}(e, t)$, as illustrated in Figure 5.1.

---

[8] I have switched to a consideration of 'now' rather than 'today' merely for simplicity. That is, 'now' typically refers to a particular time while 'today' refers to the twenty-four hour period surrounding a belief or utterance. Hence, the truth conditions of 'now' are simpler to spell out, though the analogous framework for 'today' is apparent. See section 5.5 for more detail on temporal ranges.

Act I:

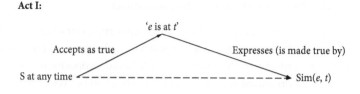

Act II:

FIGURE 5.1. Two ways to relate to the same content

Kaplan provides some clues as to why the two acts lead to different actions:

It is the manner of presentation, the character and not the thought apprehended, that is tied to human action. When you and I have beliefs under the common character of 'A bear is about to attack me', we behave similarly...Different thoughts apprehended, same character, same behaviour. When you and I both apprehend that I am about to be attacked by a bear, we behave differently...Same thought apprehended, different character, different behaviours. (Kaplan 1989, p. 532)

When you and I both accept as true 'A bear is about to attack me', the propositions we respectively believe have different truth conditions yet we are both prompted to run. The reason, in part, is that we have grammatical knowledge concerning the indexical, 'me', namely that the referent of 'me' is the speaker/believer. So, if you find yourself believing something about 'me', then you believe something about yourself. Similarly, when you find yourself believing something about 'you', a different set of behaviours is (usually) appropriate since in most contexts of utterance/belief the referent of 'you' is not the speaker/believer.

Now recall (PT2):

(PT2)   For all t: 'e is now' uttered or thought at t is true iff e and t are simultaneous

This plus the transitivity of simultaneity entails that any act that is simultaneous with e must occur at the same time as the thought that 'e is now' is true. However, if we consider 'e is at t', the time of utterance or thought is semantically irrelevant:

(PT3)   For all t, t^*: 'e is at t' uttered/thought at t^* is true iff e and t are simultaneous.

Therefore, one does not commit oneself to believing that anything simultaneous with e must also be simultaneous with any particular act of accepting 'e is at t' as true and, knowing this, one sees that 'e is at t' cannot be cognitively useful in the way that indexical sentences can be, which is just as Perry pointed out (Perry 1979). In other words, if I want to *A* when *e* occurs (for example enter a cinema when a movie starts) I must refrain from *A*-ing until I accept that '*e* is now' is true and I must begin to move when I do accept this. However, knowing (PT3), I know not to let any propositional attitude mediated by '*e* is at *t*' influence my decision to act. This is why one will typically behave differently depending on which sentence is used to express a given propositional content. So, relating oneself to a tenseless content via a tensed sentence can prompt one to behave and believe in ways that won't arise with a tenseless sentence. Thus far, there appears to be no need to resort to tensed content (i.e. anything other than tenseless relations).

5.4 Indexicals, perception, and causation

I have argued thus far that the cognitive significance of present-tense beliefs is the result of, first, our knowledge of the linguistic principles—(PT1), (PT2), etc.—that govern temporal indexicals and, secondly, the employment of logico-semantic rules, such as the transitivity of simultaneity, that enable us to time our actions appropriately (more on this in section 5.6). But notice that these rules are tenseless: they can be truthfully believed at all times. Concerned by this, William Lane Craig writes:

> On a B-theoretic ontology, all times are equally real. So why does *it is 4:30 at 4:30* present itself as 'now' to someone and only to someone at 4:30? Why is the person tenselessly existing at 4:30 thus distinguished from his fellows? The obvious answer is that 'is presented' is not tenseless, but tensed, and there is a uniquely present moment, other times being . . . unreal. Because 4:30 really is present, the cognizer comes to believe that 'It is now 4:30', not just a tenseless proposition. (Craig 1996, p. 257)

Present-tense beliefs concerning events seem subject to a similar worry: why does '*e* is simultaneous with *t*', a relation that holds tenselessly, present itself as 'now' at and only at *t*? What is required, for the B-theorist, is a tenseless account of how one is triggered to form present-tense beliefs at just the right times.

To begin, notice that present-tense beliefs are not, in general, formed at will or randomly but, rather, in response to perceptual stimuli from our environment. One is taught not to believe that 'now is *t*' is true until one sees a clock face that reads '*t*', or until one perceives an event that one knows to be simultaneous with *t*. As we are educated we become the kind of beings who refrain from accepting 'now is *t*' or '*e* is now' as true until certain perceptual experiences occur. So, the primary trigger for present-tense beliefs is perception. As perception is a causal process, it follows that the B-theorist must provide an account of the relation between events in our environment and present-tense beliefs concerning that environment.[9]

---

[9] I am assuming that what we mean by 'perception' entails that *S* perceives *x* only if *S* and *x* are in causal contact (of some kind) with each other. The point, in brief, is that it is part of our concept of perception that causal (at least counterfactual) dependence holds between the act of perception and the object perceived.

Let us start with present-tense beliefs about the time; call them 'clock-time beliefs'. These are beliefs of the form 'now is t' (is true), 'it is t' (is true), 'the time is t' (is true), and so on. These beliefs are formed in one of two ways: by looking at a clock that reads 't', or perceiving an event that one knows to be simultaneous with t.[10] For instance, when I see a clock face that reads '4:30', I believe 'it is now 4:30 p.m.' or 'it is now 4:30 a.m.' to be true depending on what other perceptual experiences are had at that time (daylight or darkness, for example). I don't, of course, perceive 4:30 directly. Rather, I form a belief about the current time upon perceiving something—an image on a clock face—that I know to be correlated with that time. On the other hand, I may have read the night before that construction crews will be working on the sidewalk outside my home at 4:30 p.m. the next day. Upon hearing their trucks pull up I may be prompted to accept 'it is now 4:30 p.m.' as true. Clock-time beliefs prompted by looking at a clock are typically formed non-inferentially. Those formed by perceiving other events may cause one to believe without inference that 4:30 is now but one may, in addition, run through a little chain of reasoning: the trucks are pulling up now, so it must be 4:30 (since the trucks pulling up and 4:30 are simultaneous).

The upshot is that if we are well trained, then clock-time beliefs will be the effects of events that impact our perceptual faculties. But notice that an event's effects are usually transmitted by media that are sufficiently speedy that if one sees or hears them, then one sees or hears them as they happen.[11] Moreover, such transmissions typically degrade with distance and time so that we don't feel the effects of events that are not close enough to cause effectively simultaneous perceptual beliefs. In short, if e is at t, our act of seeing or hearing e will occur at t and not later because the range within which we are able to perceive events (unaided) is quite small when compared to the distances light or sound waves can travel in extremely short times, and because the signals degrade quickly relative to our perceptual capacities. Since we may assume that backward causation, if possible, is exceedingly rare, similar reasoning informs us that we won't see or hear the effects of e prior to t.

If we consider the other three senses, the story is not significantly different. Taste and touch require bodily contact so only the time required for signals to travel from nerve endings in our skin to our brains will separate the perceptual effects of an event

---

[10] Some people can determine the time rather accurately with something analogous to an internal clock. They may observe a clock at t, then n hours later know that the time is $t + n$. I think, however, that this is a special case of the account presented below. What one probably does here is learn to respond to stimuli from within one's body. For example, I might check a clock at 4:00, then one hour later say 'I think it's 5:00'. What prompted me to say that is presumably some sensation I had at the time. Upon feeling that sensation (which I associate with one hour of elapsed time based on past experience) I am led to believe that I looked at the clock one hour earlier. If this is (broadly) correct, then such 'inner' perception will be covered by the account I provide here.

[11] I will not focus on the slight time lag for it is easy to see how to make the requisite repairs, but laborious to do so.

from the event itself. Again, we can consider the two to be effectively simultaneous. Our sense of smell is the least effective. While it operates over very short distances, because olfactory-triggering particles dissipate as they spread out, these particles may linger. However, we quickly learn this and adjust our beliefs accordingly, except in cases where we suddenly detect the presence of a new smell, in which case the detection can serve as a reliable guide in forming clock-time beliefs. The general conclusion is that if we are taught properly, our clock-time beliefs will happen only at the appropriate times.

We do, of course, also form another kind of present-tense belief. Beliefs of this kind have the form: '*e* is now' (is true), '*e* is happening is now' (is true), '*e* starts now' (is true), and so on. Call these 'present event beliefs'; their story is parallel to that of clock-time beliefs. We learn not to believe that '*e* is now' is true until we perceive *e* directly, or some event *e**, perhaps the reading on a clock face, that we know to be simultaneous with *e*. Again, such beliefs can be formed inferentially or non-inferentially and since perception typically relates us to events that are effectively simultaneous with their perceptual effects, we can conclude that our present event beliefs will normally occur at and only at the time at which the event in question occurs.

Let me summarize this account schematically. First, present event beliefs:

(PE_e) $(\forall t)(\forall e)(\forall S)[(S$ is aware, at t, that e is present/now) $\leftrightarrow$

i. (*e* is simultaneous with t and is the proximate cause of S's acceptance, at t, of '*e* is now' as true)[12]

Or

ii. $(\exists e^*)(e^*$ is simultaneous with e and t, and is the proximate cause of S's acceptance, at t, of '*e* is now' as true)

Or

iii. $(\exists e^*)(e^*$ is simultaneous with t and is the proximate cause of S's acceptance, at t, of '*e** is now' as true and S knows that e^* is simultaneous with e)].

Secondly, clock-time beliefs:

(PE_t) $(\forall t)(\forall S)[(S$ is aware, at t, that t is present/now) $\leftrightarrow$

iv. $(\exists e)(e$ is simultaneous with t and is the proximate cause of S's acceptance, at t, of 't is now' as true)

---

[12] If one is worried that 'causes' is tensed, here is a paraphrase: 'Sim(*e*, *t*); *e* and S's act of acceptance of '*e* is now as true', B, are proximate; and CAUSE(*e*, *B*)'. While I assume the asymmetry of causation here, I in fact do not feel it is essential to the argument and one could re-write all of the (PE) clauses in tenseless, symmetric terms. All that I require is that the causal relation hold between *e* and B and that they be simultaneous so far as experience is concerned.

Or

v. $(\exists e)(e$ is simultaneous with t and is the proximate cause of S's acceptance, at t, of 'e is now' as true, and S knows that e is simultaneous with $t)$

Or

vi. $(\exists e)(\exists e^*)(e^*$ is simultaneous with t, and is the proximate cause of S's acceptance, at t, of 'e is now' as true, and S knows that e is simultaneous with $t)]$.

Some comments on $(PE_{e/t})$. Clause (i) corresponds to direct awareness of the presence of e, i.e. cases where one is aware of e as now but not by way of anything else. Clause (ii) corresponds to direct awareness of the presence of e^* but indirect awareness of e. In both cases, the awareness is non-inferential. Clause (iii) corresponds to direct awareness of the presence of e^* but inferential awareness of the presence of e. These may be iterated further but are the base clauses.

As I noted above, we are never directly aware of a time; we only know what time it is via an awareness of the presence of some event. Accordingly, all awareness in (PE_t) is indirect. Clause (iv) covers cases where we form the belief that t is now non-inferentially on the basis of perceptually interacting with an external event, whether this is the bouncing of photons off a clock face or something else. Clause (v) covers cases where one draws an inference on the basis of an event of which one is directly and non-inferentially aware as present. Clause (vi) covers a slightly more complicated inference. Again, iterations are possible.

Notice that $(PE_{e/t})$ summarize our ability to *correctly* form present-tense beliefs. As I am using it here, 'aware that' is a success phrase. We of course make mistakes but this is no argument against $(PE_{e/t})$ as analyses of when we get things right, so long as they work as an account of such success. Moreover, $(PE_{e/t})$ allow us to see what has gone wrong when mistakes occur, as some examples should make clear.

Imagine that one looks skyward at night and sees a sudden flash of starlight. Startled, one utters, 'A supernova is happening now!' Or, consider feeling the aftershocks of a distant earthquake and asserting, 'An earthquake is happening now!' One cannot (rightly) be aware that either the supernova or earthquake is present since both occurred well before the relevant utterances. Yet in both cases one is apparently caused by the event in question to believe it to be present.

However, consider that even if one is relatively near the epicentre of an earthquake, one does not directly experience the initial event. An earthquake is a sequence of events that starts with the movement of a tectonic plate. This transfers energy to the ground near the initial motion, which is then transferred up towards the surface where one is standing. The shifting of the earth above the epicentre is in fact a descendant of the original event and one is directly aware of this descendant, not the initial shock. If the descendant is effectively simultaneous with the original movement of the plate, then one is aware of the earthquake as present. The point, however, is that what one is directly aware of in general is the shifting of the ground that is in contact with one's feet and that is all one should, strictly speaking (according to (PE_e)), believe to be present (if one wishes to call *that* the earthquake, then so be it). Nonetheless, it is easy to see how harmless errors might perpetuate.

Similar considerations apply to the supernova example. In neither case is it true that e is the proximate cause of one's belief that e is present; rather, e^*, a causal descendant of e, causes one to mistakenly believe that e is present. In cases where the time lag between e and e^* is small, this is a harmless error (and can become entrenched in our ways of speaking). In other cases, it isn't, but fortunately these are rare.

As another example, consider a flashlight manufacturer who is testing a new switch. At t, she sees her assistant's light shining in the distance and says, 'The new switch is now in the on position'. At t, the switch is in the on position, and causes the manufacturer to believe it is in the on position. However, since all she perceptually experiences is the flash of light, she cannot be said to be aware of the switch being in the on position. This is correct, but notice that the *proximate* cause of the manufacturer's belief is not the switch being in the on position but is, rather, the flash of light. It is only the latter of which she is directly, perceptually aware. She comes to believe that the switch is now in the on position because she is directly aware of a flash of light and knows that her assistant is testing the new switch and that switches typically cause lights to turn on (effectively immediately). This case is captured by clause (ii) of (PE_e).

This does raise an additional question: what determines causal proximity? After all, is it not some neurological event in one's brain that is in fact the final link in the chain of causation from e to the belief that e is present? If so, then $(PE_{e/t})$ would apparently entail that we never perceive external events. The correct response to this lies, I believe, at the phenomenological level. Phenomenologically, it is, for example, the flash of light that is the proximate cause of the manufacturer's present-tense belief concerning the flashlight switch. There is a continuum of events from the flicking of the switch to the activation of certain parts of the brain that one might choose here, but the consideration that draws the line is phenomenological. That is, the latest event of which one is experientially aware prior to forming a present-tense belief counts as the proximate cause of that belief.

So, while there may be some event that is causally nearer than e or e^* to the act of accepting 'e is now' or 't is now' as true, e or e^* must be the phenomenologically closest event for $(PE_{e/t})$ to hold. Phenomenological proximity does not track causal proximity in all cases. This runs counter to a stance Quine suggests in 'Epistemology Naturalized':

Now that we are permitted to appeal to physical stimulation the problem dissolves; A is epistemologically prior to B if A is causally nearer than B to the sensory receptors. Or, what is in some ways better, just talk explicitly in terms of causal proximity to sensory receptors and drop the talk of epistemological priority. (Quine 1969a, p. 293)

If we replace 'epistemologically' by 'phenomenologically' in this quotation, then Quine expresses precisely the position I wish to deny. I wish to deny it because I think it is manifestly false that we are only ever aware of events in our brains or perceptual organs. Moreover, I see no reason to follow Quine in eschewing phenomenological talk, certainly not for the anti-foundationalist arguments in 'Epistemology Naturalized'; after all, I have made no reference to that venerable epistemic doctrine here.

In objection to accounts such as $(PE_{e/t})$, Thomas Nagel writes:

a tenseless description of the history of the world (including the description of people's tensed statements and their truth values) is fundamentally incomplete, because it cannot tell us which time *is* the present. (Nagel 1986, p. 59; his emphasis)

I think that the B-theorist may respond to this as follows. No historical account, analysis, or formula can tell one what time it is (present tense); for this one must causally interact with one's environment. $(PE_{e/t})$ do, however, explain *how* we are able to know what time or event is present, and this is all that can be expected of an analysis of the presence of experience. To tell the time one must employ one's learned ability to use temporal indexicals in response to perceptual stimuli, but the content of what one learns is tenseless. It is the conflation of the activation of our cognitive skills with the apprehension of tenseless facts that leads to the erroneous conclusion that we need tensed predicates to account for beliefs about time.

It might further be objected that it is coherent to suppose that a Cartesian consciousness might have an experience of presentness even though it is disembodied and lacks perceptual experiences. Would this, then, be a counter-example to the above account, which explains such experiences perceptually? The important question to ask here is what such experiences of presentness would be experiences of. Since they are, by hypothesis, not perceptions of external events, they must either be perceptions of inner events or else a third kind of experience.[13] If the first option is what the objector has in mind, then I will run an account analogous to that presented above but for perception of inner states. That is, one experiences an inner event, *e*, as present if and only if *e* causes one to believe that *e* is now, or causes one to believe that

---

[13] I ignore the possibility that such experiences are in fact perceptions of external events because, say, they were placed in the being's mind by God, who intended the creature to know of the event. In such a case it is plausible to suppose that the experience is at least counterfactually dependent on either the occurrence of the event or God's will and is, therefore, really a kind of perception. On the other hand, if the being accepts as true '*e* is now' as a result of pre-established harmony (so that this occurs simultaneously with *e*), then this belief is either counterfactually dependent on the occurrence of the event (tracing back to the beginning of time, perhaps), in which case it is analogous to perception, or it isn't, in which case it isn't really an experience *of e* at all.

e^* is now and one knows that e^* is simultaneous with e, and so on. Indeed, I intend the account above to cover such inward perception.

Let us, however, consider the second option, that the being has a third kind of experience, one that is not causally related to any other. Perhaps, without cause or explanation, such a being, at t, simply has an experience with the character 'I am now experiencing something'. This would seem to be an experience of presentness without an event to cause it and serve as its object. This appears to be both coherent and unaccounted for by ($PE_{e/t}$). Such cases can, however, be handled by making the following addition to ($PE_{e/t}$):

($PE_{n,s}$) $(\forall t)(\forall S)[(S$ has, at t, non-directed, self-referential awareness of presentness$) \leftrightarrow$

vii. $(\exists e)(e$ is simultaneous with t and is the acceptance, by S, of 'I am experiencing something now/currently/etc.' as true).

Other thought experiments may compel more amendments to ($PE_{e/t}$), but we must bear in mind that such amendments will be damaging only if they require more than tenseless relations, and thus far there is little reason to suspect that this will be the case. Moreover, so long as the account above works as an account of standard, human experience of the present, we needn't worry too much about exotic counter-examples.

There is a great deal of psychological literature on the nature of temporal experience—see, for example, Dennett (1991), chapter 6—that I have bypassed in the foregoing. This may seem to be a glaring oversight for it might be argued that we cannot rule out, *a priori*, an experimental test that demonstrates that a person came to believe that e is now without being causally connected to e. I think, however, that the question here is not an empirical one; this chapter is not intended to be an exercise in *a priori* psychology. Rather, the topic is a philosophical one, concerning whether one can rightly be said to be aware of an event without causal connection to it. In other words, the question is under what conditions it is *proper* to consider a reported awareness of e to be genuine, and this strikes me as a normative and conceptual question. That is not to say that empirical discovery is necessarily irrelevant to such disputes, just that the normative question remains, since we will invariably, in response to any empirical result, want to know what, if anything, in our understanding of the experience of time is contradicted by the result. Since ($PE_{e/t}$) is, as I argue above, an account of when we in fact perceive an event or time, i.e. when we get it *right*, the account isn't threatened by a thought experiment in which a person comes to believe that e is now without causally interacting with e. For the real question will persist: does this rightly count as being aware of e, or is it merely a kind of cognitive distortion? I have tossed my hat in the ring. My answer, as given by ($PE_{e/t}$), is clear: unless the act of awareness is causally connected to the event or time to which it is directed, it is improper to consider it an awareness of that time or event.[14]

To believe that e is now without e, or some e^* that is simultaneous with e, causing that belief, is akin to a visual hallucination, such as when one thinks one sees a pink elephant in the room; unless a pink elephant caused the visual experience, it is incorrect to consider this a case of seeing a pink elephant. Similarly, I propose that one can mistakenly believe an event to be present and that this could occur if neither that event nor one known to be simultaneous with it is the cause of the belief. This, to reiterate, strikes me as a conceptual, rather than an empirical, point.

5.5 Externalism, tense, and content

It will be worthwhile to contrast the position I have defended here with Mellor's (1981a) view that though reality is completely described by the B-series, many *beliefs* are tensed (and must be so if we are to act in a timely manner). In other words, the existence of tensed beliefs does not entail that we must describe the non-intentional world in tensed terms. Ludlow raises a question:

[W]hat would it mean to say that we have tensed beliefs but a B-theory semantics and metaphysics? If the world contains only B-theory resources, then *precisely* how do we avoid having a B-theory psychology? (Ludlow 1999, p. 96, emphasis added)

I mention this criticism for two reasons. First, I would like to emphasize that my position differs from Mellor's in that I do not claim beliefs to be tensed, or psychology to be non-B-theoretic, in any way. For beliefs to be tensed would be for their content to involve irreducibly tensed properties or predicates, that is, for their

---

[14] Suppose we perform an experiment in which we causally isolate a person, S, from a certain event type, E. We test S and discover that she can consistently report when an instance, e, of E is occurring. Would this show that non-causal perception of events is possible, or that we are wrong in assuming S has been (sufficiently) causally isolated from E? Obviously, the latter could be discovered to be the case by performing further experiments, but conceptually we know that if, for example, counterfactual dependence is sufficient for causation, then this would necessarily count as a case of (previously unknown) causation (since we must assume that she not only reports awareness of e when it occurs but fails to do so when it does not).

If, on the other hand, causation requires something more robust, such as energy transfer, then this would be a case of non-causal perception if, by hypothesis, no undetected energy is being transferred. But then it is no longer clear that a physically possible experimental outcome has been described, and physically impossible accounts of perception have no clear bearing on an account of human experience of present-ness. Certain experiments in quantum mechanics, however, suggest that instantaneous action at a distance might be physically possible, in which case events can be correlated without a signal between them; this might be considered to be a case of non-causal connection (see, e.g., Brown 1994). Still, even in such cases there is at least a nomological dependence between the kinds of events in question, and one could seize upon this to define 'causation' more broadly, to include anything underwritten by a law of nature.

In short, the claim that perception is a causal concept does not appear to be prone to straightforward empirical refutation. Whatever empirical set-up we imagine, perception or awareness of e must be reliably correlated with e. 'Reliable correlation' is, I shall assume, a sufficient placeholder for 'causes' in $(PE_{e/t})$.

semantics to be A-theoretic, which is something I deny; I do not believe that psychology needs to employ any conceptual resources incompatible with eternalism or tenseless semantics precisely because our differential response to utterances that do and do not contain tensed language can be explained tenselessly. Nonetheless, secondly, it seems clear that even though, as I've argued, Acts I and II have identical semantic contents, they may, consistently with my account, be distinct psychological states; after all, they lead, potentially, to very different kinds of actions and inferences. Accordingly, I emphasize 'precisely' in the above quotation because Ludlow might press the following sort of objection at this point: just what is it that makes the two mental states psychologically distinct? Consider the following:

> The illusion of a possible way out here is fostered by thinking that there could be psychological concepts that are, as it were, disembodied—cut off from the actual world in important ways...As Burge (1986) has argued, psychological states (particularly perceptual states) are indicated in part by relations to the external world. In this case, that means that if the world is not tensed then it is difficult to see how our perception of the world could be tensed. (Ludlow 1999, p. 96)

Psychological externalism (see Ludlow 1999, pp. 152–6) renders it difficult to make out how one could distinguish mental states without this having implications for the truth conditions of the propositions believed while in those states. If, in other words, mental states are to be distinguished by external states, then any attempt to distinguish Acts I and II seems destined to implicate a proposition with tensed content.

Now, whether or not this line is decisive against Mellor, it doesn't apply straightforwardly to what I have argued thus far, for I have not defended the existence of tensed beliefs or mental states; I deny that there are beliefs whose content demands treatment in terms of tensed predicates or properties. Rather, I explain our experience of the temporal in terms of a Kaplan-style strategy of positing different characters under which we apprehend one and the same tenseless content. Could Ludlow, however, not press a similar objection here and ask how the linguistic rules and functions that give rise to the different characters are to be individuated if not by positing tensed contents/logical forms? This line of questioning is interesting enough to merit attention, and also provides the opportunity to develop my account of temporal experience in more detail.

Now, as a first pass at a response I would draw attention again to the case of personal indexicals. If S_1 addresses S_2 with 'You are tall', S_2 may reply 'I am tall', and I think it is clear that the semantic content of each utterance is identical even though the psychological state of S_1 may very well differ from that of S_2, since they will (potentially) behave differently in light of these utterances. While one may certainly ask just *how* linguistic rules allow speakers to keep track of the difference between themselves and others, suppose one were to argue that the only way to employ or individuate the rules involves apprehending 'personal' predicates such as 'is I' and 'is you' respectively.

If we follow this line of reasoning then we would be committed to the following kind of schema:

(7)   'I am tall' said by S (at t) is true iff I am tall (at t)
(8)   'You are tall' said by S (to R at t) is true iff you are tall (at t).

There are at least two reasons to reject this. First, since the context of evaluation of an utterance by S of 'I am tall' or 'You are tall' may differ from the context of utterance, (7) and (8) may be false even when the original sentence tokens are true. In other words, the utterance may come out as false whenever somebody other than S evaluates it, and this is implausibly restrictive. Secondly, there is little motivation to accept 'personal' predicates at the level of logical form; surely all there is to being, say, Joshua Mozersky is being Joshua Mozersky. There is not, in addition, the fact that I am I, a proposition that only I can express; after all, everybody else can rightly apply such a predicate to themselves, so it can't really serve to distinguish me anyway (similarly, every time can claim the predicate 'is present' of itself, so how does that distinguish what is occurring now?). The supposition that there are well-formed predicates such as 'is I' or 'is you' that are expressed by personal indexicals has, therefore, little to recommend itself. Similarly, we should remain suspicious that Ludlow's challenge pushes us into accepting tensed predicates such as 'is now'.

Now one may nonetheless ask for some detail as to how, for example, one tells the difference between oneself and another speaker. As Perry (1979) demonstrated, if I want to know that I am the one doing the speaking, I must characterize the thought that Joshua Mozersky is talking under the character of 'I'; nothing else will do. So how do I do this? If, as I suggest, it is implausible to suppose this is done by expressing or apprehending a proposition that includes a predicate such as 'is I', then it seems the answer has to do with the causal differences that underlie my perceptions of others and myself. For example, I have visual and auditory perspectives on my own body that I share with no others and perhaps, through training, I am able to correlate certain perceptual markers with 'I' and others with 'you', 'her', 'him', etc. (this is merely a suggestion, but I think it gets the idea across).

The causal-perceptual account provided in section 5.4 is intended to furnish just such an explanation in the case of temporal experience. In other words, if some event, e, that occurs at time t, cannot be experientially singled out in virtue of satisfying the predicate 'is present', it can be singled out in virtue of having (its most immediate effects) very close to t; what e possesses is the ability to causally influence proximate objects at, effectively, t (any later than this and effects have typically faded). Put yet another way, not only is e located at t but its perceptible effects are also located (effectively) then and, in general, only then. So the predicates of e that allow us to single it out as 'present' or 'now' are the relational ones of being simultaneous with t and of having effects at (and only at) t, not the monadic predicate 'is present' (or, since Ludlow is a presentist, 'is existent'). Similarly, what underwrites the difference between two interlocutors is not that the 'is I' predicate is true of one and the 'is you' predicate is true of the other, but that they each stand in the relation of being (physically, mentally, etc.) distinct from one another.

Of course this alone doesn't answer the question of how we identify such distinguishing characteristics, but this account is intended to get us started in this direction. If we are trained to respond to certain kinds of causal stimuli with beliefs under a tensed mode of presentation, and we accept linguistic rules that combine with such beliefs to lead to certain kinds of action and inference that the rules don't license with beliefs under a tenseless mode of presentation, then, I argue, we see how we are able to single out an event amongst others that all tenselessly coexist and respond to it only at the appropriate times. Let us consider the personal case again. Suppose that S_1 is three metres to the north of the location from which 'I am tall' emanated. Given a lifetime of experience noticing the difference between hearing others and hearing herself speak, she may notice, for example, consistent differences between the two kinds of hearing (concerning, say, resonances in her sinus cavities). Accordingly, there is no reason to suppose that S_1 will not in general be able to perceive the difference between being separated from this location and being coincident with it; certainly recourse to 'personal' predicates is not required. While the actual empirical story remains to be told, what is important is that there is plenty of logical room for that story to be told without tensed (or personal) predicates.

By making present-tense experience of events dependent on causation, i.e. on events causing intentional states, I intend to rebut a second kind of objection that is lurking in Ludlow's stance:

How can a psychological property (call it *foo*) that bears no relation to tense in the actual world have anything to do with tense? It is no good to say that our abstract property foo is tensed because it is grounded in our time consciousness or temporal perception. That merely keeps the question one step removed. Then we must ask what it is about time consciousness and temporal perception that makes them tensed. (Ludlow 1999, p. 96)

We see the externalist objection lurking—Ludlow wonders how a mental act can be tensed if it fails to correspond to anything tensed in the world—but there is something else here as well, and it has been pointed out by other writers. Consider the following:

if I never know the present date, then I can never use information about the dates of events to act successfully, and there is no license to attribute to me an understanding of sentences that fix the dates of events [i.e., tenseless sentences]. It is true that, as Mellor says, anyone who knows that 'It is now *T*' is true during, and only during, *T*, knows what 'It is now' means. But only someone who already knows what 'It is now' means, can know that 'It is now *T*' is true during and only during *T*. In general, an understanding of a sentence of the form '*S* occurs in T_1' depends on understanding sentences of the form 'It is now T_2'. Thus, it cannot be that being able to think tenseless thoughts facilitates understanding tensed sentences, for it presupposes it. I think that processes of acquiring tenseless concepts and tensed concepts go along hand in hand, they are inseparable...For example, we need to know that the sentence we hear refers to the thunder that is simultaneous with it, that they occur on the same date; and we need to have some grasp of tense to understand the sentence 'Dessert will be served after the salad' concerns the meal we are attending now. (Dolev 2000, pp. 278–9)

Similar remarks are found elsewhere:

What I want to say about putatively tenseless propositions is that, in so far as these propositions could be viewed as expressing temporal truths or falsehoods at all (truth and falsehoods about 'what goes on in time'), their sense must be parasitic upon that of tensed propositions...(Teichmann 1998, p. 181)

The idea, in short, is that there can be no philosophical grounds for affording the B-series any kind of priority over the A-series since tensed concepts are at least as fundamental to our understanding of time as are tenseless notions. Put another way, the Ludlowesque objector might insist that linguistic rules such as (PT1) are in fact tensed rules and that the causal-perceptual account offered here really does just push the problem back a level.

The account I provide above is intended to address this point. To put it briefly (and somewhat crudely), we will succeed in forming temporal beliefs appropriately so long as the following all hold: we (humans) are the kind of beings that take inputs such as patterns of light, say from digital clock faces reading '4:00 p.m.', and produce outputs such as accepting 'it is now 4:00 p.m.' as true; we combine outputs such as this with other background beliefs and desires we have, such as 'if you want to do something at *t*, act when and only when it is believed that "it is now *t*" is true', and 'the movie starts at 4:00 p.m.', and 'I want to see the movie', to form further outputs such as 'I must leave now'; finally, we must be the kind of entity that, when given beliefs characterized by forms such as 'I must leave now' as inputs, produce outputs such as bodily movements. The consistency of this account shows, I believe, that Ludlow is simply wrong to argue that the only way to distinguish mental states that involve tense from those that don't is to posit belief-relations to propositions with tensed predicates and content. Background beliefs, linguistic rules, learned patterns of behaviour, and causal-perceptual sensitivity to our environments all will combine to transform tenseless contents into beliefs with tensed characters (again, the empirical detail remains to be filled in; this shows, however, that it will be consistent with tenseless theories of time).

Ludlow, Teichmann, Dolev, and others may feel that this simply sidesteps the objection, but note that nowhere do I argue that beliefs mediated by tenseless sentences are psychologically or epistemically privileged. It is perfectly consistent with what I argue here that our very first utterances and beliefs are and indeed *must* be utterances and beliefs with tensed characters. If that's the way the epistemological and psychological facts are, then so be it; it doesn't affect the arguments I have put forth. What is vital to my position is that the story of how present-tense beliefs and utterances are appropriately produced be consistent with utterly tenseless contents. Here, once again, is the outline of the story: all events exist tenselessly at their respective temporal locations; all their perceptible effects reside close by; humans are able to perceive such effects quickly; humans form beliefs with tensed characters on the basis of such effects; humans integrate such beliefs with linguistic knowledge to produce further beliefs; such further beliefs, with appropriate desires, cause action. Even if beliefs mediated by tensed sentences are psychologically or epistemically primary, then if the account above is correct, this doesn't entail that the beliefs have tensed contents.

Here is another way to view the situation. The quotations above suggest, as has often been remarked, that there is a kind of regress that threatens a tenseless account of temporal indexicals. For instance, a rule such as 'an utterance of "now" refers to the time simultaneous with that utterance' can only be successfully employed by a speaker if, on any given occasion, she can identify which token of 'now' is occurring then. If pressed she might assert, 'I mean *this utterance* of "now"', but then she must take 'this utterance' to mean 'the utterance I am hearing right now'. So, such a rule assumes that a speaker is able to know which events are present and, accordingly, presupposes a mastery of temporal indexicals and can't explain it.

In response to this line of objection I point, again, to the central role that causation plays in my account of temporal belief and utterance formation. I deny that in order for a speaker to correctly employ a rule such as 'an utterance of "now" refers to the time simultaneous with that utterance' she must first be capable of determining or knowing which utterance is the present one; rather, she needs to be *caused* to hold the appropriate belief. The move here is analogous to that made by epistemological externalists against the internalist insistence that any belief counts as justified only if appropriate evidence or reasons are in principle cognitively accessible. The externalist move is to deny that one must know that a belief is justified in order to be justified in holding it. Rather, so long as the belief is produced in the right way—for example, reliably—then the belief is justified (see, for example, Goldman 1979). One benefit of this position is that it provides a non-sceptical way to end the regress of reason giving.

I propose something similar in the case of understanding temporal indexicals. In order to successfully implement rules concerning 'now'—(PT1), (PT2), etc.—it is not necessary that a speaker first identify which utterance of 'now' is under consideration, if by this we mean she must undergo a sound process of reasoning with the conclusion that the utterance in question is that which she is currently producing or hearing. Rather, what is necessary is that the utterance she produces or hears *causes* her to accept as true 'I now hear an utterance of "now"'. This, when combined with other beliefs—perhaps she is simultaneously caused to accept as true '4:00 is now'—and the relevant rules will enable her to quickly form the belief that 'this utterance of "now" refers to 4:00', or 'it is now 4:00'. There is, in short, no need to suppose that the first step in this process is one of giving reasons or explicitly employing a rule. The procedure can be grounded in causal connections between events and believers/speakers.

There is, at any rate, a fatal flaw in any argument that tries to use the ineliminability of tensed sentences to argue for propositions that include tensed predicates. The problem is that more is essential for successful thought and action than temporal indexicals; spatial and personal indexicals, as Perry points out, are just as necessary. However, we know that objects in space are not properly characterized as exhibiting spatially tensed predicates such as 'is here' and 'is there'; 'is there' is not, in other words, a monadic predicate but, rather, a (disguised) relation holding between an object's position and that of an observer. Nor, moreover, do we have good reason to believe that predicates of selfhood and otherness apply to persons, even though 'I' and 'you' are linguistically and psychologically ineliminable and basic. In short, any argument along Ludlow's (or Teichmann's or Dolev's) lines will, quite simply, prove too much. We know, therefore, that they are invalid and an alternative account is needed. Providing such an account has been the purpose of this chapter. I turn now to some final considerations on the relation between linguistic meaning and psychological states.

5.6 Semantic objections

Howard Wettstein argues that the difficulty with any theory in which 'cognitive states are to be individuated by linguistic meanings, is revealed by examples in which synonymous utterances differ in cognitive significance' (Wettstein 1986, p. 195). William Lane Craig (2000) considers a number of such cases:

I. Informative Identity Statements:

A. Wettstein imagines seeing a performer with half-face make-up from windows on opposite sides of an auditorium and telling someone looking through one window 'He is the same person'—leading the addressee to the other window—'as he is'. The cognitive significance of the first 'he' differs from that of the second. But . . . the linguistic meaning is the same. (Craig 2000, p. 109)

B. imagine correcting someone at a New Year's Eve party in 1999 who thinks that the twenty-first century begins with the year 2000. We could say 'The present century is the same as'—waiting past midnight—'the present century'. The linguistic rules governing temporal indexicals can only treat this sentence as a triviality, thereby leaving its cognitive significance unexplained. (Craig 2000, p. 109)

II. Similar Tokens:

C. Two persons might both utter 'He is about to be attacked by a bear', where in fact a single individual is referred to, but where this fact is not obvious and hearers believe two different individuals are being referred to. In such a situation someone might believe one utterance and not the other. But since the purely linguistic meanings are identical, there is nothing to explain this difference in cognitive significance. (Craig 2000, p. 109)

D. Imagine a man in hospital, who, before falling into a coma says, 'My wife is coming to visit today.' Later that same day he suddenly comes out of the coma but believes that he has been unconscious for three weeks. Knowing his wife's faithfulness, he says, 'My wife is coming to visit today.' Both his utterances in fact refer to the same day and by the rules governing linguistic meaning should have the same cognitive significance. But they do not for the man no longer believes the first utterance he made, though he does believe the second. (Craig 2000, p. 110)

It appears that two acts of belief involving assent to sentence tokens with the same linguistic meaning can nevertheless differ in cognitive significance. So perhaps it is a difference in semantic content that explains the cognitive difference between (1) and (2) after all. However, it turns out that the interesting features of Craig's examples can be handled by the B-theorist by noting the role played by background beliefs in each case.

Consider Craig's fourth example above, concerning the man in the short-lived coma. The following aspects of Craig's description are correct: (i) the man utters two tokens of the same sentence type before and after his coma; (ii) the two tokens share a linguistic meaning (character, role) since this is determined by the sentence type to which they belong; (iii) according to the tenseless theory, the semantic content of each utterance is the same; (iv) the man has different cognitive attitudes to the two utterances. Craig concludes that (iv) conflicts with (iii), and that the difference in significance can only be due to some difference in content between the two utterances, but upon reflection we can see that this needn't be the case at all. The reason is that the man's stock of background beliefs has changed in the time between the two utterances.

Upon awaking from the coma, the man has gained a belief he lacked beforehand, namely the belief that three weeks separate his current belief/utterance from his previous one. Accordingly, if he believed before the coma that today = 1 June, then upon awakening he has the erroneous belief that today = 22 June. He also believes that his earlier utterance occurs on a different day from his current utterance. But it is precisely the point of Kaplan–Perry semantics for indexicals that 'today' refers (directly) to its day of utterance. Combine this with the incorrect belief that 'today' (uttered the second time) refers to a day three weeks later than the previous utterance, and the difference in cognitive significance is readily explained.

To put it more explicitly, the case is as follows. First, at *t*, the man enters the hospital and accepts as true:

(9)   My wife is coming to visit today.

Then, at *t**, a different time but one that occurs in the same twenty-four hour period, the man accepts as true:

(9*)   My wife is coming to visit today.

Owing to the fact that 'today' refers to a twenty-four hour period of time, we may assume that the content of each belief/utterance is identical. But, crucially, this is not all that there is to the story. The example depends on the unexpressed but nonetheless present belief, held at the time of utterance of (9*), that:

(10)   Today is three weeks later than (the day of) my last utterance.

To put it even more starkly, the man believes the following:

(10')   The utterance of (9*) is later than the utterance of (9) by three weeks.

If we assume, as Kaplan and Perry argue, that the linguistic rule governing the use of today is:

(11)   'Today' refers to its day of utterance,

then (9), (9*), and (10') together explain why someone might believe (9) but not (9*) even if the two do not differ in content. The reason is that one may believe that the day referred to in (9) differs from that referred to in (9*) and so think that the two utterances make different claims. But of course the key element of the story is that the man is *deceived*; he is wrong about the time of his second utterance. If he knew the truth, then the cognitive significance of the two utterances would not differ for him. Similar reasoning explains the difference in Craig's third example: the example rests on each speaker *believing* (wrongly) that different people are referred to by each utterance. Given the character/role of 'he', this erroneous belief explains the difference in cognitive significance. Indeed rather than confusing things the Kaplan–Perry account of indexicals renders such cases understandable.

The informative identity statement examples that Craig provides can be explained in a similar fashion, though they are slightly trickier cases owing to the rather short temporal span between utterances. Let us start with the first example: one peers into the east window of an auditorium and sees a man in heavy make-up. One then walks to the west window and sees a clean-faced man. One carelessly assumes that one has seen two people. Now an usher comes along and corrects you. At some time, *t***, the usher points to the man in make-up and utters:

(12)   He is the same as...

Now you are led to the other window and, at t^{***}, hear:

(12′)   ... he is.

The relevant linguistic and semantic facts are, respectively, that 'he' refers (directly) to the person demonstrated, and that the person demonstrated is the same in both cases. But telling someone that a person is identical to him/herself should not be informative. In this case it is. How can we explain this?

By appeal, again, to the different set of beliefs held by the informee on the two occasions, t and t^*, at which the initial beliefs are formed. The only reason one would assume there are two people in the room upon peeking into the second window is that one believes that the person seen in each instance has a uniformly covered or clear face (as the case may be). One is fooled into thinking two people are in the room only because of the assumption that neither alleged person has make-up covering only one half of his face. So, at some earlier time, t, one looks into the east window and wrongly accepts as true:

(13)   He has make-up on (*all of*) his face.

Then, at t^*, after walking around the auditorium one wrongly accepts as true:

(14)   He has no make-up (anywhere) on his face.

From these one concludes:

(15)   There are two people in the room,

and one accordingly informs the usher of this fact.

Subsequently, the usher corrects you. What has happened to your beliefs? Upon hearing the usher utter (12), one still believes that (13) is true, i.e. the man referred to is completely covered in make-up. Upon hearing (12′), one can no longer believe this for, by Leibniz's Law, if the man demonstrated at t^{***} is identical to the man demonstrated at t^{**}, then all and only the same predicates must apply to each (and, in this case, let us assume that you believe, correctly, there is no possibility of the man having cleaned all the make-up off his face in time to deceive you). But one person cannot be both completely covered in make-up and completely free of make-up at the same time. Accordingly, one realizes that one and the same man is wearing half make-up and that is what makes (12) and (12′) informative. In other words, one is told the trivial fact that man in the room is self-identical but in such a way (i.e. via such a demonstration) that one must alter one's beliefs that (13) and (14) are true. Accordingly, one must give up the belief in (15). All of this is explained within the confines of Kaplan–Perry semantics for indexicals.

Finally, let us consider the second example above, the New Year's Eve party. In this case one wrongly thinks that 2000 is the dawn of the twenty-first century. One is then corrected as follows. At t (before midnight), one is told:

(16)   This century is the same as...

then, after a pause, one is told, at t^* (after midnight):

(17)   ...this one.

Note that though 'this century' refers to the particular one-hundred year period in which one finds oneself, in this sort of example one picks out a century by in fact referring to a more specific time and claiming that it belongs to the set that runs from 1901 to 2001. That is, one's utterance of 'this' in 'this century' only indirectly refers to the entire one-hundred year period. What in fact occurs is that one directly refers to a shorter period of time, roughly corresponding to the length of the utterance, and claims that it occurs within certain temporal boundaries. One's utterance does not encompass an entire century so one can only refer to it via this combination of specific reference and general description. (One can, of course, refer to any century by means solely of a definite description, but then one doesn't place one's utterance within that century. However, such placement is precisely what one needs to do in order to be informative, as in Craig's example).

So what I think is a more precise understanding of what is going on in this example is that at a particular time, t, one hears the utterance of (16) and accepts that:

(16')   The century in which t (or (16)) occurs...

is the same as:

(17')   The century in which t^* (or (17)) occurs.

Recall that it is at the later time, t^*, that one hears (17); moreover, one is aware of this difference. Initially, however, one had the following belief:

(18) t occurs in the twentieth century and t^* in the twenty-first.

More precisely, knowing the conventional role that midnight plays in our system of time keeping, one believed that:

(18')   For all t: [(if t<midnight, 31 Dec. 1999, then t is a member of the set of times designated by 'the twentieth century') and (if t > midnight, 31 Dec. 1999, then t is a member of the set of times designated by 'the twenty-first century'.)]

But after hearing (16) and (17), one no longer believes that (18') is true, because one knows (otherwise the demonstration would not be effective) that t is earlier than midnight and t^* is later than midnight, yet both fall in the same century. One is told that the times occupied by (16) and (17) occur in the same century. So the apparently trivial identity statement in fact tells us that two moments that we thought fell in different centuries in fact fall in one.

The conclusion that may be drawn here is that where linguistic differences between sentences are not available to explain differences in cognitive significance, differences in background beliefs generally will be. So long as we subject our background beliefs to consistency constraints and metaphysical principles such as Leibniz's Law, it is clear that apparently trivial statements can in fact be informative. One may be forced into altering one's stock of beliefs as a result of such constraints, but none of the beliefs involved need be ones with tensed contents.

5.7 Conclusion

I have argued that the presence of experience (of events and times) is to be explained by an account of the cognitive significance of tenseless contents that are apprehended under a tensed mode of presentation. I have presented a tenseless, tripartite analysis of such beliefs. First, one is guided by the grammatical knowledge that 'e is present' is true iff e is simultaneous with the time of utterance; 't is now' is true iff t is simultaneous with the time of utterance; and so on. Secondly, learning and experience lead one to be causally triggered to accept present-tense sentences as true in response to appropriate stimuli. Thirdly, one endeavours to keep one's stock of background beliefs consistent and coherent. These three elements are, I claim, individually necessary but jointly sufficient to explain the presence of our experience of events and times. Hence, beliefs about the present can be accounted for by the B-theory of time.

This undercuts, I believe, a common position taken by opponents of the B-theory. Authors such as Bigelow (1991), Smith (1993), and Craig (2000) take presentness to be a primitive predicate of events, one that is not explicable in other terms, nor reducible to other entities. But the primary justification for resorting to the claim that some predicate or property is primitive and unanalysable is the combination of: (i) the fact that any attempt to spell it out in other terms ends up in circularity, regress, or else some other kind of absurdity, and (2) the meaningfulness of claims involving that predicate or property. A plausible candidate here is the concept 'true'. Attempts to define or reduce this notion to others seem bound to fail (see, e.g., Davidson 1996).

It is now clear, however, that such a situation is not the case with regard to the predicate 'is present'. I have provided, in this chapter, a non-circular, non-regressive, non-absurd schema that adequately accounts for the logical properties of the present tense and that draws only on the resources of the tenseless theory of time and the causal theory of perception. In Chapter 4, I defend the use of 'is earlier/later than' to account for the past and future tenses. We can use tenseless relations to illustrate why the present is experientially privileged, why uncontroversial entailment relations hold between tensed sentences, why the truth-value links obtain, and, hence, why what is future will be present and past. Given this, there seems to be no plausible reason to maintain that 'is present' (or 'is past' or 'is future') is a simple and unanalysable predicate that is not reducible to tenseless relations. There is, in sum, no need to suppose that the logical form of propositions concerning time involves any predicates other than tenseless relations. The tenseless theory of time, which is the second pillar of the B-theory, is well supported and secure.

6

Objects and times

6.1 Introduction

A philosophical study of the concept of time is bound to come into contact with philosophical questions concerning the nature of change. This can be seen by considering the problem of temporary intrinsics (Lewis 1986). Consider an ordinary object, such as an apple. An apple can undergo change by having its colour move from green to red to brown. Assume, for simplicity, that when the apple is any colour it is entirely and only that colour; furthermore, let us ignore worries of vagueness and take it that at any given moment the apple is exactly one of green, red, or brown. In short, 'is green', 'is red', and 'is brown' are precise, mutually exclusive, and exhaustive predicates of the apple. Since the apple changes, it exhibits all three colours; the colours are, however, mutually exclusive. This appears to be a contradiction: if the apple is green, it is not red; yet, the apple is both green and red. An unhappy conclusion threatens: it appears as though it is impossible to consistently describe change.

The air of paradox quickly dissipates, however, for one immediately realizes that the apple is green *at t*, red *at t'*, and there is no conflict here at all. As Hinchliff writes:

The solution to the puzzle may at first seem too obvious for it even to be a genuine puzzle: mention the distinct times at which [the apple] has its distinct [colours] and declare the problem solved...This solution is correct but incomplete...What is required is a theory of temporal modification which explains how change is possible (Hinchliff 1996, pp. 119–20)

In other words, a consistent account of change requires that we understand how predication (Hinchliff's 'modification') involves time. Hence, if we wish to elucidate the semantic role of time in our discourse—i.e. if we wish to have a rich understanding of the logical form of propositions involving time—we shall have to consider issues concerning objects and temporal predication. By 'temporal predication' I mean an expression of the form '*x* is *F* at *t*'. I shall assume that any predicate that an object can satisfy at some times but not others is a temporal predicate.[1]

---

[1] Some temporal predicates may be instantiated by an object at all times at which it exists; it may nevertheless remain a temporal predicate because it is *possible* for it to be instantiated at/relative to some times but not others.

The predicate 'x is F at t' is one of the most basic forms in our temporal repertoire. Since we are unable to account for the most ordinary species of change without such expressions, we are not going to get very far in our philosophical theorizing about time without an account of them. The precise understanding of (the propositions expressed by) such temporal predications remains an issue of controversy, in part because different philosophers think about change in different ways, but also because one's stance on temporal predication has implications for one's views on the nature of objects, in particular whether they persist, or survive change, in virtue of being composed of temporal parts (four-dimensionalism) or in virtue of being located at different times (three-dimensionalism). The three-/four-dimensionalism debate is regularly conducted in metaphysical rather than semantic terms (see, e.g., Sider 2001, Hawley 2001) but I believe that the most tractable and reasonable approach to the problem is via a consideration of temporal predication.

In what follows I argue that the best account of temporal predication is a relational account, according to which temporal predicates express relations between objects and times. This view, I conclude, not only has greater justification than its rivals but also can withstand the arguments brought to bear against it. I finish with a consideration of the implications of this account for the dispute between three-dimensionalists and four-dimensionalists.

6.2 Temporal predication: the contenders

The so-called 'problem' of change is a long-standing issue that occupied such ancient thinkers as Heraclitus, Parmenides, Plato, and Aristotle (McKirahan Jr. 1994). The *locus classicus* of the recent debate is David Lewis's brief but compelling discussion in his *On the Plurality of Worlds* (Lewis 1986, pp. 202–4) where he considers the idea of an object gaining and losing temporary, intrinsic properties:

Persisting things change their intrinsic properties. For instance shape: when I sit, I have a bent shape; when I stand, I have a straightened shape. Both shapes are temporary intrinsic properties; I have them only some of the time. How is such change possible? (Lewis 1986, p. 203)

Surviving an alteration involves conflicting concepts: *identity*, which is required for persistence, and *difference*, which is required for change.

Lewis (1986) believes there are three possible solutions to the puzzle of change. The first is presentism. For a presentist, the only properties any object has are those it currently instantiates so there can be no incompatibility with properties it did or will have. As I have already rejected presentism, this solution won't do (Lewis similarly finds presentism too implausible to be taken seriously as a solution to the problem of change).

The second solution is as follows: when we assert that x is F at t the proposition expressed is that a *relation* holds between x and t. In other words, the proposition expressed by 'the apple is green at noon' is that the apple stands in the green-relation to noon, which has the following, relational form:

(1) $F(x, t)$.

Then, when we assert that the apple is red at 6:00 p.m., we express a proposition of the following form:

(2) $G(x, t')$.

Clearly there is no contradiction here. Moreover, it is clear that x will retain its identity from t to t' in virtue of satisfying Leibniz's Law: it is tenselessly true of x that it bears relation F to t and G to t', so what is true of x prior to the change is true of it afterward.

According to Lewis's third, preferred solution, to claim that an object is green is not to attribute any relation to it. Rather, temporal predicates are what they appear to be: monadic but satisfied not by ordinary, three-dimensional objects but by temporal parts. This removes the contradiction from accounts of change because to say that the apple is green at t and red at t' is to express the propositions that the t-part of the apple is green:

(3) $F(p^t_x)$;

and the t'-temporal part of the apple is red:

(4) $G(p^{t'}_x)$.

On this account, change is a matter of tenselessly having temporal parts, which all exist tenselessly, to which different monadic predicates are truthfully ascribed. Therefore, the object retains its identity through time by never changing as a whole.[2]

The difference between the relational and four-dimensional accounts of temporal predication is twofold: first, according to the former temporal predication is relational in structure while according to the latter it is monadic (at least as concerns time); secondly, according to the former, ordinary, three-dimensional objects are the subjects of temporal predication while according to the latter it is instantaneous temporal parts that satisfy these predicates.

---

[2] For the stage theorist (e.g. Hawley 2001, Sider 2001), the only objects are instantaneous temporal parts; a persisting or, as four-dimensionalists put it, perduring object is in fact a collection of such parts, each of which is a counterpart of the others. This is a metaphysical difference from Lewis's view, according to which the apple is itself a four-dimensional entity spread out in time, but as concerns predication the difference isn't important, for in both cases it is temporal parts that satisfy predicates. Hence, I will consider the views together here, but separately if need be.

Much of the debate over the puzzle of change revolves around Lewis's solutions. There are, however, other accounts worth noting. According to Mellor (1998) and Sattig (2006), the phrase 'at t' in 'x is F at t' has the form of a temporal operator that modifies a tenseless predication, Fx, to form an instance of temporal predication; e.g.:

(5)   At t: Fx.

For Mellor, the operator, 'at t', provides us with the *location* of a tenseless fact:

t and t' ... are not entities that a is *related to* by F and F', but the temporal *locations* of non-relational facts, Fa and $F'a$ which constitute this change [i.e. the change of a from F to F']. (Mellor 1998, p. 91)

Sattig, on the other hand, outlines (though he doesn't ultimately defend) a similar view, which he calls the 'intensional' account of temporal predication. On the intensional account, temporal predicates such as 'is green' are, as they appear to be, monadic predicates; their extensions, however, are relativized to times because their *intensions* are functions from times to extensions, which are 'classes of ordinary objects' (Sattig 2006, p. 80).

So there are four rival positions on the nature of temporal predication that I wish to consider: the relational account, temporal parts theory, Mellor's 'locational' operators, and the intensional view. I shall argue that it is the relational account that comes out ahead on both semantic and metaphysical grounds.[3]

The strategy is as follows. First I sketch out the relational theory. I then consider some objections to it and respond to them. I move on to examine two of its competitors, Mellor's view and the intensional account. I conclude that they do not provide compelling alternatives to the relational view. Accordingly, this leaves the relational account and the temporal parts account. In Chapter 7 I examine the latter, finding it to be unconvincing. That will complete the defence of the relational view and three-dimensionalism.

---

[3] An alternative that I won't consider explicitly is the 'adverbial' view of temporal predication put forward by Haslanger (1989), Johnston (1987), and Lowe (1988). On this view, temporal predicates are not relational but their instantiations are. In other words, for an object, o, to be F, is for o to be-at-t F or, to put it adverbially, for o to be F 't-ly'. On this view, 'o is t-ly F' and 'o is t^*-ly $\sim F$' are as consistent as are 'o is actually F' and 'o is possibly $\sim F$'. But, as Hawley (2001, pp. 21–2) points out, for adverbs in general, the same trick cannot be pulled off successfully: o cannot be *silently* F but *loudly* $\sim F$. Accordingly, we are left, on this view, wondering what it is about temporal adverbs that renders otherwise incompatible claims consistent. Moreover, the 'be-at-t' locution clearly expresses a relation between an object and a time: an 'instantiation' relation rather than an 'is red at' relation. In this case, however, one has merely exchanged one relation to times for another and the resistance to the relational view is unmotivated. I shall argue, moreover, that the relational character of 'is red at t' follows straightforwardly from the logical notion of a relation. If that is right, then it will be difficult for an adverbialist to argue that 'be-at-t' expresses a relation while 'is red at t' does not. Hence, I believe that the arguments below adequately cover the adverbial view even if not addressing it directly.

6.3 The relational account of temporal predication

According to the relational account, locutions of the form 'x is F at t' express relations between objects and times. Why should one accept this view? The reason is, in fact, rather simple: such expressions appears to be relational in form, and upon further consideration, nothing seems to cast serious doubt on this verdict; hence, it ought to be believed. Let me lay this out.

To begin, let us note just what a relation is. In general, a relation is a set of ordered pairs:

In general, then, we want a relation to be a set of ordered pairs of objects. (Zehna and Johnson 1972, p. 61)

[F]irst-order propositions which can be characterized as involving a relation are characterized instead as involving the set of ordered pairs that it singles out. And the way in which they obtain their truth values is explained, not in terms of which ordered pairs exemplify certain relations, but in terms of which ordered pairs are elements of certain sets of ordered pairs. (Zalabardo 2000, p. 19)

If S and T are any sets, then any subset R of $S \times T$ is called a relation between S and T ... If R is a relation between S and T and (s, t) is an element of R, then s is said to be R-related to t. (Gemignani 2004, pp. 150–1)[4]

Accordingly, any open formula that is satisfied by ordered pairs (or triples, etc.) defines a relation.

Now, consider the proposition expressed by, for example, 'the car is parked under the bridge' or 'the boat is stuck in the house'. They are both of the form:

(6) x is F [prep] y,

where '[prep]' is a variable standing for any preposition. For a given preposition, (6) is an open formula that is satisfied by ordered *pairs*, <x, y>, of entities: for example, <car, garage>, <boat, house>. Hence, in both cases, a relation is defined. The same, I argue, applies to 'the apple is red at noon'. It, like the other two examples, is of the form of (6) so, putting to the side (for the moment) metaphysical differences between kinds of object, it clearly is satisfied by an ordered pair, <apple, noon>. In conclude that, in general, expressions of the form 'x is F at t' define relations:

(R) $F(x, t)$.

This is, as a matter of form, simply what such expressions do. That, in a nutshell, is the argument for the relational account of temporal predication. Now the question is

---

[4] Recall that the Cartesian product of sets S and T, $S \times T$, consists of all ordered pairs, (s, t), such that $s \in S$ and $t \in T$.

whether this conclusion can withstand scrutiny. Let us, therefore, examine it in more detail.

A virtue of the relational account, as noted above, is that it renders ordinary instances of change logically coherent:

(7) $F(x, t)$ & $G(x, t')$,

Recall that in (7) one and the same entity—x—is both red and green, so the relational account is compatible with *endurance*: the view that objects are three-dimensional entities that can retain their numerical identity through change.

Some, such as McTaggart (1908), argue that because (7) is a tenseless, temporally invariable proposition, it cannot be a genuine report of change. He is wrong, however, because his argument depends on the premise that an object changes only if there are propositions about it that can be truthfully expressed at some times but not others. In other words, this argument assumes that the *process* of change, whatever that turns out to be in the world, requires a *description* that changes. But I can see no reason to grant this assumption; much as an unchanging sequence of unchanging photographs can represent change, so can a tenseless, relational description of an object represent change. Recall the discussion of the representational fallacy (Dyke 2008) in Chapters 3 and 4: we mustn't confuse features of our representations with features of what they represent. It is even more dubious to engage in the inverse line of reasoning and suppose that features of the world must be features of our representations; if that were true, then only apples could represent apples, only clouds could represent clouds, etc., all of which is absurd.

So, the relational theory is suggested by the structure of temporal predication, is a coherent solution to the puzzle of change, and works with our ordinary notion of objects. Its primary entailments are as follows: if an object, o, changes from F at t to G at t', then: (i) different relations hold between o and t and t'; and (ii) the object and times exist. It does, however, have another consequence, which may strike many as far from benign: (iii) temporal predication makes no sense independent of time; there is no such thing as a having, for example, a shape *simpliciter* or atemporally.

This last point is raised as an objection by Sider (2001, pp. 99–101), but I, in fact, consider it to be a strength of the relational view. To see this, consider that there are many predicates that can be true of concrete objects but not abstract ones; for instance, 'is red', 'is cold', 'is massive', 'is loud', 'is fragrant', and so on. It is (necessarily) false that the number seven is loud or that justice is green. While the propositions expressed by such claims do not appear to be obviously nonsensical— they are not contradictory or gibberish—there is clearly something wrong with them. I think the relational account of temporal predication offers the right explanation of this. Here is why.

If the relational theory of predication is correct, then 'x is green' has the form of a relation:

(8)　G(x, t).

Next, consider the proposition:

(9)　Justice is green.

Given (8) above, (9) is equivalent to:

(10)　G(j, t).

The problem with (9) is not incoherence. The problem, rather, is that justice, being abstract, is 'outside' of space and time and, so, cannot stand in relations to times. Hence, (10) explains why (9) can't be true, given the nature of abstract objects.

A monadic account of temporal predication has a less natural time here, for if predicates such as 'is green' are monadic, then (9) has the following form:

(10′)　G(j).

This on its own does not entail that justice stands in relation to time, so thus far it remains unexplained why (9) couldn't be true. The relationalist need only appeal to the concept of abstractness and her analysis of predication to explain why (9) is false. The monadicist, on the other hand, will have to appeal to at least one further principle. This simplicity is an advantage for the former view.

A corollary to the foregoing is that to be a concrete entity is to stand in relation to time. David Lewis argues that this entails that any enduring thing 'in itself has, for example, no colour or shape' (Lewis 1986, pp. 203–4). Lewis lodges this as a complaint, but it strikes me as an advantage. To see why, consider a world without time. Any proposition of the following form will be false in that world:

(TW)　(∃t)P

After all, a timeless world is devoid of times, so *nothing* can satisfy (TW). It is, therefore, false to say, of a timeless world, w, that there is a time at which object o has shape S. In other words, nothing can have a shape in a timeless world. Lewis finds this incredible, but it strikes me as correct, for it is of the nature of a concrete object to be related to space and time.

What, however, are we to say about abstract entities, such as geometric objects? If they exist, then they exist outside of space and time, yet it might be argued that they have shapes, for example. I think, however, that if we ponder this issue we can see that, rather than *having* a shape, a geometric object, such as a square, *is* a shape. A concrete object might *instantiate* such a shape but the shape itself does not instantiate a shape. A shape doesn't have shape, just as weight doesn't have weight: if a person's weight is 75 kg, then it is the person who has weight. I think, therefore, that even if abstract entities such as squares exist, anything of which shape is properly predicated will instantiate that shape at some time or another. Hence, the relational view of temporal predicates can be retained.[5]

Here is another objection.[6] Perhaps times are abstract entities. Since one time can be earlier than another time, it turns out that abstract objects *can* stand in relations to times after all. So, the relational view's explanation of the difference between the abstract and the concrete fails. It would be unfortunate if the relationalist were forced to deny that times could be abstract entities, since that seems like a viable view, but there is something she can say here. She can point out that there is a difference between relations that are essential to a thing and those that are not. If times are abstract locations of events, then the year 2015 cannot fail to be one year later than 2014 or one year earlier than 2016, any more than the line x = 2 on a Cartesian graph can fail to be between the x = 1 and x = 3 lines. Hence, if times are abstract, then B-relations between times are essential to those times and are no more than definitions, or essences, of those times. On the other hand, it is not essential to justice or other abstract entities that they be any colour, shape, size, weight, or any other spatiotemporal property. Hence, all such relations would be non-essential. The modified relationalist view of the difference between abstract and concrete entities is, therefore the following: abstract objects cannot stand in *non-essential* relations to times, but concrete objects can.

Notice, further, that relationalism provides a nice explanation of the validity of certain pieces of uncontroversial reasoning. Suppose that an apple is green and sweet at noon. Understood relationally, this proposition is equivalent to the conjunction of the following propositions:

(11)   Green(apple, noon)
(12)   Sweet(apple, noon).

If the apple is sweet at noon and green at noon, it follows that there is a time at which the apple is both green and sweet. (11) and (12) entail just that:

(13) $(\exists t)[\text{Green(apple, } t) \ \& \ \text{Sweet(apple, } t)]$

Similarly, (11) and (12) entail that: something is sweet at noon; something is sweet and green at noon; something is sweet at some time; something is sweet and green at some time; and so on. So, obviously valid inferences are rendered transparent on the relational account.

---

[5] This doesn't commit the relational theory to Platonism about properties. To say that at object can only instantiate a shape at a time could be taken as just another way of expressing the view that to be shaped is to stand in a shape relation to a time. The relational view is consistent with the existence of universals but doesn't require them.

[6] I thank J. C. Beall for raising it.

Let me present one more consideration in favour of the relational account before turning to objections. Notice that relationalism is in fact suggested by the way in which the 'problem' of change is expressed. The crux of the challenge is that seemingly incompatible predicates can both be true of one and the same object: the apple is both green and red. In other contexts, the fact that incompatible predications seem to be true of an object is an *indication* that the predicates contain an overlooked parameter. For example: 'John is small' and 'John is big'. There are plenty of cases in which 'is small' and 'is big' can both be true of a person; John may, for example, be a small basketball player but a big human, and this tells us that predicates such as 'is small' and 'is big' are relative to a comparison class. Another example: 'that meal was terrible' and 'that meal was delicious'. We needn't assume that one of the disputants here is objectively correct; rather, 'is delicious' and 'is terrible' are relations between meals (or other foods) and individuals. A final example: 'the box is heavy' and 'the box is not heavy'; 'is heavy' is a relation between an object and a person, or a person's strength, and that is why both it and its negation can be true of one and the same object. So, rather than taking the apparent difficulty in describing instances of change consistently as a call for an unusual metaphysical or semantic theory, we ought to take it as evidence that temporal predicates are relations that involve, perhaps implicitly, times.

I conclude that the relational theory of temporal predication appears to be correct upon a surface examination, and this appearance holds up under scrutiny. It is both well motivated and metaphysically innocuous. Surprisingly, it has relatively few defenders in the literature.[7] I turn next to a consideration of the major objections to the view.

6.4 Objections and alternatives

6.4.1 *Lewis's objection*

Lewis, famously, writes:

Persisting things change their intrinsic properties. For instance shape: when I sit, I have a bent shape; when I stand, I have a straightened shape. Both shapes are temporary intrinsic properties; I have them only some of the time. How is such change possible? I know of only three solutions...First solution: contrary to what we might think, shapes are not genuine intrinsic properties. They are disguised relations, which an enduring thing may bear to times. One and the same enduring thing may bear the bent-shape relation to some times, and the straight-shape relation to others. In itself, considered apart from its relation to other things, it has no shape at all...This is simply incredible...If we know what shape is, we know that it is a property, not a relation. (Lewis 1986, pp. 203–4)

---

[7] One of the most prominent defences of the view is Mellor (1981a). He then rejects the account, in Mellor (1998); I discuss why in section 6.4.3.

This well-known passage suggests two objections to the relational account. First, that it is blatantly obvious that shape is not a relational property; secondly, that if it were, nothing would have a shape. I don't think either objection quite hits the mark.

Contrary to Lewis, I suggest that what is obvious is that we cannot know *a priori* whether the *property* of being a certain shape, mass, colour, charge, etc. is relational or not. To see this, note that properties are usually considered to be distinct from predicates in that they are physical features of objects, or are entities in the Platonic realm; either way, they are something more than predicates in a language (Mellor 1991). Let us, then, take the case of colour. What is the property of, say, being red? In particular, do we know *a priori* that it is not relational in structure? I don't think that we do. For all we know *a priori*, an object reflects red light (or has red surface features) only when it enters into some kind of quantum entanglement with physical particles at the far side of the universe. No metaphysical theory should be incompatible with this proposition, for it is an empirical matter whether or not it is true. Accordingly, it may be the case that nothing has a colour independently of its relations to other things. Similar situations might be the case with mass, charge, and shape. There may be true scientific theories of all of these properties that surprise the philosophical imagination.[8]

I think we can conclude that determining which properties there are and their natures will always be at least in part a scientific task; philosophy might help this scientific project, of course, but empirical input is required, so we cannot be sure, as Lewis is, that we know shape properties are not relations. So, Lewis's first charge against the relational account is misdirected: the physical structure of properties such as colour, charge, mass, and shape is not apparent but, as concerns the corresponding *predicates*, the relational account is well motivated.

Let us turn to Lewis's second objection. What the relational view entails is that ascriptions of mass, shape, colour, etc. are, necessarily, relative to a time. One result, as noted above, is that there is no sense to be attached to an attribution of mass, shape, or colour to an object in a timeless world. It doesn't follow, however, that, at any given time, an object lacks mass, shape, or colour. As long as an object is, say, red at *t*, then it has colour at *t*. What is the case, according to the relational view, is that no object has colour (mass, shape, etc.) atemporally/*simpliciter*, but this is perfectly compatible with an object having a shape at each moment of its existence.

Let me expand on this response a bit by considering the question of whether the relational account eliminates the distinction between the intrinsic and extrinsic. Lewis writes: 'A thing has its intrinsic properties in virtue of the way that thing itself, and nothing else, is' (Lewis 1983b, p. 197). I think that the relationalist ought to respond as follows. If *x* is red at *t*, then *x*'s being red doesn't depend on the *way* that

---

[8] Indeed, hasn't Einstein taught us that mass is a relation between an object and a reference frame?

t is. Rather, it just depends on there *being* a *t* at which *x* is red. I don't think that Lewis in particular should have much objection to this. After all, on his modal realism (Lewis 1986) for *x* to be *F* is for *x* to be *F* in some concrete world or other. Does he conclude that for any *F*, *x*'s being *F* depends in part on the 'way *x*'s world is', and so isn't intrinsic? He doesn't, of course. To be *F* is to be *F* in some *w*, even if *F* is intrinsic. Analogously, on the relational view, for any material object, to be *F* (where *F* is a temporal predicate) is to be *F* at some time, even if *F* is intrinsic to the object.

Lewis continues:

> The intrinsic properties of something depend only on that thing; whereas the extrinsic properties of something may depend, wholly or partly, on something else. If something has an intrinsic property, then so does any perfect duplicate of that thing; whereas duplicates situated in different surroundings will differ in their extrinsic properties. (Lewis 1983b, p. 197)

I think the relationalist needs to reject the first sentence: to be a material object is to occupy space and time; that is, such objects depend on there *being* space and time for their existence. Nonetheless, there may still be a difference between predicates that express what is intrinsic to an object (such as its being round) and those that express what isn't intrinsic to the object (e.g. its being to the left of *y*). Note, for instance, that on the relational view, perfect duplicates of material objects *will* be intrinsically identical so long as each instantiates all their properties at some time or another; it is just that there is no sense to be had of a perfect duplicate of a material object that is not also in time. If one nevertheless wishes to insist that, despite all this, relations to times cannot capture what is intrinsic to an object, then I think that the intrinsic/extrinsic distinction has become defined so strictly as to lose its relevance.

Finally, let me note that the Special Theory of Relativity has accustomed us to the idea that properties, even those such as an object's mass, can be *frame-dependent*. This doesn't appear to lead Lewis to conclude that mass or shape is not an intrinsic property, nor should it. The upshot is that the intrinsic/extrinsic distinction doesn't track the non-relational/relational distinction after all.[9] Accordingly, the relationalist view doesn't preclude the former.

6.4.2 *Logical form and validity*

Le Poidevin (1991) argues that the requirement that a theory of temporal predication explain obviously valid entailments

raises difficulties for a relational account of properties. If 'Reggie was lurking behind the conservatory at four o'clock' is formulated using a three-place relation:

(a)   L(a, s, t)

---

[9] This is not, in fact, all that surprising; the former appears to be a metaphysical distinction, the latter a formal one.

and 'Reggie was lurking at four o'clock' is formulated using a two-place relation:

(b)   L*(a, t)

then the validity of the inference from (a) to (b) has simply been obscured by the notation. (Le Poidevin 1991, p. 74)

I have argued that the relational account gains strength from its ability to explain valid inference, so I consider it important to respond to Le Poidevin's objection.

My response to Le Poidevin's example is suggest that the relationalist follow Davidson (1967) and construe action sentences as expressing propositions that quantify over events that may be characterized in various ways; for example as 'lurkings'. For instance, 'Reggie was lurking behind the conservatory at four o'clock' may be formalized as follows:

(14) $(\exists e)[\text{Lurks}(e, \text{Reggie}) \,\&\, \text{Behind}(e, \text{conservatory}) \,\&\, \text{Sim}(e, 4{:}00)]$.[10]

(14) straightforwardly entails:

(15) $(\exists e)[\text{Lurks}(e, \text{Reggie}) \,\&\, \text{Sim}(e, 4{:}00)]$.

None of this is inconsistent with the relationalist's account. For example, if, while lurking, Reggie is tall, we can conjoin (14) with:

(16) $\text{Tall}(\text{Reggie}, 4{:}00)$

to derive:

(17) $(\exists e)[\text{Lurks}(e, \text{Reggie}) \,\&\, \text{Behind}(e, \text{conservatory}) \,\&\, \text{Sim}(e, 4{:}00) \,\&\, \text{Tall}(\text{Reggie}, 4{:}00)]$.

This entails that somebody who lurked at 4:00 was tall then. So, I don't think that Le Poidevin's example leads to any difficulties for the relationalist.

He has, however, another objection:

Similarly, the case of Reggie's being fatter in 1972 than Edna in 1980 poses a problem for the relational account, necessitating the introduction of peculiar entities, such as, in this case, girths, or degrees of fatness, represented here by α and β:

$\text{Fat}(\alpha, \text{Reggie}, 1972) \,\&\, \text{Fat}(\beta, \text{Edna}, 1980)$ and $\text{Greater}(\alpha, \beta)$

...when we make comparisons between people at different times (or the same person at different times) we are surely talking directly about ordinary objects, not such strange entities as girths, or heights, or personalities. (Le Poidevin 1991, p. 74)

---

[10]   Where '$\text{Sim}(x, y)$' = 'x is simultaneous with y'.

I must confess that I am unsure why it is supposed to be so problematic to introduce entities such as heights or girths into one's ontology; they simply don't strike me as strange or exotic. We are, in fact, quite familiar with them and can distinguish objects that have them from those that don't. For example, it is because people, but not rocks, have girths that the following appears peculiar:

(18)   Reggie is fatter than the Rock of Gibraltar.

The problem with (18) is that Gibraltar is not the kind of entity that has girth or any degree of fatness. Recall that 'Reggie is fatter than the Rock of Gibraltar' is, in English, an incomplete sentence, short for 'Reggie is fatter than the Rock of Gibraltar is fat'. If girths or degrees of fatness can be had by people (and animals) but not formations of rock, then the problem with (18) becomes apparent. Hence, the positing of girths or degrees of fatness does genuine explanatory work.

   Le Poidevin, on the other hand, prefers a notation that

treats adverbs and temporal and spatial modifiers as *predicate modifiers*:

At(Behind(Grotesquely(Lurks(a))p))t

From which one can validly infer:

At(Lurks(a))t. (Le Poidevin 1991, p. 75)

If, however, this is correct, then how do we explain the fact that

(19)   Fatter[(At(Reggie, 1972)), (At(Edna, 1980))]

may be true while

(20)   Fatter[(At(Reggie, 1972)), (At(Rock of Gibraltar,1980))]

may not? In other words, if 'fatter than' is a relation between objects, why can't rocks, trees, or clouds be the subjects of such relations; why is it only people and, presumably, animals that can be so related?[11] The appealing answer, again, is to suppose that only such creatures have girths, or degrees of being fat. It is, of course, not right to suppose that only persons and animals can *contain* fat; many vegetables are rich in vegetable oils, and even if we consider a large, spherical conglomeration of animal fat, it is problematic to suppose that:

(21)   Fatter[(At(Reggie, 1972)), (At(conglomeration of animal fat, 1980))].

The natural take on these issues, I suggest, is that even though objects, such as balls of animal fat, have circumferences or, more generally, physical extension, only persons

---

[11] It may be that only people can be fatter than other people, and animals fatter than other animals; I make no commitment to the possibility of cross-species comparisons of girth.

and animals have girths, understood as some kind of proportionate measure of an animal's fat content in certain areas of its body. Hence, I see nothing *a priori* suspicious about the commitment to such entities.

At a certain point, Le Poidevin suggests that the problem with girths is that they are not concrete:

Admittedly, the temporal part view has one comparing temporal parts of persons, rather than persons, but at least temporal parts are, unlike girths, concrete objects. (Le Poidevin 1991, pp. 74–5)

I am not sure, however, why a girth is any more abstract than any other property, such as mass, colour, or shape, all of which can be compared.

Another advantage of postulating such entities as girths and heights is that doing so allows us to connect the positive forms of adjectives with their superlative and comparative forms.[12] If, say, being fat is a matter of having a certain girth, then we can, ignoring time for simplicity's sake, formalize 'Reggie is fat' as:

(22) $Fat(Reggie, x)$,

where x is his girth. 'Edna is fat' is similarly formalized as:

(23) $Fat(Edna, y)$.

An immediate advantage of these forms is the following. When we express the propositions that Reggie is fat and that Edna is fat, we immediately suppose there to be an answer to the question as to who, if either, is fatter. The answer will not simply depend on their weights, for a lighter person can be fatter (if, for example, shorter). (23) and (24) explain this natural supposition, for given that Reggie and Edna have girths, x and y, it seems that:

(24) $Greater(x, y) \lor Less\ than(x, y)$ or $Same\ as(x, y)$

must be true. This may require that girths can be quantified, but that seems unobjectionable (bodily fat content, for example, is usually determined by measurements taken at key points in the body; such measurements could be added to determine a number that measures one's fatness). So, the suggested line of reasoning explains why the positive form 'Reggie is fat' immediately entails the possibility of comparison.

Suppose that Reggie is as fat as John. If we commit to girths, the following form captures this proposition:

(25) $Fat(Reggie, x)$ & $Fat(John, y)$ & $x = y$.

---

[12] The arguments that follow are inspired by those concerning attributions of height found in Katz (1995).

Now suppose that Edna is less fat than Reggie:

(26)   Fat(Reggie, x) & Fat(Edna, z) & $x > z$.

It follows that John is fatter than Edna. (25) and (26) make this obvious for they, together, entail:

(27)   Fat(John, y) & Fat(Edna, z) & $y > z$.

This is another success story for the account.

If, on the other hand, we adopt:

(22′)   Fat(Reggie)

as the formalization of 'Reggie is fat' and

(23′)   Fat(Edna)

as the formalization of 'Edna is fat', there is no obvious connection to Le Poidevin's comparative form:

(28)   Fatter(Reggie, Edna)

Why (22′) and (23′) should allow for comparisons of this kind has been obscured on this view.

The commitment to girths also affords us a nice explanation of the relation between the positive and superlative forms. If Reggie is the fattest person in the room:

(29)   Fat(Reggie, x) & In(Reggie, the room) & $[(\forall y)(\text{Fat}(y, z)$ & In(y, the room)) $\supset$ Greater(x, z)].

and Edna is fat and in the room:

(30)   Fat(Edna, w) & In(Edna, the room)

then Reggie is fatter than Edna. (29) and (30) entail:

(31)   Greater(x, w).

Once again, girths have fulfilled a useful theoretical role (for a more detailed discussion of these and related issues see Katz 1995). All of this is consistent with temporal predicates being relations between objects and times. Thus far, I find that neither Lewis nor Le Poidevin has given us reason to reject the relational view of temporal predicates.

6.4.3 Mellor's 'locational' theory

At one time, D. H. Mellor was the foremost defender of the relational account of temporal predication (Mellor 1981a, 1981b). By 1998, he had changed his mind (Mellor

1998). His argument for the turnaround is as follows. If an object, *o*, is red at *t*, then *o* exists at *t*; *o*'s standing in the 'is red-at' relation to *t* does not, however, entail that *o* exists at *t*. This is because an object can stand in a relation to a time without existing at that time; therefore, 'is red' is not a relation between an object and a time (Mellor 1998, p. 93). Instead, '*x* is *F* at *t*' expresses the proposition that:

(32)   At *t*: *Fx*.

Mellor explicates this as follows: *t* is the temporal location of the tenseless fact, *Fx* (Mellor 1998, pp. 90–5). I have a number of concerns with this account.

First, notice that Mellor's complaint is that propositions of the form *R*(*x*, *y*) do not entail that *x* and *y* are co-located, and it is true that relations lack such an entailment. But notice that his preferred solution falls prey to precisely the same problem. On his view, tenseless facts are *located* at various times. However, 'being located at' is a *relation* that holds between (let us follow Mellor and assume) the fact and those times. After all, on Mellor's account there exist two kinds of entities, facts and times, which satisfy the formula '*x* is located at *y*', and this, as argued above, suffices to define a relation.

A little further reflection reveals that *many* relations in fact entail that their relata overlap spatially or temporally; for example: '*x* overlaps with *y*'; '*x* and *y* coincide'; '*x* = *y*'; '*x* is under *y*'; '*x* is to the left of *y*'; '*x* is touching *y*'; etc. Clearly this entailment must be more than a matter of logical form alone, but the point is that Mellor's account requires co-location-entailing relations as much as does the relational theory.

Mellor has a response:

real changes of properties need effects, and for them to be changes in the things to which we ascribe those properties, that is where their first effects must be... This causal test for properties is related to another one, namely that a thing's properties should be detectable just by inspecting that thing. (Mellor 1998, 87–8)

In case the relationalist is tempted by a similar solution, Mellor writes:

it is no answer to say that changeable properties too are relations which entail this [i.e. sameness of temporal location]. For what makes ['*a* is *F* at *t*'] entail that *a* is located at *t*, if not the fact that... *F*'s being a *non*-relational property requires *a* to be located wherever and whenever *a* is *F*. (Mellor 1998, 94)

This is an interesting challenge, but I don't think it can succeed against the relational account for what is, by now, a familiar reason: '*e*'s first effects are at/on *a*' expresses a *relation* between two entities, *e* and *a*, and if it can entail that the effects of *e* are co-located with *a*, then so can other relations, such as '*x* is red at *t*'. Accordingly, Mellor's causal criterion of temporal coincidence presupposes that certain relations—namely causal ones—simply are co-location-entailing, even though their logical form, like that of all relations, is $R(x, y)$. Moreover, the relationalist can help herself to Mellor's account. After all, perhaps what makes 'x is red at t' entail that x and t overlap is that becoming red has its first effects on x at t. All of this is relational in form, of course, but otherwise takes advantage of the strengths of Mellor's account.

Even if we go so far as to assume that Fa entails that F is a non-relational property of a, Mellor's view still requires that 'x is located at y', which holds between a time and a non-relational fact, entail that x and y temporally overlap. There is just no escaping it: Mellor, as much as the relationalist, must admit the existence of relations that entail co-location. But once this is admitted, there is no reason to avoid the relational view. Indeed, Mellor's account really just seems to be a version of it.

One final point. According to the relational theory, to inspect something is, necessarily, to inspect it at some time or other. Hence, while such an inspection will require the *existence* of at least one time, nothing but the object itself will have to be inspected at that time to determine its shape, colour, size, and so on. Hence, the relationalist can, if she wishes, help herself to Mellor's causal criterion of properties and change. I conclude that the relational theory of temporal predication can withstand Mellor's attacks.

6.4.4 *The intensional account*

I have argued that a predicate such as 'x is red' expresses a relation,

(33) $R(x, t)$

whose extension is a class of ordered pairs, $<x, y>$, such that x is a member of the set of objects and y is a member of the set of times. Accordingly, time is an element of the extension of the predicate. Thomas Sattig argues, on the other hand, that such predicates are monadic in form and that their intensions are functions from times to classes of objects:

> the move from the semantics of atemporal predications to the semantics of temporal predications can be informally described as building a time not into the extension of the predicate, but rather into the intension of the predicate. (Sattig 2006, p. 80)

Though this may appear to be in conflict with the relational view, I shall argue that the relationalist can happily grant that the intensions of temporal predicates are functions from times to classes of objects.

On the intensional account, where a is an ordinary object, 'a is F at t' expresses a proposition of the form:

(34)   At $t[F(a)]$.

Given that the semantic value of a name is its referent (Sattig 2006, p. 79), (34) is true if and only if the referent of 'a' is in the extension of F relative to t:

(35) 'At $t[F(a)]$' is true $\equiv$ ref('a') $\in$ ext$_t$ ('F( )')[13]

How about the right hand side of (35): what is it for an object to be in the extension of F relative to t? Sattig provides a schema:

(36) $x \in$ ext$_t$ ('F( )') $\equiv$ At $t[F(x)]$[14]

which, when combined with (35), entails:

(37) At $t[F(a)] \equiv$ ref('a') $\in$ ext$_t$ ('F( )')

As a relationalist, I simply see nothing to object to here.

To see why, recall that the reason that temporal predicates, such as 'x is red at t', define relations is because if 'x is red at t' is true, then it is satisfied by ordered pairs, $<x, t>$, of entities. Such sets of ordered pairs are the extension of the predicate. It is consistent with this view, perhaps even desirable, to say more about how the predicate operates. The intensional account can fill in here. It tells us that *the predicate* is a function from times to classes of objects.

Now, there is simply no reason for the relationalist to object to this. Indeed, it helps to explain why F is a relation. Consider that a function:

(38) $F(x) = y$

is standardly understood to define a relation, $<x, y>$, holding between classes of entities, $\{x\}$ and $\{y\}$:

[A] function from A to B is simply a special *relation* from A to B having the property that no two different ordered pairs in the *relation* have the same first coordinate. (Zehna and Johnson 1972, p. 72; emphases added)

A binary relation R from a set A to a set B is a *function* from A to B just in case every element of A bears R to exactly one element of B...a binary relation R from a set A to a set B will only fail to be a function from A to B if either some element of A doesn't bear R to any element of B or some element of A bears R to more than one element of B. Hence, to show that R is a function, it will suffice to rule out these possibilities. (Zalabardo 2000, p. 27)[15]

On the relational view, for any given time, t, there will be exactly one class of objects, $\{x\}$, that is F, and 'x is F at t' will only be defined for times, t, such that at least one object is red then, so t will stand in the F-relation to one and only one element. Accordingly if, 'x is F at t' is a relation, then F is a function from times to classes of objects. So far as I can tell, therefore, the intensional account and the relational account are natural complements in the theory of temporal predication.

The advantage of the intensional account, according to Sattig, is that it stays 'closer to the surface form of temporal predications' than does relationalism, so that it can

---

[13] Sattig 2006, p. 80; I have changed the numbering to fit in with the text of this chapter.
[14] Sattig 2006, p. 80; I have, again, changed the numbering to fit in with the text of this chapter.
[15] This is a standard definition, found in many places (for example, Gemignani 2004, p. 132).

'take seriously certain intuitions that flow from this surface form' (Sattig 2006, p. 81). The idea here is that the surface form of 'the apple is red at noon' includes an explicit temporal modifier of the form 'at t', as does (34). If, however, a predicate, 'x is F', is truly a function, as the intensionalist assumes, then the logical form of 'x is F at t' might just as well be represented by (38) or (R) as by (34); they are all equivalent. Hence, there is no genuine advantage here.

Sattig, however, continues:

> The intensional account allows shapes and colours to be properties instantiated relative to times, whereas the relational account turns shapes and colours into relations to times. The intensional account thus avoids metaphysically extravagant entities, such as shape-relations, and takes seriously the variation-intuition that change in shape is having different shapes at different times. (Sattig 2006, p. 81)

In response to this, I note, first, that the relational account does not render shapes and colours themselves into anything. The relational account is a theory of what *predicates* such as 'is red' and 'is round' express; it is not a theory of properties, at least not if these are construed as entities in the physical (or Platonic) world. A theory of properties ought to be sensitive, at least in part, to the empirical study of the relevant portions of reality, as I have argued.

A second, related point is that the relational view is, accordingly, metaphysically innocent. It does not commit to any extravagant entities such as 'shape relations'. If there exist, for example, objects and times such that the former are square-shaped at the latter, then an 'is square' relation has been defined. Nothing extravagant has been posited; only square objects and times. The fact that Sattig assumes extravagant entities are required by the relational view indicates an implicit commitment to the idea that wherever a relation has been defined, there must exist an entity, x, which *is* that relation. But, of course, this would simply rule out nominalism, or extensionalism, about relations without argument. Moreover, as I argue above, we needn't assume that for every element in our language, such as a relational term, there corresponds an entity in the non-linguistic world; such a move from the structure of language to the structure of reality is unconvincing in general (see, also, Dyke 2008, Russell 1905). Hence, defining shape predicates as relations doesn't commit one to such things as reified shape relations, only to the existence of ordinary, shaped things and times.[16]

---

[16] It is, of course, compatible with the existence of such relations. It is also possible that a proposition, such as that x is F at t, is made true by the fact that x is F at t, where this fact is an objective entity that exists in addition to x, t and the relation between them. I take the relational account of predication to be compatible with this view and its denial. It strikes me that there are different ways one might conceive of the structure of such facts—complexes of objects, and times, objects, times and relations, etc.—that may all be combined with the relational theory of predication.

Thirdly, the relational view takes seriously the intuition that change in shape is having different shapes at different times. The relationalist needn't deny that when an object changes its shape from round to square, it has different shapes at different times. She simply explains this in terms of the object standing in different relations to those times.

Finally, note that Sattig argues that the intensional account incurs the cost of 'complicating the semantics of temporal predications via the notion of a predicate's having an extension only relative to a time' (Sattig 2006, p. 81). I don't agree. The intensional account, properly understood, in fact shows how intensions and relational extensions are connected. If we combine the claim that temporal predicates express relations between objects and times with the claim that predicates are functions from times to objects, the result is an intuitive, clear, and metaphysically inoffensive theory. Whatever complication this adds strikes me as unproblematic. I conclude that the intensional view is no threat to a relational account of temporal predication; it is, if anything, its natural companion.

6.5 Change and pseudo-change

I have argued that the best account of change is provided by the relational account of temporal predication: for an object to change is for it to stand in different relations to distinct times, e.g.:

(39) $\text{Red}(x, t)$ & $\text{Green}(x, t')$

Next I want to consider the objection that the relational account is unable to distinguish pseudo-change from genuine change.[17] Consider, for example, the following Goodman-inspired predicates:

(40) x is Grue* at t iff x is green at t and $t < t'$; otherwise x is blue;
(41) x is Bleen* at t iff x is blue at t and $t < t'$; otherwise x is green.[18]

Now suppose that x persists from a time $t_1 < t'$ to $t_2 > t'$ and remains green throughout the interval. Accordingly, the following is true of x:

(42) $\text{Grue*}(x, t_1)$ & $\text{Bleen*}(x, t_2)$.

But (42) is of the same logical form as (39), i.e.:

(43) $F(x, t)$ & $G(x, t')$.

---

[17] I thank Omid Hejazi for raising this objection.
[18] See Barker and Achinstein (1960).

In this case, however, x has not changed, because its colour remains the same. It might seem, therefore, that the relational theory is incapable of distinguishing genuine change from pseudo-change.

I think that three considerations will take the bite out of this objection. First, my argument above is that all change is a matter of objects standing in different relations to different times, *not* that all instances in which an object stands in different relations to different times report genuine change. For example, the proposition that *John is to the right of Sally at noon and to the left of Sally at 1:00* does not entail that John has changed. Still, all genuine accounts of change will be relational in form.

Secondly, notice that given (40) and (41), (42) is logically equivalent to:

(42*)   Green(x, t_1) & Green(x, t_2).

(42*) clearly does not indicate genuine change. One can arbitrarily construct predicates that will allow for propositions of the form of (43) to be true even when x hasn't changed, but the trick will be to do so without the constructed predicates being logically equivalent to predicates that entail that no genuine change has occurred. Artificial predicates such as those defined in (40) and (41) give us no reason to believe this can be done.

For example, consider the following:

(44) x is Tall* = x is 6′
(45) x is Short* = x is such that Sally is 6′ 1″.

Now suppose that John is 6′ tall at t and Sally is 6′1″ at t'. In that case, the following is true:

(46)   Tall*(John, t) & Short*(John, t').

This is a case of pseudo-change, however, because (46) is logically equivalent to a proposition that is consistent with John not having changed in height at all, namely *that John is 6′ tall at* t *and Sally is 6′ 1″ at* t′.

So, playing around with predicates and times in an attempt to construct propositions that have the same form as (39) but are not reports of genuine change is bound to fail because of the equivalence that will have to hold between predications of pseudo-change and predications of non-change. The only way to resist this charge would be to take predicates such as x is Grue* or x is Tall* as basic or indefinable (or, at the very least, not defined in terms of ordinary predicates), and I simply fail to see how this could be defended.

One might, however, attempt to turn this argument around and insist that the equivalence of (42*) and (42) shows that when an object remains the same colour, it is justifiable to conclude that it nonetheless changes. In other words, the logical equivalence might be thought to demonstrate that we *can't* favour (42*) over (42).

This argument assumes, however, that there are no *non-logical* reasons for favouring (42*) over (42) as the true description of the situation in which an object remains green from t_1 to t_2, but there are such reasons. As noted above, Mellor points out that genuine physical changes have effects. What (42) and (42*) both report is a situation in which such effects are lacking: the 'change' from Grue* to Bleen* has no effects at all; hence, there is reason to conclude that (42*) gets things right.

Thirdly, note that this problem isn't unique to the relational account. Suppose that 'x is green' and 'x is blue' are monadic predicates:

(47)   G(x)

(48)   B(x).

We can still define Grue* and Bleen* as per (40) and (41) above and ask whether an object 'changing' from Grue* to Bleen* is genuine change. Suppose that G(x) applies to object o from t_1 to t_2. This will still be a situation that is equivalent to Grue*(x) applying to it until t' and Bleen*(x) applying after t'. But has o really changed? Obviously not, so the problem isn't to be confined to relational predicates. If one is tempted to reply that o has changed only if a *property* has been gained or lost, then I think the relationalist can help herself to that solution, because in both cases we need to appeal to something other than the structure of the predicate to determine whether property gain or loss has occurred.

In short, though (42) and (42*) are logically equivalent, there are good reasons to think that the balance of considerations stands against (42) and in favour of (42*) as the correct description of the situation. The relational theory of temporal predication has, I conclude, the resources available to distinguish genuine change from pseudo-change.

6.6 A note on relational vs. substantive theories of time

There is an argument, from L. N. Oaklander,[19] that my view commits one to absolutism, i.e. substantivalism about time. The argument is as follows. Consider a world in which all that exists is a single object, a red apple for example; assume the apple exists for only a single instant, t. On the relational theory of predication that I defend, to be red is to stand in a relation to a time:

(49)   R(a, t).

If we consider t to be a substantive entity, independent of its material contents, then this is unproblematic. Suppose, on the other hand, that t is a set of simultaneous

---

[19] Personal communication.

events. The only plausible event in this scenario, however, is the apple's being red. Call this event A:

(50)   A = R(a).

If that is the case, however, then (49) becomes:

(51)   R(a, {A}) = R(a, {R(a)}).

This, however, is problematic for it explains an object's being red in terms of that object's being red. So it seems that the view I defend is circular given relational time, but not given substantive time, in which case it favours the latter.

   The crucial premise in this argument is that the only plausible event in this imagined scenario is the apple's being red, but I think this is doubtful. In particular, it seems to me that whenever there is the event of an apple being red there is also a more fundamental event, namely the existence of the apple. The event of the apple's existing, A′, may be glossed as follows:

(52) $A' = (\exists x)(x = a)$

This is a more fundamental event because the apple's being red entails that the apple exists but not vice versa. Hence, it is plausible that the former event is in some sense built up out of the latter. If, then, we allow for an event such as A′ in our scenario then t will consist of two simultaneous events, the apple's existence and the apple's being red:

(53) $t = \{A, A'\}$.

Now, because all members of t are simultaneous, one is free to assume that an apple can stand in a relation to t in virtue of standing in a relation to any part, or element, of t. In this particular case, the apple's being red can be a relation between the apple and A′:

(54) $R(a, t) = R(a, A') = R(a, (\exists x)(x = a))$

This formulation avoids the problematic circularity for it does not presuppose that the apple is red in explicating the redness of the apple. Rather, it entails that in the imagined case an apple's being red is a relation that holds between the apple and its own existence. This seems correct to me. For one thing, no apple can be red if it doesn't exist and (54) entails this. Furthermore, (54) entails that the apple exists at any time at which it is red, which is clearly correct. Note also that this account entails that the apple could exist at a time and not be red—e.g. at a time that consists of A′ and B = Blue(apple, A′)—which is also correct. So, the relational theory of temporal predication is, I conclude, compatible with a non-absolutist metaphysics of time and, therefore, it is neutral with respect to the metaphysical question whether times are sets of events or substances in their own right.

6.7 Conclusion

I have argued that temporal predicates appear to express relations between objects and times, and that this appearance withstands scrutiny. The relational view can parry the objections that have been raised against it. It is, in short, a natural, intuitive, and straightforward account of temporal predication that allows for objects to retain their strict identity despite changing. Given all this, it strikes me as a compelling account.

All of this assumes that temporal predicates apply to objects as ordinarily conceived: three-dimensional individuals that can be located at more than one time. Surprisingly, many philosophers find this to be an objectionable assumption. Accordingly, the next order of business is to consider four-dimensionalism. The key question is whether we have good reason to suppose temporal parts exist. I turn to that question next.

7

Temporal parts

7.1 Introduction

It is commonly supposed that objects persist in time by *enduring*: that is by being located at more than one time. According to perdurance theory, on the other hand, ordinary objects persist in time by being 'spread out' in time. On one version of this view, persisting objects are unified, four-dimensional space-time entities that are composed of temporal parts (see Quine 1950, Smart 1963, Lewis 1983a, Heller 1984). On another version, persisting objects are mereological sums of temporal parts, each of which is a distinct object standing in counterpart relations to other temporal parts (Hawley 2001, Sider 2001). For the former—traditional four-dimensionalists—temporal parts are ontologically subsidiary to the extended whole they compose; for the latter—'stage theorists'—the momentary temporal parts are ontologically fundamental and persisting entities are nothing over and above them. I will use 'four-dimensionalism' to refer to either view, since my main interest in what follows is whether we need to posit temporal parts in our ontology. I will distinguish the views as necessary, on a case-by-case basis.

Let us, then, try to get clear on the notion of a temporal part. Sider (2001, p. 60) provides the following definition:

x is an instantaneous temporal part of y at instant $t =_{df}$ (1) x is a part of y; (2) x exists at, but only at, t; (3) x overlaps every part of y that exists at t.

We can imagine extended temporal parts that cover a span of time, but I don't think any loss of generality is incurred by focusing on the instantaneous case.

For four-dimensionalists, temporal parts are the subjects of predication: locutions such as 'x is F at t' express propositions of the form x's *instantaneous temporal part at t is F*. Here temporal predicates are monadic, so this is equivalent to $F(y)$, where y takes on as a value x's instantaneous temporal part at t. So, as noted in Chapter 6, this is a competitor to the relational account of temporal predication on two fronts: the logical form of predicates and the entities that are the subjects of predication.

It is worth emphasizing that temporal parts are supposed to be genuine members of the four-dimensionalist's ontology; they are not logical fictions, nor are they mere terminological conveniences. Temporal parts are not, for instance, ordered pairs of objects and times, $<x, t>$. For one thing, even the three-dimensionalist can admit such entities; in fact, they are nothing more than her (temporal) predicates (as argued in Chapter 6). Moreover, ordered pairs of objects and times:

instantiate properties only in a derivative sense: '$<x, t>$ is F' just means 'x is F at t'. Instantiation would remain fundamentally relative to times. (Sider 2001, p. 62)

I agree, so this understanding of temporal parts is insufficiently robust to distinguish four-dimensionalism from three-dimensionalism.

Consider an instance of one of the so-called 'paradoxes of coincidence'. A statue, S, is formed from a lump of clay, L. L existed prior to S; so L and S have different histories. Moreover, L, unlike S, would survive being flattened into a pancake-like disc; so L and S have different modal properties. It seems, accordingly, that given Leibniz's Law, L and S are distinct objects (see e.g. Sider 2001, p. 142). Yet, during the time in which L is shaped into the statue S, it is absurd to suppose that two objects, L and S, exist and overlap for if so, the object ought to weigh twice as much as it in fact does. Some of the appeal of temporal parts theory derives from its apparent ability to easily handle such cases. The four-dimensionalist may (and typically does) argue that S and L, though distinct, overlap in virtue of sharing temporal parts, in particular all the parts that exist after S is created and before it is flattened. So at any given time during that period there exists only one object, namely a temporal part; it just so happens that those temporal parts are included in more than one 'larger', four-dimensional entity (or sum of temporal parts in the case of stage theory).

Suppose, however, that temporal parts are conceived of as nothing more than ordered pairs of objects and times; or else, perhaps, events in the *histories* of three-dimensional objects. Sider writes:

Temporal parts theorists often say it is possible for a statue and the lump of clay from which it is made to share spatial location because they overlap by sharing a single temporal part. But ersatz temporal parts [i.e. ordered pairs of objects and times] and slices of histories are not genuine parts of continuants, and so the overlap between the statue and lump would not be secured. (Sider 2001, p. 61)

If two objects can stand in the same relation to a time without being co-located,[1] then the ordered pair conception of temporal parts won't do the work the four-dimensionalist wants it to do; similarly, two objects can be part of the same event without overlapping. So, four-dimensionalism must be the view that temporal parts are genuine, distinct elements of our ontology; they are something other than ordinary objects, times, and the events that comprise an object's history.

---

[1] Though, as I argue in Chapter 6, it seems clear that some relations do entail coexistence. I won't push the point here, however, since my concern is to draw out the substantive ontological nature of temporal parts by the four-dimensionalist's own lights.

We've seen that David Lewis is attracted to this view in part due to his dissatisfaction with the relational account of temporal predication. Sider is as well:

Four-dimensionalism is supposed to allow an account of property instantiation that avoids both presentism and the need for relativizing property instantiation to times: instantaneous stages instantiate temporary intrinsics *simpliciter*. (Sider 2001, p. 62)

I have argued in Chapter 6 that concerns over relational predicates are unfounded, so I won't rehearse the arguments here. There are, however, four additional arguments in favour of an ontology of temporal parts that I believe are worth addressing. First, there is often assumed to be a natural analogy between spatial and temporal extension that gives genuine credence to temporal parts doctrine. Secondly, one finds a particular dissatisfaction with the conception of objects as three-dimensional entities that endure through time. Thirdly, there is the belief that temporal parts theory offers the best solutions to various paradoxes (such as the paradox of coincidence briefly mentioned above). Finally, there is an argument, due to Sider, to the effect that temporal parts theory follows from some simple, hard to deny premises.

Let me offer a quick preview. I shall argue that: (1) the spatial doctrine with which temporal parts doctrine is allegedly analogous in fact supports three-dimensionalism, if it supports anything at all; (2) the dissatisfaction with the conception of a three-dimensional object is unfounded (or, perhaps better put, founded on a tendentious idea); (3) the various paradoxes can be handled as well (or better) by the three-dimensionalist; and (4) Sider's argument is question-begging and in tension with his claim that temporal parts are genuine objects rather than mere concepts. The upshot is, I conclude, that we have no compelling reason to believe in temporal parts; three-dimensionalism is the preferred ontological position.

7.2 Temporal parts and spatial-temporal analogies

One motivation for the doctrine of temporal parts can be found in the comparison of space and time. Objects can exist at more than one time as well as in more than one place. By the latter I mean not only that an object can exist at different places at different times by moving, but that an object can exist in more than one place at one and the same time by being spread out in space. Since, let us assume, the object *as a whole* cannot occupy more than one spatial region at a time, it is tempting to suppose that the object itself does not occupy multiple locations at a given time but, rather, is composed of various *spatial* parts each of which is entirely located at a particular place at a given time.

Markosian gives expression to the idea:

It is uncontroversial that physical objects are typically extended in both space and time. But there is some controversy in the philosophy of time over whether extension in time is analogous to extension in space. Spatial extension is normally thought of as necessarily involving different spatial parts at different locations in space. (Although it should be noted that those who believe in extended *mereological simples* (i.e., objects without proper parts) would deny this.) A bicycle, for example, can be extended across a doorway in virtue of having some spatial parts inside the doorway and other spatial parts outside the doorway. (Markosian 2002)

In a similar vein, Katherine Hawley writes:

Material objects extend through space by having different spatial parts in different places. (Hawley 2004)

and Sider claims that:

US Route 1 extends from Maine to Florida by having subsections in the various regions along the path. The bit located in Philadelphia is a mere part of the road (Sider 2001, p. 2)

This suggests an apparently appealing account of spatial variation: 'Route 1 changes from bumpy to smooth by having distinct bumpy and smooth subsections' (Sider 2001, p. 2).

There are many respects in which space and time appear to be analogous: we speak of things (events) extending in time and things (objects) extending in space; times and places can both be thought of as kinds of locations; there are semantic similarities between the temporal indexical 'now' and the spatial indexical 'here'; and so on (see Taylor 1992, chapter 7 for a well-known discussion). This suggests—though controversially, as Markosian remarks in the quotation above—that there might be some traction to be gained in rendering persistence in time analogous to extension in space.

In order to evaluate this suggestion, it is important to consider whether the concept of spatial extension is usefully explicated in terms of spatial parts. While I don't doubt that objects, in many cases, contain proper parts, I do think that a *relational* account of spatial extension has advantages over the (arbitrary) spatial parts account. In the remainder of this section, I briefly outline such a relational view and outline its strengths. I conclude that if the analogy with spatial extension has any purchase it in fact counts against temporal parts.

At a given time, t, an object, o, may be extended in space. It may also exhibit spatial variation; it might be F at one end, G at the other. The question is whether these uncontroversial claims *entail* that o is composed of spatial parts and that it has one part, x, which is F and another, y, which is G. I think it does *not* and the reason is as follows. All of the relevant facts can be accounted for in terms of relations that hold between objects and places. All we need to assume is the existence of a location relation, 'located-at', that holds between objects and places.[2] Alternatively, we may

---

[2] Times too, of course, but nothing is lost and simplicity of explanation gained by ignoring that complication in what follows.

assume that objects stand in location-entailing relations to places. For instance one may argue that o is red at a point, p, as a result of standing in the 'is red at' relation to p and that 'x is red at p' entails that x is located at p. This is analogous to the case of temporal predication, as presented in Chapter 6. For present purposes, the distinction between these two relational accounts is unimportant, so I shall help myself to a (primitive) location relation in what follows.

Suppose that o extends from point s_1 to point s_2. One may wish to explicate this by saying that o has spatial parts at s_1, s_2 (and all points in between). We needn't, however, say this. Since o, s_1, and s_2 are, we may assume, all well-defined entities, we need simply suppose that o stands in the location relation to both s_1 and s_2:

(1) $L(o, s_1)$
(2) $L(o, s_2)$.[3]

Similarly, if o is, say, smooth at one end and rough at the other, this needn't entail that o contains a spatial part that is smooth and another that is rough. Rather, we may suppose that o stands in the 'smooth-at' relation to s_1 and the 'rough-at' relation to s_2:

(3) $S(o, s_1)$
(4) $R(o, s_2)$

One important thing to notice about the location relation is that it is one–many. Even at a given time, it may relate a single object to multiple locations. Similarly, regular spatial predicates such as 'is rough', 'is smooth', 'is red', and 'is green' are one–many in that they may relate a given object to many places at the same time (and many times as well).

I think that there are two sets of consideration that provide reason to favour a relational understanding of spatial extension and variation. First, it captures all the inferences we wish to make about objects in space. Secondly, it avoids certain problems that attach to spatial parts theory. Let me deal with these points in turn.

First, consider the following proposition:

(5)   The iron poker is hot at one end, cold at the other.

(5)   entails all of the following:

(6)   The poker is hot somewhere
(7)   The poker is cold somewhere
(8)   Something is hot somewhere
(9)   Something is cold somewhere
(10) Something is hot somewhere and cold somewhere else.

---

[3] One may prefer to view the relation as an 'occupation' relation, or a 'coincidence' relation, or, perhaps, an 'overlap' relation. I don't think the differences, if any, between these are germane here.

The relational account of spatial extension has no problem explaining these entailments. If the logical form of (5) is:

(5′) $H(o, s_1)$ & $C(o, s_2)$

then propositions capturing the form of (6)–(10) all follow as a matter of straightforward, deductive moves:

(6′) $(\exists s)H(o, s)$
(7′) $(\exists s)C(o, s)$
(8′) $(\exists x)(\exists s)H(x, s)$
(9′) $(\exists x)(\exists s)C(x, s)$
(10′) $(\exists x)(\exists s)(\exists s')[H(x, s)$ & $C(x, s')]$

Similarly, the relational account can explain why:

(11)   The poker is extended

entails:

(12)   The poker is located somewhere.

Since extension is a matter of standing in the location relation to more than one point, (11) expresses a proposition of the following form:

(11′) $(\exists s)L(o, s)$ & $(\exists s^*)L(o, s^*)$.[4]

This clearly entails:

(12′) $(\exists s)L(o, s)$,

which is plausibly the form of (12). So the relational account appears to explicate the right inferences about objects and locations in the right way.

It is, of course, consistent with the relational account that objects have parts that are spatially extended and, perhaps, in virtue of which they stand in location relations to places. For instance, it may very well be that the poker is composed of a body and a handle. In that case, the poker may be cold at one end in virtue of a part of the poker being cold. This will, however, result from the fact that the poker is composed of two objects, a handle and a body, and that the handle is cold, not, I argue below, from the mere fact that it is hot somewhere and cold somewhere else. For instance, suppose that:

(13)   The poker has a handle and a body and the handle is cold.

We can formalize (13) as follows:

---

[4] And all spaces in between, of course. It is unnecessary to complicate the discussion by formally representing this.

(13′) $(\exists x)A(x)$ & $(\exists y)B(y)$ & $P(x, o)$ & $P(y, o)$ & $[(\forall s)(L(x, s) \supset C(x, s))]$

where '$A(x)$' = 'x is a handle'; '$B(x)$' = 'x is a body'; '$P(x, y)$' = 'x is part of y', and '$L(x, y)$' and '$C(x, y)$' are understood as above. (13′) straightforwardly entails that the poker has a handle:

(14) $(\exists x)A(x)$ & $P(x, o)$;

and that its handle is cold:

(15) $(\exists x)A(x)$ & $P(x, o)$ & $[(\forall s)(L(x, s) \supset C(x, s))]$.

It also entails, naturally, that some handle is cold:

(16) $(\exists x)A(x)$ & $[(\forall s)(L(x, s) \supset C(x, s))]$.

Once again, it seems clear that the relational account of location has no problem with spatial reasoning even in cases where spatial parts exist.

   If, on the other hand, spatial extension is necessarily a matter of containing a spatial part, then unwelcome consequences follow. Spatial parts theory entails that any time an object is extended, it follows that it has a part, and any time there is a predicate that does not accurately describe the entirety of the object, the existence of a part is entailed. If that is the case, then:

(17)   There exists an extended, homogeneous entity

must entail:

(18)   There exist parts.

But this seems wrong, for it appears metaphysically possible that extended simples exist. The relational account, however, needn't commit to the existence of a part wherever there is an extended object or whenever a predicate applies differentially across an object, so it is compatible with extended simples. This is good for the relational account because it remains an open metaphysical question whether extended simples are possible, but spatial parts doctrine rules out one possibility on semantic grounds.

   A second problem is that spatial parts doctrine is implausibly ontologically indiscriminate. Consider a cross-section of my body with some arbitrary spatial region. Such a section might encompass my right hand, left foot, one rib, and my nose. Suppose that everything within this cross-section has a property, F, such as exhibiting a certain colour. Should the spatial 'part' so defined be counted as an *additional* element in our ontology, i.e. an addition to me, my hand, foot, rib, and so on? On the face of it, this just doesn't follow and the relational account can, as it should, remain agnostic on the existence of such additional entities. If, however, objects occupy spatial regions *in virtue* of having parts there, then it follows that the motley combination of my foot, hand, rib, and nose is an additional object that is part of me.

Now, there is a perfectly legitimate use of the term 'part of' which is *utterly* liberal in that any arbitrary portion of, say, my matter is a part of me: since such matter is not *outside* of me, it is, as we say, part of me. There is no problem with such a claim and I am not denying that any of my material content, no matter how arbitrarily selected, is a part of me in this sense. What I do consider to be a mistake is the supposition that whatever is a part of an object in this sense is *thereby* a unified entity that constitutes an independent element of our ontology.

Now, I don't doubt for a moment that we can think about my right hand, left foot, rib, and nose all at once. We could even, if we wish, give a name to this collection: Josh Jr., for example. But neither being able to think of separate things together nor giving them a name suffices for them to constitute a unified, additional entity in the world. Not every arbitrary bunch that we can gather under a single name or concept is in fact naturally individuated in the mind-independent world. Ontology is not so easy as that; it takes work to discover which kinds of object there are.

It is certainly true, for example, that right now I occupy the uneven space between the top of my shoe and the bottom of my trouser leg; there is a part of my leg that is currently exposed there. This does not mean that a proper inventory of all the entities in the room will include, not only my nose, hand, rib, foot, leg, etc., but also the spatial part that extends from my shoe top to trouser-leg bottom. That this *section* of my body is an independent, additional item in the room does not follow from my body occupying the space in question. Hence, I deny that spatial extension *entails* the existence of spatial parts.[5] Note that the point is not that it is *impossible* for collections of distinct objects to gather into, potentially unfamiliar, kinds of entities; it is, rather, that there is no evidence that this generally occurs.

The relational theory of spatial extension is, I conclude, preferable to spatial parts theory because it has fewer entailments (while explaining the uncontroversial ones), is compatible with a wider range of metaphysical views, and is not implausibly ontologically profligate.

7.3 Three-dimensionalism

It is usually suggested that if objects are three-dimensional, enduring entities, then they are 'wholly present' whenever they exist. For example:

---

[5] There is another problem with spatial parts theory: matter can occupy space even when there may be *no* object there whatsoever. Consider the water in a lake. The water clearly occupies space and has many properties. But it is highly doubtful that the water in the lake is a unified object of any kind; a quantity of water can exist without the existence of an object that is that water (see Laycock 2006a).

[T]hings, unlike events, *are* wholly present at every moment within their B-times. (Mellor 1998, p. 86)

At any time at which it exists, a continuant is wholly present. (Simons 1987, p. 175)

[F]or any (continuant), *x*, and any time, *t*, if *x* exists at *t* then *x* is 'wholly present' at *t*. (Sider 2001, p. 63)

I characterized endurance theorists as claiming that persisting objects are wholly present whenever they exist. This is naturally understood as the claim that the whole object is present whenever it exists, that all of the object's parts are present whenever it exists.[6] (Hawley 2001, p. 25)

I think, however, that the phrase 'wholly present' is inappropriate in the context of these discussions. Not only does it lend itself to unnecessary conceptual confusions, but whatever truth is implicit in the employment of the phrase can be captured just as well without it. It is, accordingly, of no use to the three-dimensionalist and I shall argue that she is better off to simply drop it from her repertoire.

The main reason for resisting the phrase is that it encourages an understanding of three-dimensionalism that threatens to render it: (i) if not logically contradictory, at least trivially false; (ii) trivially true; or (iii) utterly mysterious. A few more quotations will help to set the stage. Sider, for example, asks:

What is it for *x* to be 'wholly present' at *t*? The idea is presumably that every part of *x* exists at *t*. (Sider 2001, p. 64)

Lawrence Lombard writes:

[I]f a thing persists, say, from a time, t, to a time, t', then at any time between t and t' during which it exists it has *all* of its parts. (Lombard 1986, pp. 69–70)

Here is Katherine Hawley:

A persisting object is wholly present whenever it exists, because there is no sense in which it has (as opposed to will have or has had) parts which do not then exist. (Hawley 2001, p. 27)

One way of reading these glosses on 'wholly present' makes it seem as though three-dimensionalism is inconsistent with gain and loss of parts. For if endurant *x*'s 'whole presence' at *t* entails that all of *x*'s parts are at *t*, then *x* cannot, at *t*, have lost a part that it had beforehand.[7]

On the other hand, one may gloss the quotations as follows. In being wholly present at *t*, all the parts of *o* at *t* are at *t*. In other words, when *o* is wholly present at *t*,

---

[6] Merricks (1999) and Crisp and Smith (2005) also define three-dimensionalism in terms of objects being 'wholly present' at each moment at which they exist.

[7] Might the idea be that if if *x* is wholly present at *t*, then *x* has all of its parts at *t* in the following sense: it has all of its parts *tenselessly*, so that it would be true to claim, at *t*, that *x* has (tenselessly) all of its parts? Perhaps, but this is consistent with those parts not existing at *t*, in which case the doctrine becomes the, in my opinion, harmless understanding of three-dimensionalism defended below.

it has, at *t*, all of its parts that are parts of it at *t*. This appears to be a trivial truism. Similarly, one may understand the notion of *o*'s whole presence at *t* entailing that *o*'s entire temporal extension is at *t* as the claim that if *o* is wholly present at *t*, then all of *o* that exists at *t* is at *t*. Again, this is undeniable and, it is worth adding, is acceptable to the four-dimensionalist, which surely indicates that something has gone wrong in understanding three-dimensionalism.

There is a way of understanding the three-dimensionalist theory that inherits none of the foregoing difficulties and allows one to either use 'wholly present' in an innocent sense or, better, do without the phrase entirely. To see this, consider the version of three-dimensionalism that I have defended to this point, according to which all temporal predicates are relations that hold between objects and times. The extensions of temporal predicates are ordered pairs, and one member of those pairs is an ordinary *object*, not a temporal part. We may understand an object existing at a time in a number of ways. First, it may exist at *t* in virtue of standing in a relation, such as 'is red at', to that time and the relation is existence-entailing (though, as argued above, this may not be a matter of logical entailment). Secondly, it may exist at *t* in virtue of standing in the 'is located at' relation to *t*, in which case every object stands in the location relation to every time at which it exists (and vice versa). Thirdly, one may suppose that 'exists at' is a relation that objects bear to certain times and that standing in that relation to a time trivially entails that the object exists at a time (though, again, this is not in virtue of the logical form of the relation). In any case, it is an *object* that stands in the relevant relation to time, and that is as far as the metaphysical commitments of the theory need to go. There is, in other words, no need to invoke a notion of 'whole presence', and the debate over how to define the phrase is something the three-dimensionalist may simply bypass. To be present at a time is just for an ordinary object to stand in a relation to that time.

While the four-dimensionalist insists that an object, *o*, 'is red at *t*' in virtue of having a *t*-part that is red *simpliciter* (i.e. monadically), the three-dimensionalist, on the other hand, insists that it is the *object* that 'is red at *t*'; one member of the ordered pair is an object in the ordinary, three-dimensional sense. There is no gap in this explanation that is crying out to be filled by some notion of 'whole presence'. Rather, three-dimensionalism is the view that relational predicates hold between times and objects, rather than times and parts (whatever temporal parts are supposed to be). No further semantic question about 'presence' or existence at a time remains to be answered.

If one wishes, this position allows for a harmless understanding of 'whole presence'. For instance, the three-dimensionalist will grant that an object that persists from *t* to *t'* exists 'as a whole' at both *t* and *t'* because the *object*, rather than a temporal part, bears the relevant relations to both times. This does not, however, entail that everything that is ever a part of the object exists between *t* and *t'*, for something that stands in the '*x* is a part of *y*' relation to *o* at one time may not stand in such a relation to *o* at another time. So I reject atemporal parthood; parthood is always a relation between an object, a part, and a time.

Nor does the object existing 'as a whole' at *t* entail that it is false that the object exists at an earlier time, *t**, or a later time, *t'*. For example, it may be tenselessly true that *o* bears the 'is red at' relation to *t**, the 'is green at' relation to *t'*, and the 'is yellow at' relation to *t*. Since it is *o* that bears these relations, it is *o* that is located at each of those times.

In short, the idea behind three-dimensionalism is that when *o* is said to be or exist at *t*, then it is *o* that stands in the relevant relation to *t*, not some part of it. In *that* sense, it is perfectly right to say that 'all' of *o* stands in the relation to *t*, or that if something happens to *o* at *t* it happens to *o* 'in its entirety'. So there is an unproblematic understanding of 'wholly present' that three-dimensionalism can happily commit to, as it entails nothing implausible or incoherent. However, the phrase itself is unusual, somewhat confusing, and prone to misunderstanding, so the three-dimensionalist is, I conclude, better off without it; it truly seems only to have been coined to contrast three-dimensionalism with its rival, which allows four-dimensionalism to set the terms of the debate; but there is no reason for the three-dimensionalist to follow suit here.

I imagine one might object that a question remains: do ordinary objects endure by re-locating themselves in their entirety from one time to another, or do they 'perdure' by being 'spread out' in time?' I will reply with a question: 'what does it mean for an object to be spread out/extended in time?' If it means 'the object (tenselessly) has temporal parts located at different times', then I will respond 'no: objects are not spread out in time'. If, however, it means that an object (tenselessly) bears existence entailing relations to more than one time, then the answer is 'yes, objects are "spread out" in time, at least those that persist are'. We might as well, however, reply by indicating that the better claim is that the object endures from one time to another.[8]

In the end, Hawley comes to define endurance, which applies only to three-dimensional objects, as follows:

[A]n object endures if and only if (i) it exists at more than one moment and (ii) statements about what parts the object has must be made relative to some time or other. (Hawley 2001, p. 27)

I find nothing to disagree with here and, indeed, find it to be a nice way of capturing three-dimensionalism as I understand it. My only complaint is that when she contrasts endurance theory with its four-dimensionalist rivals, Hawley reverts to the troublesome locution. For example:

---

[8] Some might worry that this eliminates any distinction between three-dimensionalism and four-dimensionalism, as they appear to be notational variants of each other. If so, however, then this is in three-dimensionalism's favour, for it is the metaphysically less exotic theory; hence, it ought to be preferred as the ontology underlying the two, equivalent sets of notation.

Perdurance theorists think that, although the chair exists at different times, it does so not by reappearing in its entirety but by having different temporal parts at different times. Both stage theory and perdurance theory contrast with endurance theory, according to which the chair and I are wholly present whenever we exist. (Hawley 2001, p. 68)

Perhaps, here, '*x* is wholly present' is intended just to be shorthand for (i) and (ii), in which case, fine. It is, however, a misleading phrase, so I suggest we simply drop it.

Having said all this, it may be worthwhile to compare the understanding of three-dimensionalism that I have outlined with some 'requirements' that Crisp and Smith (2005) believe any adequate definition of 'wholly present' must satisfy. This will help elucidate the extent to which I believe three-dimensionalism can answer the questions it must answer. They write:

If a definition of 'is wholly present at' is to yield a substitute expression capable of filling the functions these writers wish 'is wholly present at' and cognates to fill, then, it will need to satisfy this requirement:

(R1)   It makes sense to say that an object is wholly present at more than one region of space or spacetime.

It 'makes sense' to say *p*, let us say, iff *p* isn't formally contradictory or so obviously false that any reasonable person who understood it would be inclined to reject it. (Crisp and Smith 2005, p. 321)

I have defined three-dimensionalism as the view that objects rather than temporal parts satisfy temporal and spatial predicates. On such a view, an object can stand in an existence-entailing relation to more than one time or place; since it is the object, rather than a part, that stands in the relevant relation, the object can be at more than one place or space-time region and the spirit behind (R1) is preserved.

Here is another requirement:

(R4)   It makes sense to say both that eternalism is true and that an object that is wholly present at every time at which it exists gains and loses parts over time. (Smith and Crisp 2005, p. 322)

If '*x* is wholly present at *t*' is understood as I prefer, then (R4) can be satisfied. Eternalism is the view that concrete truthmakers for claims about the non-present can and do exist (not all in the present, of course). Accordingly, past and future three-dimensional objects exist tenselessly. Nonetheless, it is those objects, rather than temporal parts, that stand in existence-entailing relations to times. Moreover, 'parthood' is, for the three-dimensionalist, a relation between an object, a part, and a time. Since these relations hold tenselessly, an object can gain and lose parts just as it can, for example, change colour or size (e.g. by bearing the 'has *x* as a part' relation to *t* but not *t'*).

Consider the following three 'requirements' that Crisp and Smith list:

(R7) It makes sense to say that an object is wholly present at one and only one time.

(R8) It makes sense to say that an object with proper parts at a region or time is wholly present at that region or time.

(R9) It makes sense to say that an object is wholly present at a region smaller than the whole of spacetime. (Crisp and Smith 2005, p. 324)

Three-dimensionalism, as I've explicated it, has no problem with the spirit behind these claims. If an object only stands in existence-entailing relations to one time, then (R7) can be accommodated; if it stands in such relations to fewer than all the times, then (R9) is satisfied; since an object can stand in the parthood relation to another object, namely its part, and a time, then (R8) can be agreed to happily.

On the other hand, the following is a 'requirement' that I reject:

(R2) It makes sense to say that an object is wholly present at a time or region and is such that its only parts are parts *simpliciter*. (Crisp and Smith 2005, p. 321)

I see nothing to recommend an atemporal notion of parthood. If temporal predicates are relations to times, then having something as a part is also a relation an object bears to a time and a part, because parts can be gained and lost. If an object never gains or loses parts, then it and its parts stand in the parthood relation to all times at which the object exists, but this does not render the parthood relation atemporal. Something might also be an essential part; a part without which an object is no longer what it was. For example, perhaps a person's brain is an essential part. Nevertheless, it does not follow that the person stands in an atemporal parthood relation to her brain. Rather, it is the case that, necessarily, at every moment at which she exists, she stands in the parthood relation to her brain and that time.

Now consider:

(R3) It makes sense to say that an object with no parts *simpliciter* but with parts-at-a-region (or parts-at-a-time) is wholly present at a region or time, and it makes sense to say that such an object is wholly present at a temporally extended region without being wholly present at any one time. (Crisp and Smith 2005, p. 322)

The first part of this is easy for the three-dimensionalist to accommodate, since the essence of the view is that parthood is partly a relation to times and that objects rather than parts stand in relations to times. The second is less straightforward. It is intended to capture four-dimensional persistence, in which an object *as a whole*—i.e. all its parts considered—occupies a temporal span/region, namely that corresponding to its lifetime, rather than a particular time. In that case, the second conjunct ought to be rejected by the three-dimensionalist, or else reinterpreted along the lines I suggest above.

Crisp and Smith's remaining requirements, (R5) and (R6), depend on accepting the coherence of controversial theses, in particular the propositions, first, that distinct objects can coincide and, secondly, that objects can perdure without having temporal parts (Crisp and Smith 2005). I consider the former below and bypass the latter, since I aim to reject perdurance.

Overall, I think the above considerations show that the work that philosophers typically try to do with the phrase 'is wholly present at' can be restated and then captured in a non-troublesome manner by three-dimensionalism as defined here and in Chapter 6. Accordingly, the three-dimensionalist can steer clear of the definitional debates over that unusual phrase.

7.4 Three-dimensional objects and 'paradoxes' of composition and coincidence

I have argued that spatial extension does not entail the existence of spatial parts; analogously, endurance does not entail the existence of temporal parts. I have also argued that the relational account of temporal predication provides an unproblematic account of persistence in time (without the need to appeal to a notion of 'whole presence'; a notion that suggests confusion).

In this section I briefly consider some arguments to the effect that four-dimensionalism better handles certain puzzling cases than does three-dimensionalism. I do not address the various puzzles and their solutions in full detail. Rather, I present what I take to be the core thinking behind the four-dimensionalist solution and then counter-argue that three-dimensionalism is at least as well situated to solve the apparent problem. If I am right, then one more kind of reason to believe in temporal parts has been removed.

7.4.1 Coinciding entities

Recall the 'paradox' of coincidence noted in section 7.1: a statue, S, is made from a certain quantity or lump of clay, L; since S and L have different histories and different modal properties, $S \neq L$. During S's lifetime, however, it exists exactly where L does. So it seems that for at least a brief period we are committed to distinct objects coinciding, which is absurd. The four-dimensionalist responds that

the statue and the lump are like a road and one of its subsegments. (Sider 2001, p. 152)

That is, they overlap by sharing temporal parts (as two roads overlap by sharing spatial parts), which are singular, so this is not a case of problematic coincidence. This is, it is argued, a superior explanation to that which can be offered by a three-dimensionalist (Sider 2001, pp. 154–88).

I think that the premise that S is distinct from L (presumably at all times) because it differs in its historical and modal properties is tendentious, so the way this paradox is set up is problematic. Compare the following line of reasoning. Suppose that Roger is a man and a husband. But Roger would still be a man even if he were never married; he would, however, not be a husband. Moreover, Roger was a man before he was a husband. So, the man and the husband are different people since they have different modal and historical properties. While married, however, Roger is not two people. So, there must be two distinct people that share a part during the marriage.

The conclusion is not compelling and the reason, I suggest, is that 'is a husband' is a predicate that relates Roger to t (at which he is married) as does 'is a man'. Roger stands in both relations to t, and there is no conflict in one entity standing in two relations to a given time; nor is there a conflict in assuming it does not stand in both relations to all times at which it exists.

We may treat a quantity of clay similarly. A certain lump of clay may stand in the 'is statue-shaped' relation to t but not to t'. The fact that the mass of clay survives the loss of its statue-shape results from the nature of masses of clay—they are not dependent on being any particular shape. Statues are dependent on particular shapes in virtue of the fact that statues just are masses of clay (or some other material) shaped a certain way. S just is L standing in the relevant shape relation to t:

(19) $S = T(L, t)$

where '$T(x, y)$' = 'x is statue-shaped at y'. Clearly, then, S exists only at the times at which L stands in T to t. L, owing to the nature of substances such as clay, is not governed by any such equation. For some material to be a lump of clay is not for it to stand in any *particular* shape relation; so long as it has any shape it may continue to be a lump of clay.

So, if L stands in the T-relation to t and the T'-relation to t' (where T' represents some non-statue-shape relation) then L exists at t and t'. If L stands in the T-relation to t and the T'-relation to t', then S exists at t but not at t'. These are, in part, the result of facts about statues and masses of clay and they can be captured by a relational theory of shape-predication. On this account, there is no temptation to suppose there are two objects existing at t, as opposed to one. The three-dimensionalist view is not threatened by such alleged cases of coincidence if temporal predicates are relational in character.

The three-dimensionalist can, therefore, offer a solution to cases such as the lump and the statue; her solution is really dissolution. In general, when an object, x, is composed of some quantity of material at t, then x just is that quantity of matter standing in the right kind of relations to t. The same will hold for an object that is composed of genuine parts, such as a car. A car is more than the mereological sum of its parts; to form a car, those parts must, in addition to existing, be arranged in a certain way (where this 'certain way' may have to be characterized, at least in part, functionally but will include, e.g., relations of physical contact). When those parts form a car, they stand in the relevant relations to a time; this is not the case of two objects—a collection of parts and a car—coinciding, even though the parts can outlive the car (that a plurality can satisfy a predicate does not entail that the plurality is an object). Accordingly, this (style of) solution appears to be generally available to the three-dimensionalist and seems at least as good as the solution offered up by temporal parts theory.

7.4.2 Undetached parts

Let us consider another alleged paradox, the 'paradox of undetached parts'. Sider writes:

> We begin with a cat, Tibbles, and a certain proper part of Tibbles, Tib, which consists of all of Tibbles except for the tail. Tibbles and Tib are obviously numerically distinct. But suppose now that Tibbles loses her tail; it seems that both Tibbles and Tib survive: Tib because nothing has happened to it beyond having something external to it detached, and Tibbles because cats, like trees, can survive the loss of certain parts . . . Tibbles and Tib are distinct; but they coincide after detachment. (Sider 2001, p. 142)

To avoid positing distinct but coinciding entities, the four-dimensionalist supposes that

> Tibbles and Tib are like a road in which one lane merges into the main road. (Sider 2001, p. 152)

In other words, what are distinct beings prior to detachment become one object—rather than two coinciding ones—in virtue of sharing temporal parts afterward. So long as a single entity, a temporal part, can be a component of more than one 'larger' entity or sum of parts, 'paradoxes' of undetached parts are easily handled. Can the three-dimensionalist offer a response that has equivalent virtues? I think so.

It seems to me that the worrisome part of Sider's set-up is the claim that Tibbles and Tib are 'obviously numerically distinct'. Presumably, Sider means to claim that they are numerically distinct objects; but if they are anything, they are cats. We might, then, wonder *when* they are distinct cats. It seems clear that they could be distinct only prior to detachment, for Tib exists afterward, and if Tibbles survives, so does she. In this case, however, the solution seems to entail that distinct cats (partially) overlap at a time (i.e. *prior* to detachment), which is what we are hoping to avoid.

Let us consider the road analogy for a moment. Imagine a road, R, that has three lanes at one point, p, but only two lanes at another, q. We are generally inclined to agree that R can exist at both p and q, so that the 'loss' of a lane hasn't destroyed the road, much as the loss of a tail hasn't destroyed Tibbles. Let us call the three-lane portion of the road 'Ribbles' and the two-lane portion 'Rib'. Are we inclined to agree that 'Ribbles and Rib are obviously numerically distinct?' Well, at p they clearly aren't numerically distinct *roads*, for there exists only one road there. So, if this is a case where one road 'survives' the 'loss' of a lane, then it is simply the *lanes* that exist as numerically distinct at p. But the two lanes that continue on at q are not, at p, a numerically distinct road from R; Ribbles and Rib do not constitute two different roads at p for there is, by hypothesis, only one there.

So, should we suppose that there are two distinct cats, Tibbles and Tib, at times prior to the loss of Tibbles's tail (say at t)? If Tib is a distinct cat from Tibbles at $t'<t$, then at t' Tib coincides with most of a distinct cat, which is implausible. The question is, why suppose that Tib exists at t'? One can, of course, conceptually or logically divide a cat, prior to the loss of its tail, into a cat with a tail and a cat without. But such *logical* division should not be confused with *ontological* distinctiveness. We have reason to deny that Tibbles and Tib are numerically distinct at $t' < t$ for the same reason we have to deny coinciding entities in the first place.

Here is an alternative solution. A tail, u, stands in the parthood relation to a cat, c, at a certain time, t'; that same tail does not stand in that relation to c at t:

(20) $P(u, c, t')$
(21) $\sim P(u, c, t)$.

This is just an instance of ordinary change, such as an apple altering its colour. In this case, a single cat bears various relations to times and a tail. 'Tib' is not a genuine, additional kind of object in our inventory. If 'Tib' refers to the cat that exists at t, without a tail, then 'Tib' just is Tibbles, as she is at t, but perhaps given a new name to reflect her new shape. Prior to t, 'Tib' is an object of *thought*, and the process by which Tibbles loses her tail but retains her identity is non-mysterious, on the relational, three-dimensional view of objects. In a similar vein, we might suppose that R has a particular lane, l, as a part at p but not at q.[9]

Heller (1984) presents an argument, designed to show that his body ('Body'), less his left hand ('Body-minus'), exists prior to losing the left hand, since his body continues to exist both before and after the loss. Since his body exists at both times, but what exists before the loss is different from what exists afterwards, we must identify his body with the entire, four-dimensional entity that stretches from times prior to his hand loss to times after. I suggest the three-dimensionalist respond to

---

[9] On the other hand, we might suppose that 'has a tail' is a relation that Tibbles stands in to t' but not to t, so that the loss of her tail is formalized as follows:

(20') $T(c, t')$
(21') $\sim T(c, t)$

This could be done if there is reason to suppose that tails aren't genuine objects. Either solution is available to a three-dimensionalist. Since my aim here is simply to sketch out ways the three-dimensionalist might handle 'paradoxes' that temporal parts are enlisted to solve, I won't spend time adjudicating between alternative three-dimensionalist solutions.

this argument much as I do to the Tib/Tibbles example, namely by suggesting that there is no reason to suppose that Body-minus exists, in addition to Body, prior to the loss of its left hand, at *t*, just because Heller's body survives and lacks a hand after *t*. Rather, Heller's body stands in the parthood relation to its left hand and times prior to *t* but does not do so to times after *t*.

7.4.3 *Fission and fusion*

Suppose that a person, Ted, has his brain severed in two and each half is placed in a new body; assume, further, that each half-brain resumes, in its new body, mostly normal functioning and has sufficient psychological continuity with Ted prior to the operation such that if it were the *only one* to survive, then we would conclude that Ted had survived the operation. Call the new, post-operative people respectively Fred and Ed. If only Fred existed after the operation, then we would say that Ted survived. Similarly, if only Ed existed, then we would conclude that Ted survived. Hence, it seems that this is a case in which one person, Ted, at *t* is identical to two people, Fred and Ed, at *t′*. This is surely a conclusion we would like to avoid, since identity is presumably a one–one relation.

The four-dimensionalist appears to have a nice solution to such difficulties. Sider writes:

Whenever distinct material objects coincide, they are never at that time wholly present, but rather overlap in a shared temporal slice or segment. Coincident objects are therefore no more mysterious or objectionable than overlapping roads ... Fred and Ed are like a road that forks. (Sider 2001, p. 152)

If Fred and Ed are distinct people at *t′*, but both are identical to Ted, then it seems that two people in fact existed at *t* < *t′*. This is clearly absurd, argues Sider, unless whoever exists at *t* is a part of two larger entities that overlap then because each has that person-part (or -stage) as a part at *t*. Once again, let us look at how a three-dimensionalist may respond.

Note that the appealing aspect of the four-dimensionalist solution is that there exists only one entity at *t*; one person-stage or one temporal part of a person. This stage or part happens, however, to belong to two distinct entities; either two different four-dimensional objects or sums of stages. Notice that what makes Ted part of both Fred and Ed is that he stands in the requisite psychological relations to both. If only Fred had any memory or character continuity with Ted, then we would have little reason to suppose that Ed and Ted are parts of one and the same, persisting *person* (at least, such a psychological continuity assumption appears to be implicit in Sider's set-up of the problem).

In that case, however, it is psychological continuity that is essential to personal survival and the physical object—body, brain, or both—seems to matter primarily as a vehicle for psychological states. It seems, however, that a collection of psychological states is not an object, as ordinarily understood. Since we may assume that Ted's body is destroyed when each half-brain is placed in a new body, if Ted does in fact survive the operation, then it must be because Ted is not a body; he is a superset of sets of mental states, connected by memory and other psychological relations. Psychological continuity, unlike strict, numerical identity, appears not to be one–one; two streams of continuity can branch off from one. On this view, however, a person appears to be more like a process, or sequence of events, rather than a particular individual or object.

Note, however, that such a conclusion is compatible with three-dimensionalism, which needn't deny that events/processes have temporal parts and that psychologically continuous processes could 'split' much as a road does; a three-dimensionalist needn't, in other words, deny that a single person can stand in the psychological continuity relation to two later persons.

It seems, therefore, that the account of personal identity that underlies at least Sider's account of fission cases is something that is available to a three-dimensionalist. It remains possible, of course, to reject this view of personal identity and identify a person with a particular body, or to insist that only one of Fred or Ed is identical to Ted, or to offer some other response to possible cases of fission. My point is simply that, on the version of the fission thought experiment that motivates temporal parts theory, personal 'identity' is equated with psychological continuity, which is clearly capable of branching, but of a kind of branching that a three-dimensionalist can accept.

This would, to repeat, make the 'identity' in 'personal identity' quite unlike other occurrences of 'identity', which are one–one. This applies equally, however, to three-dimensionalist and four-dimensionalist accounts of the view. So I think that the solution that the four-dimensionalist offers is no better (though perhaps no worse) than that available to the three-dimensionalist. Similar considerations apply to imagined cases of personal 'fusion' as well where, for example, the memories of one person are preserved by 'downloading' them into the brain of another.

7.4.4 Some tentative conclusions

I have only very briefly examined a number of apparent paradoxes associated with objects, time, and change. I think, however, that a general conclusion can be tentatively reached, namely that three-dimensionalism can offer solutions to the puzzle cases that are at least as plausible as those of the four-dimensionalist. Perhaps, in some cases, these solutions are better viewed as *dis*solutions of the problems, but they are no less appropriate responses for that reason.

I have not, obviously, offered a general account of 'objecthood' here, roughly appealing to a notion along the lines of 'distinct individual'. I have suggested no general stance on when certain parts compose or constitute an object and when they do not. I have not defended any particular account of the conditions under which something is a cat, an apple, or a statue nor how much loss or gain of parts something can sustain while remaining the same object (or even the same kind of object). There are clearly important issues here.

For instance, Tibbles can survive the loss of her tail, but how many parts can she lose before she ceases to exist? Would the loss of her head do the job? Perhaps; though if that head were kept alive in a vat of nutritive fluid, the appropriate conclusion might be that Tibbles survives and remains a cat; after all, she is alive, conscious, retains her memories, and has typically feline DNA. So, it is not perfectly clear at which point Tibbles fails to exist; I do not know for how many parts, x, it must be the case that:

(22) $\sim P(x, y\ t)$

before there is no longer any Tibbles to be the value of the variable y.

This, however, is a question that the four-dimensionalist must address as well. The four-dimensionalist insists that Tibbles can survive the loss of a tail because she is a temporally extended entity, or sum of stages, with tailed and tailless temporal parts/stages. It is surely the case, however, that Tibbles can eventually be destroyed. Precisely how much change must she undergo before what remains is no longer a temporal part of her? How different must one temporal part be from Tibbles's previous temporal part in order to no longer count as part of her, or count as part of the sum of stages that is her? Must it be a headless temporal part? A temporal part that is dead? What? The four-dimensionalist faces the same challenges as the three-dimensionalist. So, three-dimensionalism appears to suffer no relative disadvantage.[10]

7.5 The argument from vagueness

Thus far I have defended three-dimensionalism as the appropriate ontological viewpoint, and a natural companion to relational temporal predication, by arguing that there is no convincing motivation for an ontology of temporal parts. There is one final argument, deriving from Sider, that I want to consider: the 'argument from vagueness' (Sider 1997, 2001).

Sider begins by arguing that whenever some entities exist, so does their mereological sum or fusion. Imagine a case in which it appears uncontroversial that some entities, the x's, compose a further entity, y. For example, imagine all the subatomic

---

[10] I suspect that the answers to these sorts of questions will differ for different kinds of object, and will generally involve substantive, empirical considerations. For instance, retaining a certain DNA structure and biological functioning may allow a cat to survive extreme loss of parts; a house, on the other hand, may be destroyed by relatively less loss. I suspect that a case-by-case analysis will be required.

particles, the x's, out of which Tibbles, y, is composed right now; in this case, the particles compose a further object, a cat. Now consider a case in which Tibbles is incinerated so that all of her subatomic particles are dispersed; in this case, it might be supposed that the subatomic particles, which exist, do not compose any other object; they do not have a fusion (Sider 2001, pp. 122–3). We can, however, now imagine connecting these two cases by a series of cases, each of which is extremely similar to its adjacent cases

in all respects that might be relevant to whether composition occurs: qualitative homogeneity, spatial proximity, unity of action, comprehensiveness of causal relations, etc. (Sider 2001, p. 123)

Sider claims that if not every class of objects has a fusion, then there would have to be a 'sharp cut-off' in this sequence of cases, on one side of which composition occurs, and on the other it does not; he argues that it is absurd to suppose there exists such a line, for each case can be made arbitrarily similar to its adjacent cases:

It would involve saying, for example, that although certain particles definitely compose a larger object, if one of the particles had been 0.0000001 nanometers displaced, those particles would definitely have failed to compose any object at all. (Sider 2001, p. 124)

He concludes that such a cut-off is arbitrary and so cannot be plausibly defended. Since clearly fusion occurs in some cases it must, therefore, occur in all.

Sider notes that his argument depends on the following premise:

P_3:   In any case of composition, either composition definitely occurs or composition definitely does not occur. (Sider 2001, p. 125)

This is why the cut-off would have to be 'sharp'; if there were vague cases of composition, then there might be no sharp cut-off, which would make restricted composition less arbitrary.

Sider's defence of this premise comes from an appeal to the linguistic theory of vagueness; i.e. the claim that vagueness cannot be 'in the world' but is simply the result of semantic indecision (i.e. of not having settled on one from a range of precisifications of our predicates). Sider argues that, given the linguistic theory of vagueness, it is absurd to suppose that it could be indeterminate whether composition occurs because then 'it would be vague how many concrete objects exist' (Sider 2001, p. 127). Sider concludes that this is impossible. His argument is as follows.

First, note that one can construct what Sider calls a 'numerical sentence'; for instance the sentence that exactly two concrete objects exist:

$\exists x \exists y [Cx \ \& \ Cy \ \& \ x \neq y \ \& \ \forall z(Cz \rightarrow [x = z \lor y = z])]$. (Sider 2001, p. 127)

where 'Cx' = 'x is concrete'. Secondly, Sider argues that this cannot be a vague sentence:

First, note that numerical sentences have no syntactic ambiguity. Secondly, note that the concreteness predicate, 'C', presumably has precise application conditions since it was defined by a list of predicates for fundamental ontological kinds that do not admit of borderline cases...So if any numerical sentence is to be indeterminate in truth value, it must be because one of the logical notions is vague. (Sider 2001, p. 127)

Sider argues (2001, pp. 128–30) that logic cannot be a source of vagueness, since there are not alternative ways of making the meaning of logical terms precise. He concludes that how many objects exist cannot be a vague matter since numerical sentences cannot be vague; hence it cannot be vague whether composition occurs (as this would entail that how many objects exist might be an indeterminate matter). Accordingly, P_3 is secured.

Having done this, Sider then considers instances of diachronic identity. Suppose that an object, x, persists from times t to t'. Let us consider the class of objects that compose x at t: the subatomic particles of which it is made, for instance. It follows from the above reasoning that this class has a fusion, z. Moreover, z has the following properties: (i) it exists at and only at t; (ii) each part of z overlaps x at t; (iii) every part of x at t overlaps z. In other words, z is a temporal part of x (recall Sider's definition of 'temporal part' noted above). Hence, temporal parts exist.

In short, if every class of objects has a fusion—which Sider argues it must—then the objects that compose an object at t also have a fusion; by definition this fusion is a temporal part.

Even if one accepts every step of Sider's argument, it seems to me that at most it proves that one cannot have a restricted principle of *mereological* fusion. The important ontological issue, however, is whether every fusion is a genuine object, a true addition to our ontology, or might some be no more than *ersatz* objects, such as Sider's example of ordered pairs of objects and times? So the question I wish to raise is whether Sider's argument is plausible without *assuming*—rather than proving— that every fusion is a genuine object. I don't think so.

To see this, consider the following:

It may well be indeterminate whether a given class of molecules has a fusion that counts as a *person*. This is not inconsistent with P_3, for the class may definitely have a fusion which is a borderline case of a person. (Sider 2001, p. 125)

The reason Sider asserts this is apparent: the defence of P_3 involved a numerical sentence with, Sider assumes, only non-vague, precise predicates. On the other hand, the predicate 'is a person' cannot be assumed to be free of semantic indecision. So even if a class has a determinate fusion, it may not be a determinate person. It seems clear, moreover, that this observation of Sider's generalizes: it cannot be assumed that any predicate that picks out a kind of ordinary object is free of semantic indecision. So even if every class of objects has a determinate fusion, it may remain indeterminate whether the fusion is a person, chair, galaxy, electron, battery, computer keyboard, desk drawer, newspaper, and so on.

Now, if we consider the kinds of entity that are in the extensions of typical sortal predicates, then I think it is clear that they are generally more than mere mereological fusions. The reason is that, in general, the fusions can exist when the relevant objects do not. For instance, a house is not just a mereological fusion of its parts—doorknobs, window frames, bricks, electrical panels, plumbing tubes, etc.—because those same parts may be organized into a parking garage, a ship, a statue of a wolf, or a pile of garbage. While in all of these cases the same sum of parts exists, there is no house. If this is right, then we have no reason to believe that Sider's key premise, P_3, will hold for ordinary categories of object since only fusions have been precisely defined.

What this shows is that fusions, whatever they are, are not ontologically aligned with ordinary kinds of object. What sort of object, then, is a fusion, which is said to determinately exist even though it may not be a house, car, computer, teacup, cat, nose, doorknob, or any other common category of object? It is not only that a fusion may be an indeterminate instance of any ordinary object; it may determinately *not* be any ordinary object at all: Russell's nose, a teacup, a spacebar, and an office door have a fusion, but if so, this fusion won't fall under any existing sortal predicate. Fusions may, of course, be admitted as objects of *thought*, but that is not to be a distinct entity in the inventory of the world.

I am not arguing that it is impossible for such disparate entities as Russell's nose, a teacup, a spacebar, and a door to compose an object. The point is that the existence of their fusion doesn't entail this, any more than the existence of the parts of a house entails that the house exists. So the question now is: how much reason have we been given to think that every fusion bears ontological weight? I don't think Sider's argument provides any.

The reason is that if P_3 only holds for fusions, not ordinary objects, then Sider's argument appears to be question-begging. Recall Sider's example of a numerical sentence:

$$\exists x \exists y[Cx \,\&\, Cy \,\&\, x \neq y \,\&\, \forall z(Cz \rightarrow [x = z \lor y = z])].$$

This is supposed to express the proposition that exactly two concrete *objects* exist:

Now surely if P_3 can be violated, then it could be violated in a 'finite' world, a world with only finitely many concrete *objects* [emphasis added]. That would mean that some *numerical sentence*—a sentence asserting that there are exactly n concrete *objects* [emphasis added] for some finite n—would be indeterminate. (Sider 2001, p. 127)

But the predicate 'is concrete' is defined by Sider as follows:

Let us stipulatively define *concrete* objects as those which do *not* fit into any of the kinds on the following list:

sets and classes
numbers
properties and relations
universals and tropes
possible worlds and situations

If I have missed any 'abstract' entities you believe in, feel free to update the list. (Sider 2001, p. 127)

But of course, on the linguistic theory of vagueness, a concrete object exists determinately only if 'is a concrete object' is not subject to semantic indecision. Hence, Sider's argument appears to assume that the values of the variables in the numeric sentence are precisely defined entities, namely fusions; after all, imprecisely defined entities—which may very well be all of the ordinary objects we have reason to believe exist—may violate the numerical sentence (it may not be determinate how many persons exist, for example, or that there are exactly two stars, etc.). So it seems that Sider's argument in fact presupposes that fusions are what satisfy the variables in the numerical sentence and, therefore, its determinacy cannot be used to demonstrate that fusions determinately exist. Put another way, 'is an object' appears to be a vague predicate unless we assume the existence of such precise objects as fusions and, of course, such an assumption is out of place in an attempt to demonstrate their determinate existence.

I am not denying that we can define a predicate, 'is a fusion', which certain entities satisfy. My point is that the relevant ontological concern here is not whether some kind of object can be defined but, rather, whether that kind of entity exists as an additional kind of object in our ontology. Given that many kinds of object are more than mere fusions, Sider hasn't demonstrated that the existence of a fusion is sufficient for the existence of an ontologically weight bearing object. It would be an extremely implausible sort of idealism to suppose that for every collection human beings can conceive there exists a corresponding object in the world. As an example, let us briefly examine the semantics of plural reference.

There are no logical limits on which entities we can *group* together by definition or mentally. For example, flocks of geese or schools of fish. Henry Laycock writes:

Consider, for example, the many beavers presently in Lake Superior. On the one hand, it would seem counterintuitive (if not simply question-begging) to insist that *they* cannot be included under 'anything whatever'. And on the other hand, it is plain that they may be 'introduced into discussion' by way of *plural* substantival expressions, e.g. by the definite description 'the beavers in Lake Superior' or even by the demonstrative 'those beavers'. In any natural-language sense of 'singular', these phrases do not introduce something into discussion by means of 'a singular, definitely identifying substantival expression', precisely because the referring expressions in such cases are not singular but plural. The beavers in Lake Superior (it could very plausibly be said) are many things and not just one. (Laycock 2006b)

Let us assume that there are beavers in Lake Superior right now; in such a case, they exist. It remains, however, a question as to whether they exist 'as one' or, irreducibly, 'as many'.

Some philosophers have responded that the beavers do exist as a unity since the *set* consisting of the beavers in Lake Superior exists if they do. Lowe, for example, writes:

[S]ets appear to come so cheaply that it is hard to see why anyone should deny their existence who accepts the existence of their members—deny, for instance, that the set of planets exists while accepting that each of the planets exists. (Lowe 1995, pp. 523–4; see also Russell 1919, chapter 17)

Of course for Lowe sets, so construed, may very well be abstract objects in both the sense of existing outside of space and time and of not existing separately from their members (i.e. as being separable only in thought; see Lowe 1995, p. 523). If fusions exist in this sense, then the resultant notion of 'temporal part' cannot do the work that the four-dimensionalist wishes it to do, for it is not to abstract entities that predicates such as 'is red (at *t*)' or 'is round (at *t*)' are applied. So, while fusions, much as sets, are cheap and easy to come by in the abstract, they must be more than abstract if they are to amount to items in our ontology of concrete objects.

If, on the other hand, we suppose that whenever there is a plurality or grouping of objects, there *also* exists, as a matter of logic or metaphysical necessity, the set or mereological sum of those objects in some more robust, concrete sense, then we land in highly dubious waters, as Boolos warns (referring to a brand of breakfast cereal):

One might doubt, for example, that there is such a thing as the set of Cheerios in the . . . bowl on the table. There are, of course, quite a lot of Cheerios in that bowl . . . But is there, in addition to the Cheerios, also a set of them all? . . . It is haywire to think that when you have some Cheerios, you are eating a *set* . . . Maybe there are some reasons for thinking there is such a set . . . but it doesn't follow just from the fact that there are some Cheerios in the bowl that . . . there is also a set of them all. (Boolos 1984, pp. 448–9)

I believe, similarly, that Sider's argument only shows that whenever there is, say, a bowl of Cheerios there is also the fusion of those Cheerios in the Lowe-style, *abstract* sense of 'fusion', or in the sense of being an instance of a coherent definable predicate. If we are to believe that whenever there are Cheerios there is *also* an additional entity, their *concrete* 'fusion', then we must be given some substantive reasons for believing this (because, to repeat, being able to define something doesn't conjure its existence).[11] Sider's argument doesn't provide these because, as I argue above, P_3 begs the question in favour of the existence of fusions as concrete objects.

---

[11] To take an example, there are reasons to believe that in addition to the molecules that compose Sider at some time, *t*, there exists a *person*, Theodore Sider. After all, most collections of molecules are unable to form intentions, have thoughts, take actions, write books, formulate arguments, and so on. Those that do

So, despite Sider's argument, one can plausibly follow Boolos and Laycock and insist that not all groups of objects constitute a further object: *some* fusions are genuine objects; others are irreducibly plural and do not constitute a unit or individual in any concrete sense. And, indeed, there are good grounds, beyond those provided by these authors, for insisting on restrictions here. One reason, for example, to be suspicious of fusions as *objects* is precisely how many fusions there are; Sider's position would greatly multiply the number of kinds of object in the world, and in the absence of a compelling argument for this explosion, it ought to be resisted.

Unrestricted composition also sits uncomfortably with the substantive delimitations of objecthood that we insist on in other areas of enquiry. Not every collection of entities is a chemical element, or a biological entity, or a physical particle, etc. Yet, the principle of unrestricted composition tells us that every collection of entities is an object in some very general sense; it is just not a sense that plays any role in our empirical investigations into the world. Accordingly, unless fusions do compelling philosophical work, we have no reason to reify them. I have argued in the foregoing that the philosophical work done is far from compelling: three-dimensionalism can do the work that needs to be done. I conclude that despite Sider's efforts, belief in temporal parts remains unmotivated.[12]

7.6 Conclusion

I think that the foregoing discussion shows that there is little to compel one toward an ontology of temporal parts. I do not think that it is *impossible* that temporal parts exist, simply that nothing that we believe entails that they exist and the philosophical issues that appear to most commonly motivate their acceptance can be solved just as well by a less exotic account. I can't find any problem that is addressed by the positing of temporal parts that can't be solved just as well three-dimensionally.

---

seem to constitute a substantive kind of entity, a person, that is more than just the sum of molecules, which could exist without the person.

[12] In discussing temporal ontology Le Poidevin (1991) sketches out what he calls the 'minimal thesis', which is simply the view that objects are extended in time rather than 'wholly located' at every moment of their existence. He argues that this does not entail that the concept 'object' is derived from a conceptually or epistemically more basic notion, 'temporal part'. Nor, he argues, does it entail that temporal predication is monadic in form; the minimal thesis is consistent with relationalism, the temporal operator view, what have you (Le Poidevin 1991, p. 62). Hence, it might seem that we can be four-dimensionalists without temporal parts. I remain unconvinced. It seems to me that to say objects are 'extended' in time is just to say that they persist, that is they endure by standing in existence-entailing relations to more than one time. To suppose that temporal extension is more than this, namely perdurance, strikes me as unmotivated, given the arguments presented above.

If one combines the relational account of temporal predication with three-dimensionalism, one is well positioned to handle the philosophical problems of change as well as the apparent paradoxes of coincidence, fission, fusion, etc. Three-dimensionalism may be elucidated without recourse to the phrase 'whole presence' and is consistent with substantive, empirically determined restrictions on our ontology. I conclude that there is no compelling case for the existence of temporal parts.

8

The B-theory and the passage of time

8.1 The passage of time

For the past century, B-theorists have focused much of their efforts on *denying* that time passes. For example, D. C. Williams writes:

McTaggart was driven to deny the reality of time because he believed that while time must combine the dimensional spread with the fact of passage, the B-series with the A-series, every attempt to reconcile the two ended in absurdity. Broad can only cling to the hope that a better reconciliation may yet be found. My present thesis would resolve the antinomy by rejecting the extra idea of passage as spurious altogether. (Williams 1951, p. 462)

Williams's paper is a classic; widely read and quoted. So is another, by J. J. C. Smart:

It is clear, then, that we cannot talk about time as a river, about the flow of time, of our advance through time, or of the irreversibility of time without being in great danger of falling into absurdity. (Smart 1949, p. 485)

Another very important B-theorist is, of course, D. H. Mellor, who writes:

One author, however, I will acknowledge: J. E. McTaggart, who proved the unreality of tense and of the flow of time. (Mellor 1981a, p. 3)

More recently, the B-theorist Simon Prosser writes:

There is no real passage of time. What we refer to by 'the passage of time' is an illusory feature of conscious experience. (Prosser 2007, p. 81)

Now, I take myself to be a B-theorist but I think that the denial of passage is very much a mistake; a mistake that contributes to the apparent plausibility of the A-theory. What is the source of this mistake? There are, I think, two apparent ones. The first is the acceptance of McTaggart's argument that passage entails the A-theory; the second is the comparison of temporal passage with *motion*.

Concerning the first, return to the quotation from Mellor 1981a. McTaggart's argument against the passage of time is just his argument against the A-series, namely that it is incoherent (McTaggart 1908). Mellor has no objection to this strategy:

What is wrong with McTaggart is not his attack on time's flow but his view that change requires it. (Mellor 1998, p. 72)

If McTaggart's attack on time's flow is fine, then the passage of time entails the mind-independent reality of the A-series, for McTaggart's argument is against the latter directly. Indeed, in his own argument against the reality of passage, Mellor presents a version of McTaggart's argument against the A-series (Mellor 1998, pp. 72–8).

But this strikes me as odd. After all, McTaggart's assertion that the A-series is essential to time is the *target* of Mellor's argument. If one rejects McTaggart's conception of time and change, why retain his conception of temporal passage? I certainly agree with Mellor that any account of change that depends on the existence of a mind-independent A-series is doomed, but this only entails that time doesn't pass if temporal passage entails the existence of an objective A-series. I see no reason to believe this.

Let us turn now to the second motivation for denying passage. Here, again, is Smart:

Contrast the pseudo-question 'how fast am I advancing through time?' or 'How fast did time flow yesterday?'. We do not know how we ought to set about answering it. What sort of measurement ought we to make? We do not even know the sort of units in which our answer should be expressed. 'I am advancing through time at how many seconds per—?' we might begin, and then we should have to stop. What could possibly fill the blank? Not 'seconds' surely. In that case the most we could hope for would be the not very illuminating remark that there is just one second in every second. (Smart 1949, p. 485)

The concept of temporal *motion* is taken to reduce to the trivial idea that one second is one second in duration, which can hardly provide any substantive elucidation of temporal passage. Huw Price raises a similar concern:

Indeed, perhaps the strongest reason for denying the objectivity of the present is that it is so difficult to make sense of the notion of an objective flow or passage of time. Why? Well, the stock objection is that if it made sense to say that time flows then it would make sense to ask how fast it flows ... Some people reply that time flows at one second per second, but even if we could live with the lack of other possibilities, this answer misses the more basic aspect of the objection. A rate of seconds per second is not a rate at all in physical terms. It is a dimensionless quantity, rather than a rate of any sort. (Price 1996, p. 13)

Once again, the concept of temporal motion is, underneath the surface, a truism that cannot be equated with a genuine process.

On a related note, Smart further raises the concern that if time flows, then it must move, and if it moves it must move with respect to time:

...just as we thought of the first time-dimension as a stream, so will we want to think of the second time-dimension as a stream also; now the speed of flow of the second stream is a rate of change with respect to a third time-dimension, and so we can go on indefinitely postulating fresh streams without being any better satisfied. Sooner or later we shall have to stop thinking of time as a stream. (Smart 1949, p. 484)

Hence, the concept of temporal motion leads to an absurd conclusion. Williams expresses the same worry:

For as soon as we say that time or the present or we move in the odd extra way which the doctrine of passage requires, we have no recourse but to suppose that this movement in turn takes time of a special sort: time$_1$ move[s] at a certain rate in time$_2$, perhaps one second$_1$ per one second$_2$, perhaps slower, perhaps faster. Or, conversely, the moving present slides over so many seconds of time$_1$ in so many seconds of time$_2$. The history of the new moving present, in time$_2$, then composes a new and higher time dimension again, which cries to be vitalized by a new level of passage, and so on forever. (Williams 1951, pp. 463–4)

A common line of argument is detectable: temporal passage is a kind of temporal motion and the latter idea is either trivially uninformative or ontologically absurd. The question is, why hold this view of temporal passage? Thinking of time as something that moves is, on the face of it, rather bizarre. We certainly shouldn't accept it simply because the word 'passage' usually connotes movement. The passage of time may be some other kind of process.

So I see many B-theorists falling into the trap of thinking of temporal passage as either an objective A-series or else as motion, neither of which is appealing. I want to suggest a third alternative: the passage of time is the *B-theoretic ordering of events* by the (semantically basic) 'is earlier than' relation; that's it. On the B-series, first one thing happens, then another. That is temporal passage. As I argue above, genuine change occurs in the B-theory, but if real change occurs in time, then time passes. Indeed, there is no more to temporal passage than just ordinary occurrences of change.

If the B-theorist admits, as all do, that moments and events are ordered by an 'is earlier than' relation, then little sense can be made of the denial of temporal passage, other, that is, than the denial of metaphysical *theories* of temporal passage: branching future histories; a moving, absolute NOW; the accretion of 'slices' of reality; and so on. These are, I have argued, all models of time that collapse under their own ontological weight. But there is no reason to suppose that such rejection entails the unreality of temporal passage.

Consider that I know of no B-theorist who denies that people *age* and die; or who denies that we are the *descendants* of earlier, pre-human ancestors; or that the Sun has *depleted* some of its nuclear fuel since yesterday; and so on. The B-theory gives one no reason to deny any of this. On the B-theory, I have aged in the past year because the time of my writing this sentence is later than my last birthday; I am the descendant of my parents in part because my birth is later than theirs; and the Sun's fuel has depleted since yesterday because it has less fuel today than yesterday. If one has in mind a conception of temporal passage that is so rich that none of the foregoing suffices, then I am happy to give it away. Since the B-theory is compatible with genuine change and process, I remain quite content with a conception of temporal passage as the ordering of events.

This is why the relational theory of temporal predication presented in Chapters 6 and 7 is of such importance to my view. Since change can be understood relationally, the B-theory needn't deny real change. *Things* change, according to the B-theory, and events really happen one after another. The world is genuinely temporal and dynamic. However, the B-theory offers a perspective on the world that is not wedded or limited to that of any particular time, such as an absolute present (whatever that could be). The proposition that an object, *x*, changes from red to green by standing in the 'is red at' relation to one time and the 'is green at' relation to another combines the two desiderata of, first, supporting the idea that objects can retain their identity through change and, secondly, framing that idea in a tenseless language that allows us to consider all times, objects, and events in a single model.

Michael Dummett is one philosopher who believes that the existence of time entails that any theory of the world is necessarily limited to or restricted by the temporal perspective of the present:

Now if time were real, then, since what is temporal cannot be completely described without the use of token-reflexive expressions, there would be no such thing as the complete description of reality. There would be one, as it were, maximal description of reality in which the statement 'The event *M* is happening' figured, others which contained the statement 'The event *M* happened', and yet others which contain 'The event *M* is going to happen'. (Dummett 1978b, p. 356)

John Campbell expresses a similar point (without agreeing with it):

Someone who opposes realism about the past insists that we are immersed in time: our present temporal perspective is not simply one among many. (Campbell 1994, p. 247)

The B-theory that I defend is intended precisely to be a theory of time that is independent of temporal perspective. This is part of why I feel it is important for the B-theorist not to deny the passage of time: the latter, understood as realism concerning change and processes in time, is too difficult to deny, so denying it lends unnecessary credibility to the A-theory. Temporal passage does not require a theory that is restricted to the perspective of the present, because change (Chapters 6 and 7) and the experience of the present (Chapters 4 and 5) can be explained in temporally 'impersonal' terms. Hence, I echo Horwich:

... change is always variation in one thing with respect to another, the totality of absolute facts about those functional relations remaining forever constant. (Horwich 1987, p. 25)

This proposition at the very heart of my version of the B-theory.

So, as I intend it, a B-theory that includes temporal passage is a contribution to the project of providing an explanation of the spatiotemporal world, and our place in it, that is neither perspectival nor incomplete. In light of this, consider Prosser, who argues that there is no possibility of experiencing temporal passage:

By 'epiphenomenal' I mean that the passage of time neither causes nor in any sense influences or determines physical events. Insofar as physical events can be accounted for, the account is in terms of physics or at least in terms of what supervenes on the physical, and no appeal to the passage of time plays a role in any such account. (Prosser 2007, p. 79)

I agree with the essence of Prosser's account for I consider the passage of time to be nothing other than the temporal ordering that applies to ordinary, spatiotemporal events. I deny that the passage of time is anything over and above this; in particular, as noted above, I deny that it is some kind of temporal motion or change in time itself. So, in that sense, what 'the passage of time' refers to is simply not the kind of thing that can have an influence on physical events; the phrase instead ought to be understood as a general description of the fact that things change and that times and events stand in *temporally asymmetric* relations to each other. Obviously, that events stand in an *earlier than* relation to each other cannot itself be the cause of anything. Therefore, the passage of time isn't the direct cause of anything. However, we can experience the sequence of events in our environment: we can experience one event while remembering another; in each case, the experience is, at least in part, the effect of events in our surroundings. It is in this way that we experience the passage of time because passage is nothing over and above the sequence of occurrences. So, Prosser is right to argue against temporal passage as a kind of *motion* or *flow* that exists in addition to the regular course of events. He is wrong, I think, to conclude that this means time doesn't pass; it is simply that passage is a summary concept for the temporally ordered sequence of events in the universe: change entails a B-series ordering and the latter entails the passage of time; so the existence of change suffices for the existence of passage.

I conclude that the B-theory allows us to understand how time, change, and passage can be real and is able to explain them in a way that is independent of temporal perspective. I turn next to some thoughts on the direction of time, in a B-theoretic context.

8.2 The direction of time

The most prominent defenders of the B-theory tend to argue that the unreality of temporal passage entails that time lacks any inherent direction. If I am right that the only sense in which time does not pass is the illegitimate A-theoretic sense, then it ought to be compatible with the B-theory that time has a direction. The natural assumption would be that the direction of time will be captured by the *earlier than* relation, but more needs to be said about this.

Paul Horwich writes:

The fact that *now* coincides with progressively later and later events indicates nothing about the structure of time. In particular, it does not imply that time has an 'arrow' or directional character of any sort. For, as we have seen, 'now' is an indexical expression, like 'here', so there is no metaphysical significance in the variable location of its referent. (Horwich 1987, p. 37)

Horwich proceeds 'to conclude, from what we know at the moment, that time is probably isotropic' (Horwich 1987, p. 57). Horwich, like other B-theorists, rejects the A-series *and* temporal passage (1987, pp. 15–25) but we see in the above quotation that he moves from there to a rejection of temporal asymmetry or direction: he does not take the existence of the B-series to suffice to define an arrow of time.

Before Horwich, C. D. Broad argued that the passage of time is required in order for time to have a direction (or 'sense' as he called it; Broad 1923, p. 57). If we visualize a line, then we need to place an arrowhead on the line to properly represent time. But, argues Broad, 'the meaning of the arrow-head is only supplied by reference to something which is at one point *before* it gets to another' (1923, p. 57). As a result, we cannot use the concept of direction to explain the asymmetry of time, because direction presupposes temporal ordering. Broad then argues that:

...the intrinsic sense of a series of events in Time is essentially bound up with the distinction between past, present, and future. A precedes B because A is past when B is present. (Broad 1923, 58)

Now, for Broad, the distinction between past, present, and future is dependent on the notion of 'absolute becoming', which is much like Tooley's accretion of facts:

...the change of an event from present to past turned out to depend on the fact the sum total of existence increases beyond the limits which it had when our given event came into existence...Let us call...[this] kind of change *Becoming*. (Broad 1923, p. 67)

For Broad the direction of the timeline depends on the difference between before and after, which depends on the difference between past, present, and future, which in turn depends on becoming.

Broad considers the passage of time to be necessary for temporal direction, while for Horwich the existence of the B-series is insufficient for temporal direction. Both agree, in other words, that more than the B-series is required for time to have a direction. Huw Price, too, is suspicious of objective direction:

In saying that the sun moves from east to west or that the hands of a clock move clockwise, we take for granted the usual convention that the positive time axis lies toward what we call the future. But in the absence of some objective grounding for this convention, there isn't an objective fact as to which way the sun or the hands of the clock are 'really' moving. Of course, proponents of the view that there is an objective flow of time might see it as an advantage of their view that it does provide an objective basis for the usual choice of temporal coordinate. The problem is that until we have such an objective basis we don't have an objective sense in which time is flowing one way rather than the other. In other words, not only does it not seem to make sense to speak of an objective *rate* of flow of time; it also doesn't make sense to speak of an objective *direction* of flow of time. (Price 1996, p. 13)

For Price, even if temporal passage were real, which he denies, there would remain the question as to which direction time is flowing *objectively*. We assert that the NOW moves from the past to the future, but in virtue of what would this motion be *from* the past and *to* the future, rather than the other way around? Perhaps, counters Price, the direction of time is a perspectival matter and not something intrinsic to time itself (Price 1996, p. 15).

Now I think that Broad's perspective is the most easily addressed here for he, like McTaggart, assumes that before/after must be explicated in terms of past/present/future though, unlike McTaggart, that the latter three must be explicated in terms of absolute becoming. But we have already seen (Chapter 2) reasons to reject Broad's picture, so I think we should agree that before/after is conceived of in the B-theoretic sense, i.e. as an asymmetric relation between concrete events. What, however, are the prospects of a B-theoretic account of temporal direction?

Philosophers such as Price and Horwich believe that the B-series lacks the resources to ground an objective direction of time because they believe that something more than the ordering of events by the 'is earlier than' relation is required for temporal direction, and this is because in the absence of this extra something there would be no objective basis for preferring one direction on the timeline, as opposed to the other, as *the* direction of time. To use an analogy, an arrow printed on a traffic sign is asymmetric but it doesn't inherently point toward its head; it would be perfectly acceptable to adopt a convention in which arrows point *away* from their head and *toward* their tails (so that when one wants to indicate in which direction one should travel to get to Toronto from Montreal, one displays an arrow whose head is closer to Montreal and whose tail is closer to Toronto). Such a representational convention, inverted from our own, could work just as well, so there is no objective sense in which an arrow has a *direction* (even if it is asymmetric); something else, in particular human conventions, is required. Similarly, authors such as Price and Horwich argue that in the absence of some additional feature, which *cannot* be provided by McTaggart's A-series, even an asymmetric timeline must not be thought to have an inherent direction.

Horwich and Price go further and argue that there is no further feature available because the laws of nature are all time-reversal invariant. That is, if process A to B to C is physically possible, then so is process C to B to A.[1] Moreover, the second law of

---

[1] More accurately, what is possible is, in fact, the process C^i to B^i to A^i, where X^i represents the temporal inverse of X. Suppose a process, P, involves an object moving from p_1 to p_2 (A), then p_2 to p_3 (B), then p_3 to p_4 (C). The temporal inverse of P, P^i, is not the object moving from p_3 to p_4, then p_2 to p_3, then p_1 to p_2. The latter process involves a series of discontinuities that the former process lacks, and may be ruled out even given time

thermodynamics, which states that entropy always increases in the future direction, is taken to be a statistical generalization that is the result of the fact that the first moment of time, the Big Bang, is a low entropy and, therefore, low *probability* condition and that, therefore, there has to be, as a matter of simple probabilistic reasoning, a *gradient* of *increasing* entropy in the temporal direction away from the Big Bang (Horwich 1987, pp. 59–76). Much, however, as an arrow has no objective direction despite the asymmetry between its two ends, so an entropy gradient has no objective direction. The 'direction' from low entropy to high entropy is, for someone such as Price, *not* an objective feature of time but simply a reflection of human perspective on time, a perspective that arises because natural selection took advantage of that gradient in producing us and, in particular, our cognitive capacities (Price 1996).

What all such criticisms of temporal direction overlook is the possibility that the direction of time may be an inherent feature of the timeline that is not reducible to or explicable in other terms such as entropy. My suggestion is that it is an *irreducible* and *built in* feature of the world that it is objectively directed along its temporal dimension. In other words, the direction toward what we call the future truly is *later* and not just later in relation to us.

A fundamental reason for believing this is that it seems that the mere *existence* of an entropy gradient is in fact inexplicable without presupposing an objective direction of time. The view of philosophers such as Price and Horwich is that because the Big Bang is an improbable, low entropy state, it follows straightaway that any states that are, from our perspective, later must be in a higher entropy state because *any* change in the state of the universe must, with overwhelming probability, increase entropy; any change in a low probability condition will, in all likelihood, result in a more probable condition. This, of course, is fair enough. But if there is no objective temporal order, then it is just as legitimate to view the universe as evolving from our future to our past, in which case violations of the second law of thermodynamics are ubiquitous. After all, if we take it as a given that the first moment of time is associated with a very low entropy state, then viewed from what *we* would call the later-to-earlier direction the universe is undergoing a very *improbable* evolution from higher to lower entropy. It is only probable that the moments of time after the Big Bang have greater entropy if the universe is truly evolving *from* the Big Bang *to* subsequent moments. If, on the other hand, there is no fact of the matter as to whether the universe evolved from the Big Bang to that next state or vice versa, then there is no fact of the matter as to whether an improbable or probable transition exists, in which case the entropy gradient remains unexplained because it is indeterminate whether the universe is evolving in accordance with the laws of probability or in regular violation of them.

---

symmetric laws of nature. P^i is, rather, the object moving from p_4 to p_3, then p_3 to p_2, then p_2 to p_1. So in addition to inverting the order of the sequence of events, A, B, and C, we must also invert the velocities of the object during those events if we wish to describe the genuine time reversal of the original process.

In other words, it is on the assumption that the universe evolved *from* the Big Bang *to* later instants that probabilistic reasoning can be employed to explain the existence of an entropy gradient. Similarly, if it is assumed that the universe truly evolves in this direction, the fact that entropy decreases in relation to the later-to-earlier direction poses no problem, for that imagined direction of time doesn't represent actual processes in nature. So the statistical understanding of the second law of thermodynamics seems to presuppose that time has a direction and appears unsuited to explaining this fact (see Maudlin 2007, pp. 128–38).

Consider, once again, that human observers are the evolutionary products of natural selection, which is a sequence of processes that started long before consciousness arrived on the scene and, therefore, long before our perspective existed to, as Price argues, endow time with its apparent directionality. But if natural selection, like all physical processes, acts in accordance with the second law of thermodynamics, and the latter, as I suggest above, depends on, rather than defines, the direction of time, then the world was evolving in time, from earlier to later, independently of human perspective.

So I think we have reason to believe that the direction of time is ontologically fundamental, a basic feature of the universe that explains why the world evolves in accordance with probabilistic and statistical laws rather than vice versa. There is, moreover, no reason for the B-theorist to be concerned with this suggestion. We can imagine that each point in time—space-time, ultimately, of course—comes with a built-in orientation, which we might think of as like a vector,[2] which distinguishes the earlier from later direction with respect to that point. There are various ways this idea might be cashed out,[3] but what I think we can conclude is that the commitment to objective temporal direction is acceptable to the B-theorist.

Kurt Gödel famously argued that the relativity of simultaneity implied by Einstein's Special Theory of Relativity entails that there is no universal lapse of time between any two events and that, therefore, the passage of time, and consequently all change, is merely a subjective illusion of observers, our projections onto a changeless world (Gödel 1949, pp. 557–8). Note, however, that the B-theory rejects presentism, so there is no need to find an absolute, universal NOW that dissects all of spatiotemporal reality. The B-theory does not, therefore, entail that there is a single, universal temporal order defined across all of space and time, which is good because Einstein's theory informs us that there is none. Rather, what the B-theory entails is that for any

---

[2] Robert Weingard suggests that every point in space-time has associated with it a vector that determines a temporal orientation; he argues that there is a '*distinguished, irreducible* everywhere continuous time-like vector field, the *Time Ordering Field* (TOF)' (Weingard 1977, p. 128, original emphasis). This field ensures that for any point in space-time, the past and future orientations are distinguished. This strikes me as the right way to think about it.

[3] Causal theories of time define temporal order in terms of causal priority, so perhaps each time is associated with an inherent causal orientation (see Frisch 2013 for an overview of these debates). In this case, the causal asymmetry is the feature of reality that grounds the direction of time. Such a view is perfectly amenable to the B-theory, so I am happy to leave it as a viable alternative.

frame of reference, genuine change, process, and temporal order are well-defined concepts; the fact that such concepts don't relate every event in the universe to every other can be granted. Hence, the B-theorist needn't follow Gödel in denying the reality of temporal passage.

I conclude that the B-theorist can happily talk of time's passage and direction, knowing that doing so will not commit her to anything in conflict with the core tenets of her theory.

8.3 General summary and conclusion

Philosophers who write about time tend to divide into the *A-theorists* and the *B-theorists*. I have defended a version of the B-theory, which I take to be the combination of two views. The first is an ontological doctrine, eternalism, which states that location in time is existentially irrelevant; in other words, when something occurs or exists has no bearing on whether it should be considered by us to be real. The second is a semantic view, according to which the function of *tense*, in both language and thought, is merely to locate one element in or of time with respect to another; the semantics of tensed utterances and thoughts is tenseless. The A-theory is typically the denial of one or both of these views, insisting that what is real varies with time or that tense is semantically basic, or at least prior to tenselessness.

Philosophers who write about persistence tend to divide into the *endurantists* and the *perdurantists*. The former take objects to be three-dimensional entities that are able to remain numerically the same as they persist in time. The latter view objects as four-dimensional entities that are composed of temporal parts. A variation of this view is *stage theory* according to which objects are not the occupants of large volumes of space-time but, rather, the instantaneous temporal stages that can be mereologically tied together by counterpart relations. On either four-dimensional view persisting objects don't change *as a whole* from time to time since change is a matter of distinct properties attaching to distinct temporal parts.

If one examines the literature on time and persistence one is struck by the fact that B-theorists tend almost exclusively to be perdurantists while endurantists tend almost exclusively to be A-theorists. One could plot this situation as follows:

	A-Theory	B-Theory
Endurantism	Many occupants (Prior, Makosian, Craig, Bigelow, Ludlow...)	Few occupants (Mellor, Mozersky)
Perdurantism	Few if any occupants; compatible with Tooley's views.	Many occupants (Quine, Lewis, Hawley, Sider, Heller, Balashov, Smart...)

It seems that those who see time as an extended component of the four-dimensional manifold of space-time (i.e. those sympathetic to eternalism) tend to believe that objects within space-time are perduring entities, while those who see objects as three-dimensional enduring wholes tend to see the universe as an entity that is in some way divided along tense lines. In this book, I have tried to provide motivation for stepping into the upper-right box in this chart.

Part of the reason for this is that it just seems to be where the arguments lead. Another part of the motivation stems from the sense that temporal parts are mysterious entities and that belief in them is not sufficiently motivated. The result is, I think, an interesting and satisfactory picture that merits exploration.

Defenders of the A-theory, such as Quentin Smith (1993), William Lane Craig (2000), Peter Ludlow (1999), Yuval Dolev (2000), and others, argue that there is something ineliminable and basic about tense that the B-theory, to its detriment, just can't explain. I think that there is a striking similarity between these arguments and arguments for irreducibly *subjective* or *personal* facts. Many philosophers (e.g. Chalmers 1995, Jackson 1986, and Nagel 1986) have argued that conscious, first-person experience cannot be accounted for in objective, third-personal terms. The impersonal, objective description of the world is incomplete, on these views, missing something that only a new kind of explanation could provide.

The arguments I respond to in Chapter 5 strike me as similar: in arguing that a purely tenseless, eternalist ontology lacks the resources to explain the experience of the present, one is essentially arguing that a *temporally* impersonal theory is fundamentally incomplete and inadequate.

In response, some B-theorists allow for tensed *propositions* or semantic *contents* but explicate them tenselessly. For example, Michelle Beer argues that tensed propositions ('A-propositions') are distinct from tenseless propositions but are 'co-reporting' with tenseless ones in that they refer to one and the same event on the B-series, as does the tenseless proposition (Beer 1988; see also Butterfield 1985). L. Nathan Oaklander, on the other hand, expresses doubts about the Kaplanesque account I defend above, writing: 'no tenseless sentence can state all the truth conditions, that is, give the complete "meaning" of a tensed sentence' (2004, p. 287); he argues, however, that tensed contents are merely subjective and do not correspond to any A-facts (2004, p. 284). These are fascinating theories and I am a great admirer of them. I do, however, go further than they do: on my account, there is no such thing as a tensed proposition or content; tense amounts to nothing more than sentences (or terms, or utterances, or thoughts) with reflexive characters and tenseless contents. Hence I believe that it is possible to explicate our ability to navigate the temporal world without recourse to anything that is tensed other than, of course, surface grammar.

Thomas Nagel writes:

> But even when all that public information about the person TN has been included in an objective conception, the additional thought that TN is *me* seems clearly to have further content. And it is important that the content is startling. (Nagel 1987, 60; emphasis in original)

I think Nagel is wrong. 'I am JM', when uttered by me, expresses no personal or subjective content; rather, it expresses the simple identity *that JM is JM* (I believe, for reasons like those I provide in Chapters 4 and 5, that 'I' is an indexical that refers directly to its utterer/thinker). An utterance of 'I am JM', however, can only express the proposition *that JM is JM* when JM is the one who utters it. Someone else must either utter 'JM is JM' or 'you are JM' to express the same thing. This is simply a function of the rules for indexical expressions.

Now, of course, to complete the story one will have to explain how it is that someone comes to learn these different rules of application for personal indexicals *without* appealing to private, subjective facts such as the alleged fact that JM is *me*. My solution will mirror the arguments in Chapter 5: the characters of personal indexicals, combined with one's ability to perceptually distinguish utterances originating in one's own body from those originating elsewhere, will, I believe, do the trick. The point I wish to make here, however, is that the tenseless account of the language and experience of time is a piece of a larger picture, the picture that views human beings as evolved parts of the spatiotemporal world, with no central, 'Copernican' place. Subjective perspective is just one part of the spatiotemporal world standing in relation to another part. The arguments of this book are intended, in part, to make this a bit more plausible.

In sum, I have argued that the combination of eternalism, tenseless predication, and endurance results in a view that is simple, powerful, and makes the best sense of objective change and temporal passage. This is also a combination that is largely overlooked. I hope to have encouraged the reader to give it further consideration.

References

Adams, R., 1979, 'Primitive Thisness and Primitive Identity', *Journal of Philosophy* 76: 5–26.

Adams, R., 1989, 'Time and Thisness', in J. Almog, J. Perry, and H. Wettstein (eds.), *Themes from Kaplan*, Oxford: Oxford University Press: 5–26.

Alston, W., 1994, *A Realist Conception of Truth*, Ithaca, NY: Cornell University Press.

Austin, David F., 1990, *What's the Meaning of 'This'?* Ithaca, NY: Cornell University Press.

Baia, A., 2012, 'Presentism and the Grounding of Truth', *Philosophical Studies* 159: 341–56.

Barbour, J., 1999, *The End of Time*, Oxford: Oxford University Press.

Barker, S. F., and Achinstein, P., 1960, 'On the New Riddle of Induction', *Philosophical Review* 69: 511–22.

Barnett, D., 2005, 'The Problem of Material Origins', *Noûs* 39: 529–40.

Beer, M., 1988, 'Temporal Indexicals and the Passage of Time', *Philosophical Quarterly* 38: 158–64.

Belnap, N., Perloff, M., and Xu, M., 2001, *Facing the Future: Agents and Choices in our Indeterminist World*, Oxford: Oxford University Press.

Bigelow, J., 1991, 'Worlds Enough for Time', *Noûs* 25: 1–19.

Bigelow, J., 1996, 'Presentism and Properties', in J. E. Tomberlin (ed.), *Philosophical Perspectives*, x: *Metaphysics*, Oxford: Blackwell: 35–42.

Boghossian, P. A., 1990, 'The Status of Content', *Philosophical Review* 99: 157–84.

Boghossian, P., and Velleman, D., 1989, 'Colour as a Secondary Quality', *Mind* 98: 81–103.

Boolos, G., 1984, 'To Be is to be a Value of a Variable (or to be Some Values of Some Variables)', *Journal of Philosophy* 81: 430–49.

Bourne, C., 2004, 'Future Contingents, Non-Contradiction, and the Law of Excluded Middle', *Analysis* 64: 122–8.

Bourne, C., 2006a, 'A Theory of Presentism', *Canadian Journal of Philosophy* 36: 1–24.

Bourne, C., 2006b, *A Future for Presentism*, Oxford: Oxford University Press.

Broad, C. D., 1923, *Scientific Thought*, London: Kegan Paul.

Broad, C. D., 1968, 'Ostensible Temporality', in R. M. Gale (ed.), *The Philosophy of Time*, Atlantic Highlands, NJ: Humanities Press.

Brogaard, B., 2012, *Transient Truths*, Oxford: Oxford University Press.

Brooks, R., 1991, 'Intelligence without Representation', *Artificial Intelligence* 47: 139–59.

Brower, J. E., 2010, 'Aristotelian Endurantism: A New Solution to the Problem of Temporary Intrinsics', *Mind* 119: 883–905.

Brown, J. R., 1994, *Smoke and Mirrors: How Science Reflects Reality*, London: Routledge.

Burge, T., 1986, 'Individualism and Psychology', *Philosophical Review* 95: 3–45.

Butterfield, J., 1985, 'Indexicals and Tense', in Ian Hacking (ed.), *Exercises in Analysis*, Cambridge: Cambridge University Press: 69–87.

Cahn, S. M., 1967, *Fate, Logic and Time*, New Haven: Yale University Press.

Callender, C. (ed.), 2002, *Time, Reality and Experience*, Cambridge: Cambridge University Press.

Cameron, R. P., 2011, 'Truthmaking for Presentists', in Karen Bennett and Dean Zimmerman (eds.), *Oxford Studies in Metaphysics*, vi, Oxford: Oxford University Press: 55–102.

Cameron, R. P., 2013, 'Changing Truthmakers: Reply to Tallant and Ingram', in Karen Bennett and Dean Zimmerman (eds.), *Oxford Studies in Metaphysics*, viii, Oxford: Oxford University Press: 362–74.

Campbell, J., 1994, *Past, Space and Self*, Cambridge, Mass.: MIT Press.

Carroll, L., 1976, *The Complete Works of Lewis Carroll*, New York: Vintage.

Chalmers, D., 1995, 'The Puzzle of Conscious Experience', *Scientific American* 273: 80–6.

Chisholm, R., 1990, 'Referring to Things that No Longer Exist', *Philosophical Perspectives* 4: 545–56.

Cohen, J., 2004, 'Color Properties and Color Ascriptions: A Relationalist Manifesto', *Philosophical Review*, 113: 451–506.

Craig, W. L., 1996, 'The New B-Theory's *Tu Quoque* Argument', *Synthese* 107: 249–69.

Craig, W. L., 1998, 'McTaggart's Paradox and the Problem of Temporary Intrinsics', *Analysis* 58: 122–7.

Craig, W. L., 2000, *The Tensed Theory of Time: A Critical Examination*, Dordrecht: Kluwer Academic Publishers.

Crisp, T., 2005, 'Presentism and Cross-Time Relations', *American Philosophical Quarterly* 42: 5–17.

Crisp, T., 2007, 'Presentism and the Grounding Objection', *Noûs* 41: 90–109.

Crisp, T., and Smith, D., 2005, 'Wholly Present Defined', *Philosophy and Phenomenological Research* 71: 318–44.

Davidson, D., 1967, 'The Logical Form of Action Sentences', in Davidson 1980: 105–22.

Davidson, D., 1980, *Essays on Actions and Events*, Oxford: Clarendon Press.

Davidson, D., 1996, 'The Folly of Trying to Define Truth', *Journal of Philosophy* 93: 263–78.

Dennett, D., 1991, *Consciousness Explained*, Boston: Little Brown and Company.

Devitt, M., 1997, *Realism and Truth*, 2nd edition, Princeton: Princeton University Press.

Diekemper, J., 2007, 'B-Theory, Fixity and Fatalism', *Noûs* 41: 429–52.

Dolev, Y., 2000, 'The Tenseless Theory of Time: Insights and Limitations', *Review of Metaphysics* 54: 259–88.

Dowe, P., 2009, 'Every Now and Then: A-Theory and Loops in Time', *Journal of Philosophy* 106: 641–65.

Dummett, M., 1978a, 'The Reality of the Past', in *Truth and Other Enigmas*, Cambridge, Mass.: Harvard University Press: 358–74.

Dummett, M., 1978b, 'A Defence of McTaggart's Argument against the Reality of Time', in *Truth and Other Enigmas*, Cambridge, Mass.: Harvard University Press: 351–7.

Dummett, M., 2000, 'Is Time a Continuum of Instants?', *Philosophy* 75: 489–515.

Dummett, M., 2002, 'Truth and the Past', *Journal of Philosophy* 100: 5–53.

Dummett, M., 2004, *Truth and the Past*, New York: Columbia University Press.

Dyke, H., 2008, *Metaphysics and the Representational Fallacy*, New York: Routledge.

Eddon, M., 2010, 'Three Arguments from Temporary Intrinsics', *Philosophy and Phenomenological Research* 81: 605–19.

Efird, D., and Stoneham, T., 2005, 'The Subtraction Argument for Metaphysical Nihilism', *Journal of Philosophy* 102: 303–25.

Einstein, A., 1961, *Relativity: The Special and General Theory*, New York: Crown Trade.

Fine, K., 2005, 'Tense and Reality', in *Modality and Tense: Philosophical Papers*, Oxford: Oxford University Press: 261–320.

Fine, K., 2006, 'The Reality of Tense', *Synthese* 150: 399–414.

Fischer, J. M., 1994, *The Metaphysics of Free Will: An Essay on Control*, Walden, Mass.: Blackwell.

Frege, G., 1918, 'The Thought: A Logical Inquiry', reprinted in P. Strawson (ed.), *Philosophical Logic*, Oxford: Oxford University Press, 1967: 17–38.

Frisch, M., 2013, 'Time and Causation', in Heather Dyke and Adrian Bardon (eds.), *The Blackwell Companion to the Philosophy of Time*, Malden, Mass.: Wiley-Blackwell: 282–300.

Gallois, A., 1997, 'Can an Anti-Realist Live with the Past?', *Australasian Journal of Philosophy* 75: 288–303.

Gemignani, M. C., 2004, *Basic Concepts of Mathematics and Logic*, Mineola, NY: Dover Publications.

Gödel, K., 1949, 'A Remark about the Relationship between Relativity Theory and the Idealistic Philosophy', in P. Schilpp (ed.), *Albert Einstein: Philosopher-Scientist*, La Salle, Ill.: Open Court: 555–62.

Goldman, A., 1979, 'Reliabilism: What is Justified Belief', in G. S. Pappas (ed.), *Justification and Knowledge*, Dordrecht: D. Reidel.

Goodman, N., 1947, 'The Problem of Counterfactual Conditionals', *Journal of Philosophy* 44: 219–36.

Goodman, N., 1955, *Fact, Fiction and Forecast*, Cambridge, Mass.: Harvard University Press.

Hare, C., 2007, 'Self-Bias, Time-Bias, and the Metaphysics of Self and Time', *Journal of Philosophy* 104: 350–73.

Haslanger, S., 1989, 'Endurance and Temporary Intrinsics', *Analysis* 49: 119–25.

Hawley, K., 1998, 'Why Temporary Properties are not Relations between Physical Objects and Times', *Proceedings of the Aristotelian Society* 98: 211–16.

Hawley, K., 2001, *How Things Persist*, Oxford: Oxford University Press.

Hawley, K., 2004, 'Temporal Parts', in Edward N. Zalta (ed.), *The Stanford Encyclopedia of Philosophy* (*Winter 2004 Edition*), <http://plato.stanford.edu/archives/win2004/entries/temporal-parts/> (accessed 15 September 2012).

Hawley, K., 2009, 'Identity and Indiscernibility', *Mind* 118: 101–19.

Heil, J., 2003, *From an Ontological Point of View*, Oxford: Clarendon Press.

Heller, M., 1984, 'Temporal Parts of Four-Dimensional Objects', *Philosophical Studies* 46: 323–34.

Higginbotham, J., 1995, 'Tensed Thoughts', *Mind and Language* 10: 226–49.

Hinchliff, M., 1996. 'The Puzzle of Change', in James E. Tomberlin (ed.), *Philosophical Perspectives 10: Metaphysics*, Oxford: Blackwell: 119–36.

Hinchliff, M., 2000, 'A Defense of Presentism in a Relativistic Setting', *Philosophy of Science* 67 (Proceedings): 575–86.

Horwich, P., 1987, *Asymmetries in Time*, Cambridge, Mass.: MIT Press.

Hughes, G. E., and Cresswell, M. J., 1982, *An Introduction to Modal Logic*, London: Methuen.

Jackson, F., 1986, 'What Mary Didn't Know', *Journal of Philosophy* 83: 291–5.

Jaszczolt, K., 2009, *Representing Time*, Oxford: Oxford University Press.

Johnston, M., 1987, 'Is There a Problem about Persistence?', *Proceedings of the Aristotelian Society* (suppl. vol.) 61: 107–35.

Kaplan, D., 1989, 'Demonstratives', in J. Almog, J. Perry, and H. Wettstein (eds.), *Themes from Kaplan*, Oxford: Oxford University Press: 461–563.

Katz, B. D., 1983, 'Perils of an Uneventful World', *Philosophia* 18: 1–12.

Katz, B., 1995, 'Making Comparisons', *Mind* 104: 369–92.

Keller, S., 2004, 'Presentism and Truthmaking', in Dean Zimmerman (ed.), *Oxford Studies in Metaphysics*, i, Oxford: Oxford University Press: 83–104.

Kim, J., and Sosa, E. (eds.), 1999, *Metaphysics: An Anthology*, Oxford: Blackwell Publishers.

Krauss, L., 2012, *A Universe from Nothing: Why There is Something Rather Than Nothing*, New York: Free Press.

Kripke, S., 1980, *Naming and Necessity*, Cambridge, Mass.: Harvard University Press.

Kripke, S., 1982, *Wittgenstein on Rules and Private Language*, Cambridge, Mass.: Harvard University Press.

Laycock, H., 2006a, *Words without Objects*, Oxford: Oxford University Press.

Laycock, H., 2006b, 'Object', in Edward N. Zalta (ed.), *The Stanford Encyclopedia of Philosophy* (*Winter 2006 Edition*), <http://plato.stanford.edu/archives/win2006/entries/object/> (accessed 1 May 2008).

Le Poidevin, R., 1991, *Change, Cause and Contradiction: A Defence of the Tenseless Theory of Time*, London: Macmillan.

Levin, M., 2007, 'Compatibilism and Special Relativity', *Journal of Philosophy* 104: 433–63.

Lewis, D., 1973, *Counterfactuals*, Cambridge, Mass.: Harvard University Press.

Lewis, D., 1983a, 'In Defence of Stages' (Postscript B to 'Survival and Identity'), in *Philosophical Papers*, i, New York: Oxford University Press: 76–7.

Lewis, D., 1983b, 'Extrinsic Properties', *Philosophical Studies* 44: 197–200.

Lewis, D., 1986, *On the Plurality of Worlds*, Oxford: Blackwell.

Lewis, D., 1992, 'Critical Notice: Armstrong, D. M., *A Combinatorial Theory of Possibility*', *Australasian Journal of Philosophy* 70: 211–24.

Lockwood, M., 2005, *The Labyrinth of Time*, Oxford: Oxford University Press.

Lombard, L., 1986, *Events: A Metaphysical Study*, London: Routledge & Kegan Paul.

Lowe, E. J., 1988, 'The Problems of Intrinsic Change: Rejoinder to Lewis', *Analysis* 48: 72–7.

Lowe, E. J., 1995, 'The Metaphysics of Abstract Objects', *Journal of Philosophy* 92: 509–24.

Lucas, J. R., 1989, *The Future*, Oxford: Basil Blackwell.

Ludlow, P., 1999, *Semantics, Tense and Time*, Cambridge, Mass.: MIT Press.

Łukasiewicz, J., 1967, 'On Determinism', in S. McCall (ed.), *Polish Logic*, Oxford: Clarendon Press: 19–39.

Łukasiewicz, J., 1970, 'On Three-Valued Logic', in *Selected Works*, ed. L. Borkowski, Amsterdam: North-Holland Publishing Company: 87–8.

MacFarlane, J., 2003, 'Future Contingents and Relative Truth', *Philosophical Quarterly* 53: 321–36.

Mackie, P., 2003, 'Fatalism, Incompatibilism, and the Power to Do Otherwise', *Noûs* 37: 672–89.

McCall, S., 1994, *A Model of the Universe*, Oxford: Oxford University Press.

McCall, S., 1998, 'Time Flow does not Require a Second Dimension', *Australasian Journal of Philosophy* 76: 317–22.

McKeon, R., 1941, *The Basic Works of Aristotle*, New York: Random House.

McKinnon, N., and Bigelow, J., 2012, 'Presentism, and Speaking of the Dead', *Philosophical Studies* 160: 253–63.

McKirahan, Jr., Richard, D., 1994, *Philosophy Before Socrates*, Indianapolis: Hackett.

McTaggart, J. M. E., 1908, 'The Unreality of Time', *Mind* 17: 457–74.

McTaggart, J. M. E., 1921, *The Nature of Existence*, ii, Cambridge: Cambridge University Press.

Markosian, N., 2002, 'Time', in Edward N. Zalta (ed.), *The Stanford Encyclopedia of Philosophy (Winter 2002 Edition)*, <http://plato.stanford.edu/archives/win2002/entries/time/> (accessed 1 May 2008).

Markosian, N., 2004, 'A Defence of Presentism', in Dean Zimmerman (ed.), *Oxford Studies in Metaphysics*, i, Oxford: Oxford University Press: 47–82.

Maudlin, T., 2007, *The Metaphysics within Physics*, Oxford: Oxford University Press.

Maudlin, T., 2012, *Philosophy of Physics: Space and Time*, Princeton: Princeton University Press.

Mellor, D. H., 1981a, *Real Time*, Cambridge: Cambridge University Press.

Mellor, D. H., 1981b, 'McTaggart, Fixity and Coming True', in Richard Healey (ed.), *Reduction, Time and Reality*, Cambridge: Cambridge University Press: 79–98.

Mellor, D. H., 1991, 'Properties and Predicates', in *Matters of Metaphysics*, Cambridge: Cambridge University Press: 170–82. (Page references to the reprint in Mellor and Oliver 1997.)

Mellor, D. H., 1998, *Real Time II*, London: Routledge.

Mellor, D. H., and Oliver, A. (eds.), 1997, *Properties*, Oxford: Oxford University Press.

Merricks, T., 1999, 'Persistence, Parts and Presentism', *Noûs* 33: 421–38.

Merricks, T., 2009, 'Truth and Freedom', *Philosophical Review* 118: 29–57.

Meyer, U., 2005, 'The Presentist's Dilemma', *Philosophical Studies* 122: 213–25.

Meyer, U., 2006, 'Worlds and Times', *Notre Dame Journal of Formal Logic* 47: 25–37.

Minkowski, H., 1908, 'Space and Time', reprinted in A. Einstein, H. A. Lorentz, H. Minkowski, and H. Weyl (eds.), *The Principle of Relativity*, New York: Dover, 1952.

Moyer, M., 2008, 'Why We Shouldn't Swallow Worm Slices: A Case Study in Semantic Accommodation', *Noûs* 42: 109–38.

Nagel, T., 1986, *The View from Nowhere*, New York: Oxford University Press.

Nagel, T., 2012, *Mind and Cosmos: Why the Neo-Darwinian Conception of Nature is Almost Certainly False*, Oxford: Oxford University Press.

Nerlich, G., 1998, 'Falling Branches and the Flow of Time', *Australasian Journal of Philosophy* 76: 309–16.

Normore, C., 2006, 'Ockham's Metaphysics of Parts', *Journal of Philosophy* 103: 737–54.

Oaklander, L. N., 1990, 'The New Tenseless Theory of Time: A Reply to Smith', *Philosophical Studies* 58: 287–93.

Oaklander, L. N., 1991, 'A Defense of the New Tenseless Theory of Time', *Philosophical Quarterly* 41: 26–38.

Oaklander, L. N., 1994, 'Bigelow, Possible Words and the Passage of Time', *Analysis* 54: 244–8.

Oaklander, L. N., 2004, *The Ontology of Time*, Amherst, NY: Prometheus Books.

Oaklander, L. N., and Smith, Q. (eds.), 1994, *The New Theory of Time*, New Haven: Yale University Press.

Olson, E., 2006, 'Temporal Parts and Timeless Parthood', *Noûs* 40: 738–52.

Olson, E., 2009, 'The Rate of Time's Passage', *Analysis* 69: 3–9.

Parsons, C., 1971, 'A Plea for Substitutional Quantification', *Journal of Philosophy* 68: 231–7.

Parsons, T., 1980, *Nonexistent Objects*, New Haven: Yale University Press.

Paul, L. A., 1997, 'Truth Conditions of Tensed Sentence Types', *Synthese* 111: 53–71.

Paul, L. A., 2010, 'Temporal Experience', *Journal of Philosophy* 107: 333–59.

Perry, J., 1977, 'Frege on Demonstratives', *Philosophical Review* 86: 474–97.

Perry, J., 1979, 'The Problem of the Essential Indexical', *Noûs* 13: 3–21.

Perry, J., 1988, 'Cognitive Significance and New Theories of Reference', *Noûs* 22: 1–18.

Pojman, L. (ed.), 2003, *The Theory of Knowledge: Classical and Contemporary Readings*, 3rd edition, Belmont, Calif.: Wadsworth Publishing.

Price, H., 1996, *Time's Arrow and Archimedes' Point: New Directions for the Physics of Time*, New York: Oxford University Press.

Price, H., 2011, *Naturalism without Mirrors*, Oxford: Oxford University Press.

Price, H., and Weslake, B., 2009, 'The Time-Asymmetry of Causation', in Helen Beebee, Peter Menzies, and Christopher Hitchcock (eds.), *The Oxford Handbook of Causation*, Oxford: Oxford University Press: 414–43.

Priest, G., 2008, *An Introduction to Non-Classical Logic*, Cambridge: Cambridge University Press.

Prior, A., 1968, *Papers on Time and Tense*, Oxford: Clarendon Press.

Prior, A. N., 1962, *Changes in Events and Changes in Things*, Lawrence, Kan.: University of Kansas Press.

Prior, A. N., 1967, *Past, Present and Future*, Oxford: Oxford University Press.

Prior, A. N., 1970, 'The Notion of the Present', *Studium Generale* 23: 245–8. (Page references to the reprint in van Inwagen and Zimmerman 1998.)

Prior, A. N., 1996, 'Some Free Thinking about Time', in B. J. Copeland (ed.), *Logic and Reality: Essays on the Legacy of Arthur Prior*, Oxford: Oxford University Press. (Page references to the reprint in van Inwagen and Zimmerman 1998.)

Prosser, S., 2007, 'Could we Experience the Passage of Time', *Ratio* 20: 75–90.

Putnam, H., 1967, 'Time and Physical Geometry', *Journal of Philosophy* 64: 240–7.

Putnam, H., 1975, 'The Meaning of "Meaning"', in *Mind, Language and Reality: Philosophical Papers Volume 2*, Cambridge: Cambridge University Press: 215–71.

Putnam, H., 1978, *Meaning and the Moral Sciences*, Boston: Routledge and Kegan Paul.

Putnam, H., 1980, 'Models and Reality', *Journal of Symbolic Logic* 45: 464–82.

Putnam, H., 1981, *Reason, Truth and History*, Cambridge: Cambridge University Press.

Quine, W. V. O., 1948, 'On What There Is', in Kim and Sosa 1999: 4–12.

Quine, W. V. O., 1950, 'Identity, Ostension and Hypostasis', *Journal of Philosophy* 47: 621–32.

Quine, W. V. O., 1960, *Word and Object*, Cambridge, Mass.: MIT Press.

Quine, W. V. O., 1969a, 'Epistemology Naturalized', in *Ontological Relativity and Other Essays*, New York: Columbia University Press. (Page references to the reprint in Pojman 2003.)

Quine, W. V. O., 1969b, 'Natural Kinds', in *Ontological Relativity and Other Essays*, New York: Columbia University Press.

Rietdjik, C., 1966, 'A Rigorous Proof of Determinism Derived from the Special Theory of Relativity', *Philosophy of Science* 33: 341–4.

Rudd, A., 1997, 'Realism and Time', *Philosophical Studies* 88: 245–65.

Russell, B., 1903, *The Principles of Mathematics*. (Page references to the 1996 edition, published by W. W. Norton and Company.)

Russell, B., 1905, 'On Denoting', *Mind* 14: 479–93.

Russell, B., 1915, 'On the Experience of Time', *Monist* 25: 212–33.

Russell, B., 1919, *Introduction to Mathematical Philosophy*, London: George Allen & Unwin Ltd.

Sanson, D., and Caplan, B., 2010, 'The Way Things Were', *Philosophy and Phenomenological Research* 81: 24–39.

Sattig, T., 2006, *The Language and Reality of Time*, Oxford: Oxford University Press.

Savitt, S., 1991, Critical Notice of Paul Horwich's *Asymmetries in Time*, *Canadian Journal of Philosophy* 21: 399–417.

Shoemaker, S., 1980, 'Causality and Properties', in P. van Inwagen (ed.), *Time and Cause: Essays Presented to Richard Taylor*, Dordrecht: D. Reidel Publishing Company.

Sider, T., 1997, 'Four-Dimensionalism', *Philosophical Review* 106: 197–231.

Sider, T., 1999, 'Presentism and Ontological Commitment', *Journal of Philosophy* 96: 325–47.

Sider, T., 2001, *Four-Dimensionalism: An Ontology of Persistence and Time*, Oxford: Clarendon Press.

Sider, T., 2006, 'Quantifiers and Temporal Ontology', *Mind* 115: 75–97.

Simons, P., 1987, *Parts: A Study in Ontology*, Oxford: Oxford University Press.

Skow, B., 2009a, '"One Second Per Second"', *Philosophy and Phenomenological Research* 85: 377–89.

Skow, B., 2009b, 'Relativity and the Moving Spotlight', *Journal of Philosophy* 106: 666–78.

Skow, B., 2012, 'Why Does Time Pass?', *Noûs* 46: 223–42.

Smart, J. J. C., 1949, 'The River of Time', *Mind* 58: 483–94.

Smart, J. J. C., 1963, *Philosophy and Scientific Realism*, London: Routledge.

Smart, J. J. C., 1980, 'Time and Becoming', in P. van Inwagen (ed.), *Time and Cause: Essays Presented to Richard Taylor*, Dordrecht: D. Reidel Publishing Company.

Smith, Q., 1987, 'Problems with the New Tenseless Theory of Time', *Philosophical Studies* 52: 371–92.

Smith, Q., 1988–9, 'The Logical Structure of the Debate about McTaggart's Paradox', *Philosophy Research Archives* 24: 371–9.

Smith, Q., 1990, 'Temporal Indexicals', *Erkenntnis* 32: 5–25. (Page references to the reprint in Oaklander and Smith 1994.)

Smith, Q., 1993, *Language and Time*, Oxford: Oxford University Press.

Smith, Q., 1994a, 'Williams's Defense of the New Tenseless Theory of Time', in Oaklander and Smith 1994: 111–14.

Smith, Q., 1994b, 'The Truth Conditions of Tensed Sentences', in Oaklander and Smith 1994: 69–76.

Smith, Q., 1994c, 'Smart and Mellor's New Tenseless Theory of Time: A Reply to Oaklander', in Oaklander and Smith 1994: 83–6.

Smith, Q., 2002, 'Time and Degrees of Existence: A Theory of "Degree Presentism"', in Callender 2002: 119–36.

Stein, H., 1968, 'On Einstein–Minkowski Space-Time', *Journal of Philosophy* **65**: 5–23.

Stoneham, T., 2009, 'Time and Truth: The Presentism-Eternalism Debate', *Philosophy* **84**: 201–18.

Strawson, P. F., 1992, *Analysis and Metaphysics*, Oxford: Oxford University Press.

Tallant, J., 2009, 'Ontological Cheats Might Just Prosper', *Analysis* **69**: 422–30.

Tallant, J., 2010, 'Still Cheating, Still Prospering', *Analysis* **70**: 502–6.

Taylor, R., 1962, 'Fatalism', *Philosophical Review* **71**: 56–66.

Taylor, R., 1992, *Metaphysics*, 4th edition, Englewood Cliffs, NJ: Prentice Hall.

Teichmann, R., 1998, 'Is a Tenseless Language Possible?' *Philosophical Quarterly* **48**: 176–88.

Thomason, R. H., 1970, 'Indeterminist Time and Truth-Value Gaps', *Theoria* **36**: 264–81.

Tooley, M., 1997, *Time, Tense and Causation*, Oxford: Oxford University Press.

Torre, S., 2010, 'Tense, Timely Action and Self-Ascription', *Philosophy and Phenomenological Research* **80**: 112–32.

Turner, J., 2010, 'Ontological Pluralism', *Journal of Philosophy* **107**: 5–34.

van Inwagen, P., and Zimmerman, D. (eds.), 1998, *Metaphysics: The Big Questions*, Oxford: Blackwell Publishers.

Weingard, R., 1977, 'Space-Time and the Direction of Time', *Noûs* **11**: 119–31.

Weiss, B., 1996, 'Anti-Realism, Truth-Value Links and Tensed Truth Predicates', *Mind* **105**: 577–602.

Wettstein, H., 1986, 'Has Semantics Rested on a Mistake?' *Journal of Philosophy* **83**: 185–209.

Williams, C., 1990, 'The Date Analysis of Tensed Sentences', *Australasian Journal of Philosophy* **70**: 198–203.

Williams, D. C., 1951, 'The Myth of Passage', *Journal of Philosophy* **48**: 457–72.

Wittgenstein, L., 1957, 'Notes on Logic', *Journal of Philosophy* **54**: 231–45.

Woods, J., Irvine, A., and Walton, D., 2004, *Argument: Critical Thinking, Logic and the Fallacies*, Toronto: Pearson.

Wright, C., 1993, *Realism, Meaning and Truth*, Oxford: Blackwell Publishers.

Yourgrau, P., 1987, 'The Dead', *Journal of Philosophy* **84**: 84–101.

Zalabardo, J. L., 2000, *Introduction to the Theory of Logic*, Boulder: Westview Press.

Zehna, P. W., and Johnson, R. L., 1972, *Elements of Set Theory*, 2nd edition, Boston: Allyn and Bacon, Inc.

Zimmerman, D., 1998, 'Temporary Intrinsics and Presentism', in van Inwagen and Zimmerman 1998: 206–19.

Index